Dr Claudia Herbert was one of the first specialist trained Trauma Therapists in the UK having trained at the Traumatic Stress Clinic in London in 1991. She is a Chartered Consultant Clinical Psychologist, Cognitive-Behavioural Psychotherapist, EMDR Consultant, Schema therapist, Applied Psychology Practice Supervisor (RAPPS) and International Trauma Specialist and Author. She is also trained in several body-oriented approaches and has been interested in combining traditional Eastern Healing Approaches with modern Western Psychology for a long time. She is the Clinical and Managing Director of The Oxford Development Centre and the Cotswold Centre for Trauma Healing.

The aim of the **Overcoming** series is to enable people with a range of common problems and disorders to take control of their own recovery programme.

Each title, with its specially tailored programme, is devised by a practising clinician using the latest techniques of cognitive behavioural therapy – techniques which have been shown to be highly effective in changing the way patients think about themselves and their problems.

Many books in the Overcoming series are recommended by the UK Department of Health under the Books on Prescription scheme.

Other titles in the series include:

OVERCOMING TRAUMATIC STRESS

2nd Edition

A self-help guide using cognitive behavioural techniques

OVERCOMING

CLAUDIA HERBERT

ROBINSON

ROBINSON

First published in Great Britain in 2017 by Robinson

Copyright © Claudia Herbert, 2017

Previous edition *Overcoming Traumatic Stress* written by Claudia Herbert and
Ann Wetmore and published by Robinson, an imprint of
Constable & Robinson Ltd., 2008

1 3 5 7 9 10 8 6 4 2

A CIP catalogue record for this book
is available from the British Library.

Important Note
This book is not intended as a substitute for medical advice or treatment.
Any person with a condition requiring medical attention should consult a
qualified medical practitioner or suitable therapist.

ISBN: 978-1-47213-613-8

Typeset in Bembo by Initial Typesetting Services, Edinburgh
Printed and bound in Great Britain by
CPI Group (UK) Ltd, Croydon CR0 4YY

Papers used by Robinson are from well-managed forests
and other responsible sources

Robinson
An imprint of
Little, Brown Book Group
Carmelite House
50 Victoria Embankment
London EC4Y 0DZ

An Hachette UK Company
www.hachette.co.uk

www.littlebrown.co.uk

Dedication

To my three children who have been my most profound teachers in this world; to all those professionals and colleagues who have guided, inspired and encouraged me in my work; to my personal teachers, who have accompanied me on my own developmental path over the years, and Uschi May, especially, whose unwavering crystal-clear vision coupled with profound compassion has kept me on my path; to all my close and loyal friends; to my PA Clare Hadland for her loyalty and her support in helping with the formatting of the revised edition and last, but most importantly, to my clients for trusting me with their recovery and healing journeys – I am so immensely grateful and have learnt so much. May it never finish…

C. H.

Contents

PART THREE

ADDENDUM – USEFUL GUIDANCE

Foreword

If you have experienced a traumatic event – or experienced events as traumatic even when others might not see them in that way – you may feel very alone with the consequences. The sudden shift in perspective on yourself – and often on your relationships and the world in which you live – leave you in a landscape for which you may have no preparation. The intensity of emotional responses to apparently innocuous stimuli, the inability to tolerate certain themes, the feeling of loss of control of your body's level of activation, the disturbance of sleep and the intrusive images – all of these can represent a shift from the known to the unknown.

In this book you will find responses to traumatic incidents, disasters and experiences that confront a person with possible loss, injury or death. However, if you have suffered early-life abuse, this book is perhaps not for you. This is very important, as if you are suffering from complex post-traumatic disorders you may feel more alone if you do not find that you are benefiting from what you read here.

Events that are stressful but do not meet criteria for trauma are also discussed. This is helpful for those deeply affected by occurrences in life which are experienced as relatively harmless by others. The reactions you experience are described here in clear language that will help you to make sense of your situation. The author's knowledge and understanding are expressed with empathy and concern. The stories of those who have suffered, written in their own words, and with whom you might identify, may help reduce your confusion as you recognise that your responses are not at all strange, unknown or inexplicable.

The impact your trauma has on partners, friends and families is also covered in detail. For example, if you and they are struggling to understand why you survived a major, life-threatening event but feel angry, preoccupied, vigilant or fearful rather than the gratitude and relief expected of you. You are encouraged to try exercises throughout, which are designed to bring in self-compassion and aware-ness of present safety. There is guidance on discovering how appropriate the body's physiological state is to present cir-cumstances – or how much it has been triggered by internal or external stimuli related to past trauma. When triggers are active the need to use resources, from within the self or from the environment, increases, and you will be given detailed guidance on how to do this.

For those seeking ways to change their thinking about themselves in relation to traumatic experiences, this book provides helpful exercises for clarifying and modifying thinking patterns and coping responses. Those who find themselves stuck in ways of behaving that are not helpful in their everyday life will be able to find out why they are doing this and learn other ways of responding. Compassionate imagery is used creatively to diminish self-criticism. And not all is dependent on verbal skills, non-verbal ways of processing through narrative are given, as are practical ways of coping with intrusive imagery and nightmares.

Within these pages you will find a detailed and comprehensive discussion of anger and its often troublesome manifestations and helpful tips for coping with panic. Mindfulness of your emotional states is encouraged as a way of counteracting numbness and restoring contact with yourself and others. The limitations of using substances such as alcohol for emotion regulation are practically addressed.

The author's deep understanding of emotional responses to trauma ensures the relevance of all the exercises detailed in this book, even when they involve complex practices, ideas and thinking styles. The awareness of what is needed at an emotional level for the human being's healing from adverse experience directs the various approaches with consistency and strength. You will inevitably resonate more with some practices than others, but there is an underlying congruence in the text throughout the book that will ensure that those able to spend time working through it step by step will benefit.

If you are a psychotherapist involved in treating trauma, the impact it has on you is helpfully covered too, with guidance on how to identify the need for changes in your work-life balance. While it is a privilege to be a trauma psychotherapist it can be particularly demanding in organisations which do not value the work, especially if it takes longer than managerial expectations propose for those most severely traumatised. Here you will find sound guidance on steps towards self-care and self-nurturing.

If you are looking for practical ways to overcome the effects of traumatic stresses as they infiltrate many areas of your life this book will help you on your journey of healing, guiding with wisdom and kindness.

Frank Corrigan, MD, FRCPsych

Co-author of *Neurobiology and treatment of traumatic dissociation; toward an embodied self* (Lanius, U.F., Paulsen, S. and Corrigan, F.M. (Eds): New York, 2014: Springer)

Co-author of *The Comprehensive Resource Model: effective therapeutic techniques for the healing of complex trauma* (Schwarz, L., Corrigan, F.M., Hull, A.M., Raju, R. London, 2016: Routledge)

PART ONE

UNDERSTANDING TRAUMATIC STRESS

1

When trauma strikes

In the grip of trauma

Terrible events are hard to deal with. Sudden, traumatic experiences can shatter people's lives and leave a profound mark on the way they feel about themselves and their lives. Traumas hurt! Often they not only cause terrible physical injuries but emotional injury as well, which can be far more painful and take much longer to heal. The effect of trauma can be a lingering feeling that your world has changed utterly. Despite hearing or reading about terrible events all the time via television, radio or newspaper, people often cannot really believe that such things could happen to them. You probably felt relatively safe in your own world and were at least able to cope with problems as they came along. Suddenly, even little things can feel overwhelming and there is a sense that everything is no longer within your control. It is as if your bubble of safety has burst. All the beliefs you held about yourself, others and your world before the trauma seem to have changed and are no longer felt to be true[1]. You are in the 'grip of trauma'.

3

What is a traumatic event?

Although everyone encounters many intensely upsetting and stressful situations during the course of their lives, not all of these would be considered *traumatic* events. *An experience can be described as traumatic when a person's normal ability to cope has been completely overwhelmed by a terrible event*, such as the one described below:

> On Saturday, 5 October 1997, 2 p.m. Francine picked up her friend Jim to go for a walk in the woods. It was a lovely and sunny autumn afternoon. As they were driving towards the woods, Francine noticed that all the colours were so vivid around them and despite the hint of cool air which had already turned some of the leaves brown, she thought that this would be a lovely treat for them. They drove along a clear stretch of country road, when she saw a car coming over the brow of a hill some way ahead of them. She noticed that the other car was starting to swerve and pull further and further out onto their side of the road. She thought that the driver must surely soon notice them and pull back into the other lane. As she started to slow down, she felt her heart pounding. She heard Jim swearing from his passenger seat. The driver of the other car didn't seem to have noticed them. He didn't seem to be aware even that he was on the wrong side of the road, heading straight towards their car. Thoughts started to race through Francine's mind: Was he dead or had he passed out? . . . Should she pull over into the other lane? . . . But what if he had fallen asleep at the wheel and would wake up to pull over onto his side of the road

4

in the last minute? He would drive into them and kill them. She thought that she was too young to die ... she felt angry ... she felt terrified ... she wondered if she should pull over into the ditch on her side of the road. But what if he drove straight into them there? He didn't seem to wake up ... he was coming closer and closer... she didn't want to die ... and then the bang, this awful crushing noise of metal. She heard Jim scream and felt herself pulled up into the air, her head hit the inside of the roof of her car. She felt dazed, confused and couldn't move ... then she looked over to Jim ... he was totally slumped forward, he was moaning, blood trickled from his head. She heard herself asking: 'Jim, Jim, are you alive, can you hear me? Stay with it, stay alive! ... don't leave me!'

Francine

There are many ways in which traumas can occur. An event would be considered traumatic if it relates to **actual or threatened death, serious injury or sexual violation**. This can occur in different ways, such as *a person experiencing or witnessing an event that involved actual or threatened death, serious injury or sexual violation.* A person may also experience trauma if *they learn that an event involving actual or threatened death caused either by violent or accidental means occurred to a close family member or one of their close friends. First-hand repeated experience or extreme exposure to aversive details of a traumatic event is also considered a trauma.* This could, for example, apply to police officers, first responders or the emergency services[2].

5

In the example above, both Francine and Jim experienced an event that would be classified as a trauma. They had a road traffic accident, which could potentially have led to death and/or serious injury. Francine responded with extreme fear and experienced the threatened death of both Jim and herself as there was nothing either of them could do to prevent the accident from happening.

For the purposes of this book, Francine's and Jim's story ends there. In reality, however, the subsequent rescue operation, the nature of the injuries, the experiences in hospital, the reactions of family, friends and professionals, and possibly the resulting legal proceedings could have been further sources of traumatisation. *Sometimes the after-effects of a trauma can even be experienced as more traumatic than the initial traumatic event itself.* A person, for example, may suffer serious injuries which require one or more painful and life-threatening operations frequently carrying with them further stressful complications. In addition, other people's unhelpful responses after a traumatic event can sometimes be sources of further stress – if others cast blame on the person, belittle the impact of the event or if there is an expectation that they should recover from an event far quicker than they are actually able to. Sometimes, comments or reactions of others increase the impact of the initial trauma and lead to increased symptoms of traumatisation. The way in which insurance settlement claims procedures or legal proceedings are currently set up can also significantly impact on a person's recovery process.

Different types of traumatic events

There are many different types of traumatic events happening much of the time all over our world and it is impossible to list them all. Some of these, such as road traffic accidents, are called *traumatic incidents*. Larger-scale events are often called *disasters* and these can be divided into three categories: man-made, natural disasters, and acts of intentional violence, crime or terrorism[3]. Man-made disasters imply that the trauma had occurred because of a human error or an error made by a machine or a system, designed by humans. Some examples of man-made disasters include:

- Transport disasters, by train, coach, underground or subway, ski or mountain gondolas
- Air disasters, such as the Germanwings Airbus crash in the mountains of southern France in March 2015
- Maritime disasters, such as the recent migrant ship disasters in the Mediterranean Sea, for example, off the coast of Libya in April 2015 drowning an estimated 400 people; the Norman Atlantic Ferry that caught fire in the Adriatic Sea in December 2014
- Fires and gas explosions, such as the Kiss nightclub fire in Brazil in January 2013, or the Kaohsiung gas explosions in Taiwan in July 2014

- Severe electric shocks due to electric power lines
- Building or other structural collapses, such as, the partial collapse of Terminal 2E at Charles de Gaulle Airport, Paris in 2004: or the Mecca crane collapse, killing 111 people in September 2015
- Mine or tunnel collapses, such as at the Gleision Colliery in South Wales in 2011; the Soma Mine disaster in Turkey killing 301 people in 2013; the Chuo expressway tunnel collapse in Japan 2012
- Environmental disasters, like the nuclear catastrophes in Chernobyl, Russia in 1986; the Fukushima Daiichi nuclear disaster, Japan in March 2011

Natural disasters constitute another category of trauma, and examples of this include:

- Earthquakes and tsunami, such as the Tōhoku earthquake and tsunami in Japan in March 2011; the Nepal earthquake in April 2015
- Floods, such as those in parts of the UK in 2007; or the North Indian floods in June 2013, which killed more than 5,000 people

- Land- or mudslides, such as in northwest China in October 2015
- Hurricanes, like Hurricane Katrina, New Orleans in August 2005, or cyclones, such as Cyclone Nargis, Bangladesh in May 2008 that caused about 138,000 deaths
- Forest fires, such as the massive California wildfires in the USA, in 2007, 2008 and 2016; or the May 2016 massive wildfires in Fort McMurray, Alberta, Canada that resulted in the evacuation/relocation of thousands and took a month to get under control; or those in southern Europe in summer 2016
- Volcano eruptions, avalanches, such as eruption of the Calbuco Volcano in Chile in June 2015; or the avalanches on Mount Everest in April 2015 or in the French Alps on the Écrin massif in September 2015
- Epidemics or pandemics, such as Ebola, Marburg or Reston Virus; Swine Flu; Mad Cow disease; Avian flu and others

The third category of trauma refers to acts of intentional violence, crime, terrorism, or war, of which several examples are:

- Terrorist Acts, such as 9/11 in New York and Washington, DC in 2001; London bombings on 7/7/2005; Paris Attacks on 13/11/2015; suicide bombings such as at the Manchester Arena after a concert on 22/05/2017 and terrorist insurgency around the world
- Acts of domestic violence, such as physical assault, sexual violation, threat of abuse
- Stabbings and arson attacks
- Hold-ups and robberies
- Shootings and mass shootings, such as the 2011 shooting on the island of Utoya, Norway, killing sixty-eight campers, or other recent ones in America, Europe and other parts of the world
- Rape, sexual abuse, incest, organised child abuse
- Serial infidelity, intentional deception and unprotected sex, exposing partners to risk of life-threatening sexually transmitted diseases[4, 5]
- Abduction, human trafficking
- Acts of inhumanity, such as torture, pillage, mass executions
- Hostage-takings, solitary confinement
- Acts defying human rights, such as those conducted by oppressive regimes or dictatorships

- Forceful displacement or mass migration in response to political violence, human rights violation or war, such as those part of Europe's migration crisis in 2015
- Wars and military conflicts, such as in some Middle Eastern, Asian and African countries

Man-made disasters and the traumas caused by acts of intentional violence, crime, violation of human rights, terrorism or war are usually even harder to adjust to and come to terms with than natural disasters.

Other life events that can be considered as trauma

Some life events, although not outside the range of typical human experience, confront people with the threat of physical injury or death such that they can be considered as trauma. Such events might include miscarriage; a life-threatening illness, for example, myocardial infarction (MI)[6], cardiac arrest, cancer, stroke, HIV; medical accidents or surgical complications; domestic accidents, house fires or the accidental or violent death of close others.

Other life events can cause extreme stress to people but would not be classified as trauma. This would include job loss and unemployment, redundancy, insolvency, the end of a long-term relationship or divorce and other experiences that cause significant unease, distress and discomfort but do not involve threatened or actual serious injury, death or sexual violation. These events might cause people to suffer from what is termed Adjustment Disorder, which is part of the category known as Trauma- and Stressor-related Disorders[2] and is described in more detail in Chapter 3.

Your experience of trauma

Many people live through very upsetting life events or witness them happening to others. Perhaps you have, too. The following checklist[7] will help you to recognise which traumas you have experienced and how they have affected you.

Please read every item below and check the boxes which apply to you.

> *You experienced this – and it still feels awful for you or causes you upset or disturbance.*

> > *You observed it happen to close others or learned about it happen to close others – and it still makes you feel awful or upset.*

> > > *You experienced this – but it does not feel disturbing for you now.*

A ☐☐☐   a fire, an accident or an explosion. At home or in a car or a plane, on a boat or at a factory or farm, an office or place of work, or other

B ☐☐☐   some kind of natural disaster, like a flood, earthquake, storm, hurricane or avalanche

C ☐☐☐ an attack during which you were hit, kicked, beaten, stabbed, held at gunpoint or hurt in some other (non–sexual) way by someone who was known to you

D ☐☐☐ as above, but an attack by someone you did not know

E ☐☐☐ being in a war or some other combat situation – or a terrorist attack, or other disturbance such as a riot

F ☐☐☐ being taken hostage, part of human trafficking or being in prison, or being a prisoner of war

G ☐☐☐ experiencing torture, either physical or psychological, while in someone else's control

H ☐☐☐ some kind of serious, life-threatening illness

I ☐☐☐ when you were over 16, being physically or psychologically forced, persuaded or tricked into some kind of sexual action, against your will

J ☐☐☐ as above, but when you were under 16

K ☐☐☐ the traumatic death of another person

L ☐☐☐ experiencing displacement or migration from your home or country due to threats of death, actual death/s of family members or close friends, serious injury or sexual violation

M ☐☐☐ some other experience, not covered by the categories above (briefly describe the experience)

And now describe which experience bothers you most. If you checked any of the events, either in the left or the middle columns, write their code letters in the box below, in order of seriousness (worst first)

Pay specific attention to those events that still bother you and refer back to them as you work through the rest of the book.

Loosening the grip of trauma

To overcome the effects of trauma it is necessary to examine the experience or events that still affect you and work to change the distressing responses produced since the event. To cope with what has happened you need to understand your reactions and how the experience affected you. This will help you to face up to memories, thoughts and feelings which may have been deeply buried in response to the trauma and may now be hindering you from getting on with your life.

Here is how Harry felt after surviving a serious house fire at his home:

After I had survived the actual trauma, I thought it was all over — but it was then when it all really began. For many months I was unable to get the images from the fire out of my mind. It was as if every day parts of the trauma were happening again. I wanted to forget it, to put it behind me, to move on with my life, but it was as if the trauma wouldn't let me. Worse still, not only were my days filled with terrifying reminders of what had happened to me, but even when I tried to get some rest from it through sleep at night it wouldn't leave me. I was haunted by repeated, recurring nightmares which seemed so real that I often woke up screaming and crying, convinced it was happening all over again. I experienced terrifying body sensations, such as feeling the heat from the fire, the smell of the burning, choking and being unable to breathe. Even though it was all over, I felt as if I was still in it. Whatever I did, it felt at the time that I just couldn't move forward but was totally trapped by the trauma. It all felt so real that I was convinced that I was going mad.

Harry

Many people have the same, or very similar reactions and fears as Harry. People's responses after a trauma are often strong and overwhelming. It can feel very hard for people to get the trauma out of their head and they may ruminate or dwell on different aspects of their experience over and over again. It might feel as if the traumatic event has taken over and this can be so distressing that it is quite common for people to feel that 'they are going mad' or 'losing complete control over their life'. Sometimes these thoughts and the overwhelming nature of the trauma can be so unbearable that people start isolating themselves from others more and more. They may feel very alone with their distress. Such reactions are common and understandable responses to trauma. *You may be relieved to hear that you are NOT alone in experiencing these feelings.* What's more, if you are experiencing such reactions you *can* be helped to heal and recover from your trauma.

Working through a trauma can take many forms. Some people are able to do this by themselves, but many may benefit much more from specialist trauma therapy. There are no hard and fast rules. What works best for one person may not work for another. The one factor that is common to all recovery from trauma is that, as you start to regain control, the trauma will gradually loosen its grip and it will start to feel easier for you to cope with life again.

Harry sought out specialist trauma therapy and describes here his process of recovery.

At the beginning of the process:

> It was as if the trauma had made me fall into a very deep, waterless well. It felt very dark and lonely while I was down there and it took me a long time before I developed the courage to start climbing up its sides to get out of it. When I first started the climb I felt that I had no knowledge of what was waiting for me at the top. The higher I was able to climb, the more I feared that something at the top might make me fall down to the bottom again. It was as if I had lost all trust in my ability to cope with what was out there for me in the world. Sometimes, this fear even made me want to climb back towards the bottom of the well again. This was because I knew that if it came to another fall it would not be quite so deep to go down. At the same time, I knew that I had to continue ascending, because the thought of staying at the bottom of this well and continuing my life in the grip of the trauma, as it had been, was unbearable.

As Harry progressed in his recovery, the images started to change:

> It felt as if I was now a fair way up from the bottom of this well. I had come to a kind of resting place, from where, for

the first time since the trauma, I could gather some strength again. From here I could start to see the sky above me and there were even days when I saw some brightness and could feel the pleasant warmth from the rays of the sun. I knew that this gave me the strength to continue with the climb out of this well. I still didn't really know what was waiting for me out there once I reached the top of this well. I imagined that it might be like a huge roundabout with several roads radiating from it. At this stage I was unsure which one of these would be the 'right one' for me to take.

Still further on in his process of recovery, Harry described:

I am now sitting on the outside edge of the well and the choice of roads available for me outside the well are only three. It does not feel as overwhelming as I thought it would be. I am now starting to feel confident enough to explore and travel along one of these roads. Before doing this, however, I had decided to cover up the well. I felt I had come out of it and I now felt strong enough to live outside the well. I knew I was travelling along a totally different road compared to the one I had travelled on before the trauma. This was because the trauma had changed me, but this was not a negative change. In many ways, it felt better. I found that I had become a much more understanding and tolerant person. I had stopped taking life for granted, my life seemed much more meaningful and of value to me now. I realised that although I would never have wished to have experienced this trauma, the process of recovering from it helped me understand myself much better and somehow made me feel internally stronger. I have become more aware of how precious life really is and I have a better sense now about the things that really matter to me in life. I will never forget the trauma, but it no longer hurts me to think about it nor does it occupy my daily life. Sometimes, I even feel that, however awful it was at the time, in the end it helped me to find a different and better meaning for my life.

Harry recovered from his trauma. The process of achieving this took him over a year from the date of the initial trauma. In his therapy Harry used many of the tools, strategies and resources outlined in this book. Harry was one of our clients, as were most of the other people, who gave permission to use their examples in this book. Their names and some specific details are changed to safeguard their confidentiality.

The aim of this book

This book is written for people (and those close to them or caring for them, including professional therapists) who feel they are in the grip of a trauma. You might be at different stages in the process of climbing out of this '*deep, waterless well*', as Harry described it. You might be at the stage where you still feel very much stuck at the bottom, where it feels dark, lonely, isolated and utterly overwhelming. Or you might have started your process of recovery and are already climbing up inside this well.

You might not even be part of this process at all, but instead are having to witness how a relative or somebody you care for is struggling to find their way out of the well. You may be able to offer a helping hand or you may feel quite powerless. You may be a therapist or a medical professional who wants to understand more about working with trauma as this is an area new to you. In this case Chapter 18 in the Addendum – Useful guidance (see page 486) might be of particular relevance to you.

Whatever your stage or your role along the path to recovery, Harry's example illustrates that recovery from trauma takes time and can be a long and uncomfortable process, during which time it can often feel that there is more darkness than light.

This book is intended as a guide to help you understand the range of reactions, thoughts and feelings that you may be experiencing. It provides you with practical advice, encouragement and strategies to help you find the confidence and courage to start or continue the challenging climb upwards towards recovery and healing. The book is written for people who have experienced, witnessed or learned about a particular catastrophic event or several events, such as a car accident or a shipping disaster, a sexual assault, a natural disaster, an act of violence, crime or terrorism, or other singular experiences of trauma. It is written for people who have been affected by trauma and can remember how their life before the trauma felt different and safer. It might also help people who have experienced other stressful life events that may not be classified as trauma but had an equally devastating effect on them. This book is likely to be of limited use for people who have suffered long-standing, repeated or complex trauma, especially if this occurred early in their life, such as childhood abuse, or enduring domestic violence. People suffering from early developmental trauma often cannot remember ever having felt safe or different and if this applies to you, you do require more specialist resources and help[8], which cannot be covered in this book. This book will not be meeting your needs sufficiently, although some parts of it could still be helpful. People who suffer from significant levels of dissociation or ongoing trauma, would benefit from working to keep safe and finding ways of leaving the traumatising situation first, before attempting to work through their experiences. This book is likely to be less useful and if this applies to you, you are advised to seek therapeutic help to support you with this.

This book is written to give helpful encouragement and useful guidance to people who suffer from trauma and other stress-related problems. It may also be useful to people who have already been diagnosed with Post-traumatic Stress Disorder (PTSD) and who may be waiting to receive therapy. It could be helpful as an adjunct to current therapy, as well as enabling those who have been affected by trauma to find out whether they might benefit from seeking professional help.

This book has grown out of the author's more than twenty-five years' experience in the field of trauma psychology. The book is based on direct clinical practice with trauma clients, supervision of other trauma professionals and consultation to organisations in relation to critical incidents. Most of the testimonials are based on real clients' experiences (whose identity has been kept confidential by altering identifying factors). Although underpinned by scientific evidence and anchored in evidence-based practice[9,10], such as Trauma-Focussed CBT (TF-CBT) and Eye Movement Desensitisation and Reprocessing (EMDR), this book moves beyond and takes into account our ever growing understanding of the neurobiology of trauma and its effect on body, mind and spirit. It incorporates third-wave CBT approaches[11, 12, 13], such as mindfulness or other body-oriented techniques and demonstrates, with practical advice and tested exercises, how to find effective ways of coping with, and finally overcoming, traumatic stress. *This book is not intended as a replacement for therapy, and may even encourage you to seek out some specialist help* (see Chapter 17 in the Addendum – Useful guidance, where seeking professional help is discussed in further detail). At the end of the book you will find some useful addresses or organisations, should you wish to contact a therapist.

How to use this book

Tips for Easy Reading

Reading a book is not the easiest task while you are in the midst of dealing with your trauma. Your levels of concentration may be poor and you may find it hard to stick with the book for very long. As this book contains a lot of information, here are some tips on how to get the most out of it:

- Don't read the book from beginning to end if that is difficult for you. Skim and browse through the book to get to know its format and content. You might find that dipping in and reading little chunks at a time is easier for you. Every person is different, and it is important that you find your own way of making the book useful to you.
- Then, if you feel up to it, read some of those passages that particularly caught your attention. Some might seem more relevant to your situation than others. Put the book down somewhere in the house where you can pick it up easily during the day to read a little bit.
- At the end of each chapter there is a checkout summary of the most important points which might help orient you to what each chapter means.
- Some people find it helpful to mark or write in their books. Maybe mark those sections that are particularly relevant or helpful to you. Have the book at your side while you try out some of the practical exercises that are described.
- Try buying yourself little index cards and write down points from the book that might be useful or meaningful to you on each card. Then carry

the cards around with you so that you can refer to them whenever you want to.

- You might have specific needs, due to injuries, physical disabilities or pain. You are advised to tailor the exercises in this book and your reading pace to suit your particular needs. Please alter and adjust these accordingly, always bearing in mind what feels comfortable and safe to you.

- You might find that parts of the book that remind you of your own experiences are rather distressing. If you feel upset, try not to worry about this, because it is quite normal and can even be part of the healing process. You might find it helps to write down your feelings or talk to a safe person close to you about them. *But if your feelings are overwhelmingly strong, please have a look at the **Cautions** section below.*

- If reading seems very daunting because you have never been a good reader, or you are in the early stages of your recovery, you could ask a safe person close to you to read the book to you. Sometimes, it can also be very helpful to work together with a close and trusted person when you are doing the exercises from the book.

- Do not read the book last thing at night or in bed. That time should be reserved for relaxation and winding down and is not the right time to read or think about traumatic events.

Cautions

If you experience any of the following responses, please put the book aside and try to do something completely different to distract yourself:

- Feeling that you are losing touch with reality, for example, sudden extreme and overwhelming memories of the traumatic event, flashbacks, dissociation or hallucinations.
- Very strong anxiety reactions, such as hyperventilation or panic attacks, an irregular heartbeat. But do remember, some anxiety is normal!
- Very strong physical reactions, such as trembling, feelings of extreme coldness or very hot flushes.
- Suicidal feelings.
- Feeling you want to harm yourself or others around you.
- Feelings of uncontrollable anger or rage.
- Fainting or feeling very dizzy.

If you do experience any of these responses while you are reading the book, and they don't seem to subside fairly easily after you have stopped reading, you should get in touch with your medical practitioner or therapist before continuing with it. Chapter 17 in the Addendum – Useful guidance can help you with finding out if you might need a therapist. The chapters in Part Two provide you with many tips on control strategies which you might find helpful to look at.

Summary checkpoints:

- Not all terrible events are classified as a trauma.
- An event is considered a trauma if it relates to actual or threatened death, serious injury or sexual violation, that you experienced, witnessed or learned of occurring to a person close to you.
- There are many different types of traumatic events and they can be thought of as falling into three categories:
  - Man-made disasters or accidents
  - Natural disasters
  - Acts of intentional violence, crime, terrorism or war
- Life-threatening illness, miscarriage, birth complications, and other similar are also traumas.
- Trauma caused by acts of intentional violence, crime, violation of human rights, terrorism or war are usually the hardest to come to terms with.
- Some events, such as ending of a relationship, job loss, insolvency or similar can cause extreme stress but would not be classified as a trauma.
- This book is written for people who have experienced, witnessed or learned about a catastrophic event or other singular traumas. It might also help people who have had other stressful life events that may not be classified as trauma but had an equally devastating effect.

- It is written for those who can remember life before the trauma feeling very differently and safe.
- This book might also benefit those caring for people who have experienced trauma, therapists, or health or medical care professionals who want to understand more about trauma and how to sustain working healthily in this field.
- If you have experienced multiple, complex or developmental trauma and cannot remember a time in your life when it ever felt safe, you will need more specialist help and resources to heal from your trauma and this book is likely to be of limited use.

2

Understanding your reactions

Common reactions after trauma

The focus of this book, and of this chapter in particular, is on *your reactions* to a traumatic life event – the disturbing and frequently overwhelming feelings and symptoms that occur in the aftermath of a terrible event.

Understanding your reactions will help to reduce your sense of isolation, of being alone with your experience. You are not alone! Current research[1] suggests that over the course of a lifetime, about 89.7 per cent of Americans experience at least one traumatic event. The majority of people experienced two or more traumas.

It is very common for most people to have some reactions in response to a traumatic experience. These can range from acute, transient reactions to severe, long-lasting symptoms. Frequently these initial reactions reduce and disappear a short while after the trauma, but for a significant number of people they can lead to more long-term consequences. It is estimated that about 9.7 per cent of women and 3.6 per cent of men in the general population exposed to a traumatic event develop over the course of their lifetime reactions that can be classified as Post-Traumatic Stress Disorder[2] or PTSD for short (A more detailed explanation of this is provided in Chapter 17 – 'Seeking professional help'on page 465). For direct victims of disasters the prevalence of PTSD is estimated to be between 30-40 per cent[3]. The likelihood of developing PTSD increases with the more traumatic events a person has been exposed to. These percentages are based on people who have attended treatment for PTSD. It could be that the percentage of PTSD is higher because people may have symptoms for many years before seeking treatment or may never seek help at all. People who have experienced intentional trauma rather than accidental trauma are more at risk of developing PTSD. The risk of developing PTSD is much higher in certain groups of people, for example rape and assault victims, combat veterans, emergency, police and rescue personnel, first responders to community disasters, journalists and photographers reporting from war[4], disaster or major conflict areas. The risk is also higher if, in addition to a recent life event, you had already experienced abuse or other trauma during your formative years of life. If the latter is the case for you it is strongly advised that you seek specialist professional help and read books on Developmental Trauma and Complex PTSD, as this book is likely to be of limited help.

PTSD is not the only response to trauma, and a range of other trauma- or stress-related conditions have been identified that can arise. These are explored in more detail in

Chapter 17 in the Addendum – Useful guidance, which explains how to seek professional help in order for your trauma-related problems to be diagnosed and treated if necessary.

When you are traumatised by a life event, you can experience a wide range of reactions which might be very disruptive to your everyday life. You may not know that they are related to the trauma you experienced, but may have noticed difficulties in your ability to cope and function and may have even wondered whether you are losing your mind.

Trauma affects body, mind, your sense of self and personality. Reactions following trauma can be divided into four main symptom groups[5]:

1 Re-experiencing the event (Intrusive reactions)

A feeling that you are experiencing the traumatic event or aspects of the event all over again. This can be through intrusive memories, thoughts and perceptions, including images, emotions and sensations, intruding into your waking or sleeping life.

2 Avoidance reactions

You make frantic efforts to avoid anything that could remind you of the trauma, or cause you to think or talk about it in any way. You may avoid distressing memories, thoughts or feelings as well as reminders, such as people, places, situations, activities, conversations or objects closely associated with the traumatic event.

3 Negative changes in mood and thought patterns

You hold persistent negative beliefs about yourself, others or the world and blame yourself or others in relation to the trauma. You can't remember important aspects of the trauma, shut down your feelings about other people and things you normally care about and keep to yourself. You may feel unusually withdrawn and emotionally numb. You may feel overtaken by strong negative emotions and find it difficult to experience more positive emotions.

4 Arousal reactions

You feel persistently aroused in a nervous, agitated sense, anxious, tense, unable to settle or concentrate, over-reacting very sharply to small things, behave recklessly or self-destructively, and, especially, have trouble sleeping.

While it is likely that many of these responses will be present immediately following a traumatic incident, for some people reactions don't occur until much later, sometimes even several weeks, months or even years. They may experience some reactions immediately but the the full range of their trauma reactions may not occur until much later. This is called delayed expression. For most people reactions follow immediately or shortly after the trauma and they usually subside during the following few weeks. If your reactions don't subside, but instead recur over and over again, you may begin to despair that you will never be like your old self again. You may feel like a *'walking alarm system'*, responding to things or events that previously had felt perfectly safe. Your thought patterns, your attitude towards yourself begins to shift as well – you might begin to believe that you have been permanently changed or damaged. You tell yourself that you *should* be coping more efficiently. You might be bothered by feelings of shame or guilt or extreme grief.

People close to you may be expecting you to get back to normal fairly quickly, and may pressure you with statements like: 'You've changed!' or 'You're not the person you were before!' While they may mean well, these statements serve to underscore your sense of feeling different and helpless. You may react by being snappy and irritable, very jumpy and easily startled (even by the smallest unexpected noises) or secretive and closed off. Or you might just keep it all to yourself, refusing to talk things over and avoiding friends or social gatherings.

The important thing to remember is that the very fact that these are unusual responses for you and an extreme change from your earlier personality or style of being suggests that they are indications of a *traumatic stress reaction*. Even if you are not experiencing all the symptoms mentioned here, you will recognise some and you may find that your own responses 'cluster' in certain areas.

The intensity of your symptoms, the severity of interference to your normal functioning and the duration of your reactions will help you and your medical practitioner determine if specialist professional treatment is needed.

It is important that you begin to understand what is happening to you, and that you resolve to get whatever help is needed to assist you in becoming yourself again.

Understanding your symptoms

It is useful to try to understand how your body responds to extreme stress. Recognising that your symptoms are continuing reactions to the overpowering stress you have experienced, and therefore unavoidable and even necessary given the circumstances, is the first step in containing them and feeling more in control.

Stress was defined by Hans Selye in 1946[6] as a demand on the human system – mental, physical or emotional – whereby overwhelming traumatic stress is perceived as an extreme demand, a threat to existence, to which the body responds by automatically mobilising *all* its coping mechanisms to provide the necessary energy for survival. What actually happens is that massive amounts of the hormone adrenaline and other internal chemicals are produced by the body in response to perceived 'danger' signals from specific parts of your brain. These are circulated to the muscles, enabling the body to move more quickly, be stronger and more tolerant to pain. The breathing changes, the muscles are tense in anticipation of action and all the physical reactions are swift.

These neurochemical processes, which humans share with animals, are aimed at activating the *'fight'* or *'flight'* responses enabling immediate survival of the life-threatening situation. If either *'fight'* or *'flight'* are not or only partially possible in a dangerous situation, more complicated neurochemical processes set in and the body might go into a *'freeze'*, *'flop'* or *'(be-)friend'* (also referred to as *'fawn'*[7]) response. 'Freeze' is a survival reaction during which the body is temporarily immobilised or numbed, similar to that of a mouse in response to an imminent attack from a cat. A *'flop'* response results in total bodily collapse, which might involve blacking out or loss of consciousness, loss of control over bodily functions, such as urinating or total disorientation. A 'be-friend' or 'fawn' response arises when survival is dependent on placating the aggressor, such as in hostage situations, childhood abuse, sexual trauma, ritual abuse, torture, domestic abuse and many others. The latter creates a condition which is better known as Stockholm Syndrome, in which a trauma survivor is torn between both positive feelings, such as empathy, concern or love, as well as negative feelings, such as anger, hate or disgust towards the abuser. The 'freeze', 'flop' or 'be-friend' or 'fawn' are reactions to very severe and often prolonged traumatic situations and frequently linked to childhood trauma or trauma related to acts of extreme violence, crime or terrorism.

If you have experienced trauma that activated these more complex survival responses, you are advised to seek specialist therapeutic help to enable you to recover from this. It would not be advisable for you to engage in any form of re-living of the trauma until your therapist has helped you to build strategies and resources that make it safe for you to do so. Your therapist could advise as to whether some of the exercises in this book are suitable given the nature of your specific trauma. You may also require more long-term therapy, tailored to developmental or complex trauma, which a suitably trained trauma therapist could assess. Chapter 17 in the Addendum – Useful guidance explains how to seek professional help. You are strongly advised to seek out your GP for a specialist referral or to make your own enquiries to find a private trauma therapist specialising in working with Complex trauma and PTSD.

Post-Traumatic Stress Reactions of high arousal have sometimes been described as 'the system getting stuck on red alert' – the emergency response fails to shut off and the body is prone to surges of adrenaline, which send messages to the brain to the effect that everything in the environment continues to be dangerous and potentially threatening – just as the trauma was. In other words, traumatised individuals 'overreact' to everything. The smallest reminder of something remotely associated with the event (a slight sound, a flash of colour, a smell) can set off a dramatic response. For example, a car backfires or there is a loud 'bang' in the street, etc., and you find yourself diving to the floor without thinking, as if your body has been 'programmed' to expect danger and to react to the slightest diversion from the ordinary as if it were life-threatening. Such behaviour could also be triggered by memory flashbacks to the actual traumatic event, or the experience of a 'replay' of all or part of the trauma before your eyes. This happens because some parts of the brain don't function normally due to the high levels of stress hormones, like adrenaline, being released. For example, the hippocampus, which processes memories, stops working properly, leading to flashbacks and nightmares of the unprocessed memories of a trauma.

What seems so real to the post-trauma sufferer may not be at all apparent to companions or onlookers. It might feel disconcerting, and at times embarrassing to you, when these dramatic over-reactions occur in public or even in front of the family. Diving under a table in a restaurant in response to a dish being dropped and smashing behind you is hard to explain, even to close friends. As a result, you may become very anxious about being in public, or in social gatherings where you feel 'exposed'. You may begin to avoid such situations or to feel panicky if they are unavoidable. Your ability to predict how you will react decreases and your confidence in your coping ability suffers as a result.

In your attempts to avoid anything that would remind you of your trauma, you might have stopped listening to the television news, reading newspapers, going to familiar places or, in particular, you might have stopped talking about how you feel. Even though research has shown that working through the trauma story and acknowledging thoughts and feelings can be the most helpful healing strategy, many trauma sufferers never admit to anyone how their experience has affected them. Instead they avoid facing what they have experienced by shutting down emotionally and constructing barriers around their feelings.

Detaching yourself from your feelings and from other people may be an unconscious, even automatic emotional response. It may seem to you as if there is no hope for the future, that things will never be different, so you begin to 'go through the motions' of existing in the present, without really feeling connected or engaged in it.

It should gradually be becoming clear that the symptoms of post-traumatic stress reactions can interact with each other in a kind of 'vicious circle' of responses which keep the cycle going.

Understanding specific reactions

It is unlikely (but not impossible) that you will have experienced *all* of the reactions discussed, so it might be helpful to pay particular attention to the ones that are the worst for you, and which bother you the most frequently.

1. *Re-experiencing the event (intrusive reactions)*

FLASHBACKS AND DISSOCIATIVE RESPONSES

Flashbacks are *unwanted memories* that are experienced *as if the event or parts of it were happening all over again.* They feel extremely real and can occur during the day, but also as dreams or nightmares during sleep. Whether waking or sleeping, flashbacks can be extremely disturbing to a person (and often to the family) because all or some of the physical sensations that were present during the original trauma are usually experienced again. They can make you feel as if you are losing control or your mind is being 'taken over' by past events. For seconds, minutes or sometimes much longer you may feel that you are again seeing, feeling, smelling, hearing, sensing and reacting to the event or specific aspects of it. Fear, horror, helplessness or other emotions associated with your trauma can also be experienced again.

Flashbacks are created because the brain links particular sensations (such as smells, sounds, feelings, bodily sensations, tastes, colours) present at the time of a trauma with danger. These are stored in specific memory systems and after the trauma become triggers, causing the flashbacks.

For example, Harry (introduced in Chapter 1) who survived the housefire would get triggered into strong flashbacks by smells of bonfires or barbecues. Although they presented no real danger to him, his brain associated those smells with his trauma in the past and automatically triggered neurochemical processes that made him feel under threat. It felt as if the situation of the housefire was happening all over again. Flashbacks and intrusive memories always follow from triggers but often these are not easy to recognise and people are unaware of their triggers. This is why these reactions can make you feel so out of control. Traumas can also lead to bodily triggers of unwanted memories or flashbacks. This can happen, for example, in trauma that occurred from behind or from a side, involved high impact or led to unconsciousness.

Moreover, flashbacks can make you feel very disoriented. At times Harry's flashbacks were so strong and felt so real that he lost connection to the 'here-and-now'. For Harry this feeling could last several minutes and sometimes as long as half an hour. He would lose track of time and feel very disoriented when he was able to re-connect to the here-and-now. When flashbacks are this strong and people loose connection to the 'here-and-now' this is an indication of a strong dissociative response. Flashbacks that are this strong are called *dissociative* flashbacks.

Commonly, dissociative flashbacks occur when people suffer from dissociation as a result of very severe and complex trauma, for example, child sexual abuse or torture. They are also linked to traumas that involved a loss of consciousness or overwhelming, incapacitating fear during which the 'freeze' or 'flop' survival reactions occurred because 'fleeing' wasn't possible at the time. In Harry's case a wooden beam had collapsed trapping him underneath, making it impossible for him to escape from the fire. He went into a 'freeze' response, when he realised that he could not escape, and by the time he was rescued he had lost consciousness.

People can experience a variety of dissociative responses and these are explained in more detail in the section on 'Dissociation' (page 63).

INTRUSIVE RECOLLECTIONS

While not every vivid memory is experienced as a flashback, most people will have trouble switching off their recollection of a traumatic event. Very simple things in daily life (even breathing heavily after hurrying or being pushed in a crowd) can become triggers that set off a whole chain of traumatic associations in an instant. This can often happen without you even being aware of the initial connection or trigger at the beginning of the chain. Be assured these are not signs that you are losing your mind! It shows that the mind is struggling to use its cognitive processes to make sense of what has happened to the world you knew *before* the trauma. Your sense of how the world *should be* has been violated. It feels as if the 'bubble of safety' that surrounded you before the trauma, and made it possible for you to get through the day, has now burst. Therefore, the world no longer feels safe and secure.

MARKED EMOTIONAL DISTRESS AND UNCOMFORTABLE BODILY RESPONSES

Another common reaction is marked emotional distress and uncomfortable bodily responses in response to reminders that symbolise or resemble aspects of the trauma. You may feel overtaken by strong negative emotional reactions, such as sadness, guilt, shame, disgust, anger, rage or others each time something makes you think about the trauma. You may also experience sudden uncomfortable bodily responses, such as heart palpitations, shortness of breath, sweating or shivering, swelling of glands, stomach aches or sickness or others. These may feel totally unpredictable and out of your control and can be very disturbing. Although they also are caused by reminders of the trauma, these can be so subtle that often you might not be aware of the triggers. You may find it hard to calm your emotions down or soothe your bodily discomfort and for some people these reactions can linger for considerable periods of time. Although very uncomfortable, these responses are not dangerous or harmful to you, but a sign that the memories of the trauma are still unprocessed by your mind, which hasn't been able to integrate what happened yet.

I had been the victim of an armed robbery. In order not to be harmed I handed the money over to the robber. For weeks after the trauma I could not forget what had happened. I could not stop myself from thinking about parts of the event, which seemed to pop into my mind at the most unexpected times. I could still remember every little thing in detail. It was like a film being replayed over and over again. I also found myself feeling all the reactions that I had had during this event and sometimes it felt as if it were happening all over again. When I thought about the trauma I re-experienced the

*shivering that I had felt, the horror and helplessness and I even
felt the anger that I had felt when the robber ran away after
having kicked an innocent customer to the ground. All this
was extremely distressing to me. It felt so out of control, as I
could never predict when these reactions would overtake me
again and how long they would linger with me.*

Ray

2. Avoidance Reactions

There are two types of avoidance reactions that people commonly experience after trauma. The first involves avoiding
the distressing memories, thoughts or feelings connected
with the trauma. The second involves avoiding or literally
keeping out of the way of *any* person, place or thing that
might be a reminder (even very remotely) of the trauma.
In particular, avoiding things that have already served as
reminders or 'triggers' and caused great anxiety or other
overwhelming feelings, such as rage, sadness, guilt or disabling grief, or that have set off a flashback.

This may also include you avoiding talking to others
about aspects of the trauma or even trying to stop yourself
from thinking about it. Sometimes people think that they
can talk to others about their traumatic experiences, but
when examined more closely it emerges that they have
found a way of talking about the trauma by not really connecting to it, which also is a form of avoidance behaviour.

Avoidance behaviour makes your world get narrower
and narrower. Frequently, you don't want to 'lose face' by

admitting that you are avoiding anything, so you make up excuses or make elaborate arrangements to avoid encountering the site of the trauma – the building, place, person or activity (such as driving after a road traffic accident). Frequently people start to avoid people close to them, such as family or friends in order not to have to talk about it or be reminded of the trauma.

For example, Ray not only felt unable to return to his work at a bank after the armed robbery, but also avoided walking past other banks or building societies, watching any news on TV or anything involving any form of violence, because this triggered uncomfortable memories, thoughts, feelings and sensations of his trauma and made him feel that it might happen all over again. Fortunately, Ray's employer sought the therapeutic help of a specialist trauma service and Ray as well as the other employees affected by the bank robbery were gradually able to resume work and overcome the effects of their trauma.

3. *Negative Changes in Cognition and Mood*

Trauma can have a considerable impact on people's belief systems, their thought processes, their mood and feeling states. This section outlines some of the changes that can be experienced as a result of trauma.

GAPS IN MEMORY ABOUT THE TRAUMA

You may struggle to recall important parts of your traumatic experience even though you were not unconscious nor under the influence of alcohol or drugs at the time. You might be aware of gaps in your memory but even with considerable effort can't recall them. You might find this disturbing because your experience feels fragmented and you know that bits of information are missing. This can feel especially disconcerting if previously your memory for events was very good. These gaps in memory happen when the traumatic event was so overwhelming that your brain at the time had to store parts of your experience in memory systems away from day-to-day conscious recall. At the time of the trauma this might have enhanced your ability to survive. Frequently, these parts of memory are not lost altogether and can be regained when you are ready to work through your trauma. You may require a course of specialist trauma therapy to help you with this. Chapter 17 in the Addendum on Useful guidance advises how to seek professional help.

PERVASIVE NEGATIVE BELIEFS OR EXPECTATIONS

Your traumatic experiences may have been so horrific that they totally changed your outlook on life. Most people will be aware from the media that bad things happen all the time somewhere in the world. Yet, when such things have happened to you, you can no longer distance yourself and the effect can be profound. You may have lost trust in yourself, others or the world around you. You may have lost your sense of safety and your belief system and expectations about yourself or others may have changed accordingly. You may now believe that 'the world is completely dangerous' or that 'nowhere is safe' or that 'nobody can be trusted'. Equally you may experience exaggerated negative thoughts about yourself. For example, you may believe that you 'are bad' or that you 'are permanently damaged'. Your thoughts may feel very strong, pervasive and totally true at the moment. Your belief system has become very bleak and focuses only on the worst. These strong, exaggerated thoughts are part of a survival reaction that hasn't yet been able to switch off. It is trying to prepare you in case such trauma should recur, even if now things may actually be safe in your life. Sometimes people have had negative lives before more recent trauma and when this is the case the trauma might further confirm and strengthen your already negative beliefs and expectations about yourself and the world.

BLAME OR DISTORTED BELIEF SYSTEMS ABOUT THE CAUSE OR CONSEQUENCE OF THE TRAUMA

It is very common for people to blame themselves for all or parts of the traumatic incident. They might think that if only they had done things differently on the day of the trauma, it might never have happened. Often they take personal responsibility for the terrible outcomes, thinking that they 'should have known' and thus could have made their decisions differently before or during the trauma. You may ruminate about the trauma and feel that somehow you or others should have done more or reacted differently for there to have been a different outcome. You may blame yourself for the way in which you responded or about things that happened in the way they did. These are very common beliefs and entirely understandable. It might help you to realise that your survival system took control and enabled you to survive under the emergency conditions that existed at the time. Even though the consequences may feel terrible to you now, your survival system did the very best it could for you at the time under those specific circumstances. The distorted beliefs that you may now be holding about yourself or others involved are an indication that your mind is still struggling to come to terms with the experiences you have been through and the changes that have arisen as a consequence.

PERSISTENT NEGATIVE EMOTIONS

Trauma can have a big impact on your emotional state. The feelings of happiness and contentment you may have experienced prior to your trauma may have given way to persistent states of low mood, sadness, fear, horror, anger, guilt or shame. These emotional states feel often difficult to control and people describe that they find it hard to 'switch out of it'. These emotional states are now described in more detail:

LOW MOOD AND SADNESS

You may experience times during which you feel over-whelmingly sad. You might feel very gloomy, but may be unable to cry and it can feel as if the sadness is stuck and won't shift. This is quite a common reaction after trauma and for some people these feelings can linger for many hours a day.

FEAR AND HORROR

The trauma may have been so horrific that you still feel terrified and frightened some of the time. It may feel to you as if these feelings are stuck in your body and at times you may literally still feel frozen in terror. These feelings can be extremely frightening, especially if they render you motionless and unable to function even though your 'here-and-now' is safe.

ANGER, RAGE AND HATRED

Your sadness may give way to bouts of anger or sometimes anger may be so strong that you cannot feel any sadness at all. Some people describe that they are consumed by seething anger, rage and hatred after certain trauma. This can be especially the case when the trauma involved acts of intentional harm, such as physical, sexual or other forms of violation.

GUILT

You may feel overly responsible for the outcome of the trauma and believe that you should have prevented certain things from happening or if you had reacted differently harm or injury might have been spared to others. You might experience strong feelings of guilt about having experienced less injury or misfortune than others who were part of the trauma. You might also feel guilt for having survived when others didn't. A belief that 'it should have been me who died. Her life was worth so much more than mine', is typical of survivor guilt.

SHAME

When trauma involved sexual assault or violation of personal boundaries, forcing the victim to be part of activities that they wouldn't have freely chosen for themself, survivors often experience shame. You may have been told as part of the ordeal, that 'it was your fault that this happened to you', or that 'you asked for this' or 'wanted or agreed to this'. You may even have been told that if you ever told anybody, that 'nobody would believe you' or 'they would think that it was your fault'. Part of you may even believe this to be true even though you were coerced or forced into the compromising position as part of your traumatic experience. Shame can be very pervasive and you may feel that you can no longer face yourself or others around you. You may not be able to even talk about or share with close others what you had to endure because your shame feels so profound. If you suffer from trauma-based shame it can be very helpful to seek specialist therapeutic help to enable you to find the inner strength and courage to share what you had to endure and to develop a more compassionate approach towards yourself.

LOSS OF INTEREST IN SIGNIFICANT ACTIVITIES

After trauma, people often struggle to motivate themselves to take part in activities that previously were enjoyable and fulfilling for them. This might relate to social activities, hobbies, sports or other interests. People describe that activities no longer hold the meaning that they previously had. If this relates to you, your range of activities may have significantly reduced compared to before your trauma and even if family members or friends invite you to take part in previously shared activities you may lack the interest and motivation to take part.

ALIENATION, DISCONNECTION AND DIFFICULTY WITH INTIMACY

Often people experience difficulty in feeling close to and communicating with others around them. They feel alienated and as if they have lost the capacity to connect to the world around them and their loved ones. You may feel pressure from friends and loved ones to revert to the person you were before the trauma, but this may not be possible. Your response to pressure to be 'normal' may be to withdraw from company and say very little and there might even be resentment towards people who expect you to 'get over it'. The changes you have been experiencing as a result of the trauma may be so overwhelming and confusing that you feel totally estranged from people who you were previously close to.

Another common experience is also to feel disengaged from other people in your surroundings, as if you are watching things from behind a glass window. You might even feel, for short periods of time, as though you are observing yourself from outside your body. Both of these feelings are dissociative responses and can feel quite disorienting as they may reinforce your feelings of disconnection from others.

Your sense of touch and ability to cope with intimacy and physical contact may be affected, too. If you jump when others touch you unexpectedly and shy away from hugging or displays of affection, this is probably because you are so caught up in trying to keep yourself together and contain your feelings that you can't respond to unexpected demands. You may feel so pre-occupied with everything going on for you that physical contact or intimacy feels just too much to you. For some people, physical contact or intimacy may also trigger reminders of their trauma, especially if this involved some form of invasion of your physical or sexual boundaries. At times when your guard is lowered (for example, during sex or when falling asleep) this may provoke feelings of sudden panic. The reason for this is that during these times you may be less able to protect yourself using avoidant strategies and as a result re-experience some of the disturbing feelings or memories of the traumatic experience.

EMOTIONAL NUMBNESS OR INABILITY TO FEEL POSITIVE EMOTIONS

Trauma can cause a sense of emotional numbness – a feeling of hollowness or of being in a void. The traumatised person may feel as though a part of them (the feeling part) has been removed or has died and they experience a sense of being shut down, without the capacity to connect to the world through feelings. This can affect your capacity to laugh, to feel happy or even your ability to cry although you may still feel very sad. Sometimes you might feel that even your capacity to love has been affected, and this can be very frightening, especially if, as a parent, you feel that your capacity to love and feel for your children has dried up.

You may feel unable to experience any positive emotion at all even though there might be things in your present life that in the past would have made you feel happy or content. Some people who have had a history of ongoing trauma originating in childhood, in addition to more current trauma, may not recall ever having experienced a sense of genuine happiness or positive emotions in their life. People who have been affected in this way are advised to seek specialist therapeutic help for complex trauma to enable them to recover and heal from their difficult life experiences.

I had to undergo complicated surgery and spent three months in a specialist hospital after a life-threatening road traffic accident. When I finally came out everybody expected me to be happy as I was learning to walk again and they thought the trauma was over now and I would be my old self. I felt totally shut down and numb, couldn't share any of their emotions of excitement to see me again and their plans for the future. I felt extremely guilty for not even being able to feel any sense of love or affection for my husband who I had always been very close to in the past and who had been loyally supporting me all throughout this time. I had lost all my previous sense of humour, optimism and lightness. I should have been grateful to have survived but all I could feel was anger, rage and gloominess. I believed that 'there was no point to life any more'. I couldn't even properly cry. When my husband tried to comfort me, I didn't want him to be physically close to me. I pushed him away and avoided his contact. I felt totally alienated from everyone around me and although physical comfort and talking might have been a relief, I couldn't bear it. This further reinforced my feelings of guilt and made me feel bad about myself because I could see how my husband was hurt by my rejection of his love and he felt helpless as he couldn't get through to me or do anything for me to make me feel better. I felt like an emotionless monster but I didn't care and even had thoughts that it might be better if 'I wasn't there any more' and that 'he'd be better off with someone else'. I had never felt so low in my life.'

Sophie

4. *Arousal reactions*

Trauma gets into the body, and the internal neuro-chemical responses may elicit strong physical sensations in you that may make you feel uncomfortably aroused and agitated.

BAD TEMPER, ANGRY OUTBURSTS AND LACK OF CONCENTRATION

It is common for people to feel much more agitated and restless after a trauma. All the jumpiness and increased sensitivity is bound to have an impact on a person's mood, temper and ability to concentrate on everyday tasks. You might be far more forgetful and often wonder what you had set out to do. Reading books or taking in written information may have become a real struggle for you. You might find yourself becoming very negative, argumentative or easily irritated, in ways that were very unlike you before the traumatic event. You could be angry with yourself for not being able to 'snap out of it'. Or you might find yourself shouting at co-workers or family members about trivial things or because they are pressing you to make simple decisions you don't feel ready or able to make. Such irritation could escalate if you feel that you have suffered because of government bureaucracy, the legal system or institutional mishandling. Often that deep-seated anger will show itself in biting sarcasm or in attempts to over-control every situation, because inside you are conscious of how difficult it is for you to concentrate and attend to details and you deeply fear making mistakes.

SLEEP DISTURBANCE

When you are highly agitated, unable to relax and constantly on the alert for danger, it is, of course, very difficult to enjoy restful sleep. In fact, disturbed sleep is a core feature reported by people who have experienced trauma and it has been found a risk factor for the subsequent development of PTSD[8]. Sleep disturbance may manifest itself in several ways: finding it very difficult to settle to sleep, waking in the middle of the night, drenched in sweat, having nightmares or recurring dreams, restless sleep with limbs moving, crying out in sleep, waking in the early morning.

> I was a pilot and twenty-six years old when one of the engines on my plane caught fire during a military air display. I was able to land the plane and was pulled out by a ground crew together with my co-pilot just before the plane exploded into a fireball a few seconds later. Immediately after the

trauma, I could not stop myself from sleeping. I felt tired and slept many hours - it was almost like being in a coma. Then, about four days after the trauma, exactly the opposite happened. I lay awake in bed for hours and could not settle to sleep. When I eventually did get off to sleep I had the most horrific dreams and kept waking up in cold sweat and terror finding it impossible to get back to sleep. I could count myself lucky if I got more than four hours sleep a night. I also became terribly irritable and found it hard to control sudden rushes of anger that kept welling up in me without any apparent reason. I could blow up over the smallest things, such as someone forgetting to close a door. After a while my friends stopped saying certain things to me and started behaving very cautiously around me. This made me feel even angrier and I became bitter and resentful towards them.

Inside myself I had lost all my previous confidence and I felt very insecure about my indecisiveness, my constant fear of danger and my complete inability to take things in around me. People often had to repeat themselves several times before I could register what they were saying. I also had totally lost my ability to remember dates and appointments and found it impossible to concentrate on reading for much longer than 10 minutes.

Peter

RECKLESS OR SELF-DESTRUCTIVE BEHAVIOUR

Trauma by its very nature confronts people with the possibility of their own or another person's death often through seemingly untimely, horrific or unjust means. Sometimes this can cause people to become more reckless with their life subsequently, taking unnecessary risks and exposing themselves deliberately to dangerous situations. For example, Peter the pilot went back to work for the security services in high risk War Zones after his trauma. Risk-taking behaviour can have several causes, such as people holding a deep-seated belief (which may not even be easily rationally accessible) that they should have died and didn't deserve to survive and that their time now is borrowed time. It can be linked to thoughts that *'death wouldn't matter'* given what they have already been through or that it would even be *'a relief from all the pain and struggle resulting from the traumatic event'*. It can also be linked to beliefs of invincibility arising from the fact that a person didn't die when others did or the nature of the trauma was such that the odds for survival were extremely slim and the person feels numb to danger now. Reckless behaviour can also be directed against others and this might be linked to a person feeling so disillusioned with others and the world as a consequence of their traumatic experiences that they have lost all sense of empathy and stopped caring. It can also be linked to feelings of extreme unprocessed anger and rage.

Sometimes people can also develop self-destructive behaviour following trauma. This is often linked to feelings of survivor guilt or guilt about not having done enough for others or shame. It indicates anger turned inwards against oneself.

If you have noticed either reckless, risk-taking or self-destructive behaviour, compromising either other people's or your own life or safety, it is strongly advised that you contact your GP and ask to be referred for specialist therapeutic help. Chapter 17 in the Addendum on Useful guidance can help you with this.

HYPER-ALERTNESS AND EXAGGERATED CONCERN FOR SAFETY

If the trauma you experienced was sudden and dramatic it is quite natural that your previous sense of safety and your ability to handle situations will have been utterly shaken. You may now be especially watchful of your environment. You may be checking things or places for safety and see potential danger in ordinary situations. This could include being especially careful about where you choose to sit when going out, for example, considering certain seats, such as the one with its back to the window, as unsafe domain. This concern might also extend to other people around you and to them you may come across as 'over-controlling' in your attempts to ensure their safety. This feeling of being on 'red alert' – assessing potential danger all the time – can be extremely draining as your senses have to work overtime to achieve this high level of security.

EXAGGERATED STARTLE RESPONSE AND PANIC ATTACKS

Sudden noises and unexpected movements can startle you severely and the physical arousal reactions that go with this can stay with you for a long time, making you feel nervous and on edge. Nervous agitation might also be experienced as shakiness, light–headedness or even lead to a full–blown panic attack. Panic attacks can occur out of the blue, seemingly without warning, and are quite terrifying. They produce physical symptoms like sudden shortness of breath, severe chest pains or a feeling of dizziness or faintness. A panic attack is another way of showing, in an extreme fashion, the result of (traumatic) stress overload. Quite frequently, it is difficult to pinpoint a direct cause and some people suffer panic attacks *after* the trauma has passed and things in their life now are safe. The occurrence of such panic attacks may signal that there are still some deeper feelings to be dealt with and you haven't yet come to terms with the events that were so frightening to you. Your memory system is still storing the unprocessed sensations of the distressing events. This makes your innate survival system react as if things are still dangerous now, including the panic attacks themselves. They reflect that your frightening experiences still need to be dealt with. Understanding that they are a sign to 'pay more attention to yourself and your healing' and *not* the onset of a disabling disease, will make them less frightening. Use the strategies in the chapters on 'Managing Reactions' to help you to gain confidence and some positive coping skills in relation to your panic reactions.

5. *Other reactions following trauma*

DEPRESSION AND TRAUMATIC GRIEF

In the early stages, following a traumatic incident, some people want to sleep all the time. This is a common immediate reaction, but if it continues for months it may signal the presence of depression.

Depression literally means 'pressed down'. It is very common for those who are grieving to go through a stage of depression. The burden of overwhelming sadness that accompanies a severe loss can be too much for some survivors to bear. They find it almost impossible to imagine life carrying on without the loved one they have lost and feel lost and helpless themselves.

Loss of a limb or limbs, or the loss of former looks through physical disfigurement, can be just as painful as losing another person through death. It can feel as if a part of yourself has died. And often, less obvious losses, such as being made redundant, losing friends and associates, a miscarriage (or therapeutic abortion), loss of physical strength or ability – or loss of faith in yourself – can be the trigger for depressed feelings.

Although some of these events may not classify as trauma they can nevertherless be experienced as traumatic. You might begin to think 'I'll *never* get beyond this' or 'I'll always feel this way' and you might minimise any efforts you have made on your own behalf. As you sink further into depression, your thinking becomes more negative and may focus on feelings of worthlessness. Self-defeating thoughts, such as: 'I've never been any good', 'I always screw things up', may become familiar patterns in your thinking. There may even be a slightly superstitious tendency in your thinking: 'Bad things happen to anyone who's around me', 'I should have expected something like this. Things were going just too well for me.'

Depressed thinking is so caught up in negative patterns that it becomes difficult to concentrate on other things. Your mind may feel as if it is racing and at the same time you experience overwhelming fatigue. Some people feel little motivation to eat, and over longer periods of time this can lead to significant weight loss, even health problems. Alternatively, others might use comfort eating to block out their distress. Memory for everyday details, appointments and even ordinary, routine activities is likely to be unreliable. The term 'burn-out' is often used to describe the experience of those who have been doing too much for too long, trying to cope with impossible demands and finally sink into a state of exhaustion. Burn-out can also be applied to people who have been trying very hard to cope after trauma, doing all the 'right things' and yet still find themselves sinking more and more into a depression.

I was a warehouse controller when I lost my right eye in an industrial accident. One of the sprung metal fittings on a piece of machinery had come undone through my own doing and hit my head, damaging my right eye. After the initial shock and a short period of hospitalization, my company offered me a different job on the factory floor which I could do with the functioning of one eye only. I tried to get on with life and continue with my work as best as I could. The accident was never really talked about any more. I tried to ignore my internal emotional reactions, because I was so ashamed of them. I felt that I should be brave, after all, accidents happen all the time in life and, if anything, this accident had been caused by my own wrong-doing. I shouldn't have fiddled with the machine when I did. However I was unable to get rid of my feelings and I noticed myself becoming more and more depressed about the loss of my right eye. I blamed myself and I didn't feel like a proper man any more. I noticed people staring at me sometimes as if I was some kind of alien. I often felt like screaming out at them, but then I would tell myself that: 'It had been my own fault ... that I only got what I deserved ... and that I shouldn't be so stupid now and pull myself together!' I felt very down and upset, but also very alone because I felt too ashamed to talk about my feelings with anybody.

Bob

DECREASED SELF-ESTEEM AND LOSS OF CONFIDENCE

As we have seen, one feature of self-blame is a very negative pattern of thinking, where you constantly put yourself down and take no credit for those things that you have achieved. Gradually, your confidence is eroded, leading to feelings of worthlessness and very low self-esteem, which may be further confirmed by the disabling effects of other reactions to the trauma. For example, you may not understand your reactions to the trauma and may belittle yourself for withdrawing from people or avoiding activities that previously you would have really liked to do. Negative thoughts lead to a sense that you are losing control, and even losing your mind: you are caught in the downward spiral of low self-esteem.

I had been a dentist, but had to give this up as a result of the severe back injuries that I sustained during a climbing excursion, when I slipped and fell, before the rope had been securely fastened by one of the fellow climbers. I had difficulties finding a suitable alternative job. Although I got some offers of work, I usually didn't last very long in the positions I started in, because of the disabling chronic pain, which would keep me off work for long periods of time. I lost all my confidence. I withdrew more and more from my previous circle of friends, because they were all so successful in their careers and I felt ashamed and embarrassed at not being able to keep up with them. I felt useless and hopeless about myself and about my abilities and prospects in my future life.

Pam

ALCOHOL, DRUGS AND COMFORT EATING

People will often use alcohol or drugs to escape or block out the painful reactions connected to their trauma and obtain a temporary respite. You might dread falling asleep, because of disturbing or repetitive dreams or fear 'losing control' by letting down your guard and becoming too relaxed. When one's sleep is disturbed over a long period, there is a strong temptation to take a pill to enhance sleep. Some people also use food and comfort eating as a way of blocking out painful feelings temporarily. For some, just the action of filling themselves with food can alleviate feelings of inner emptiness and unconnectedness.

Although such behaviour can temporarily improve things, the improvement is artificial and can have a rebound effect.

Overuse of alcohol, drugs, comfort eating or any other artificially induced 'numbing' agent can actually inhibit restful sleep and simply compound the problem.

Avoidance behaviour or emotional numbing reactions are often motivated by the desire to prevent further pain and to protect the wounded self through a very narrow interpretation of what is 'safe'. A number of factors such as guilt or self-blame or a particularly horrible detail which you are keeping secret may increase the pressure to preserve that 'numbness' as it seems safer. Again, the end result can be counter-productive and you may end up isolated and prevented from moving on with your life and your healing.

Until my rape at the age of twenty, I had been very sociable, outgoing and perfectly happy with my life. I had several close girlfriends and had good relationships with men. I had enjoyed myself at a friend's party and had trusted Matthew who was well known in the local community to take me home. On our way home we bumped into three of Matthew's friends whom I had never met before. It was then that Matthew's behaviour started to change. At first I thought that maybe I was a bit too sensitive, especially as I had drunk a bit at the party. However, slowly I became frightened by the change in Matthew's tone of voice. Cheered on by these friends, he started to become really verbally abusive towards me, calling me names that nobody had ever dared to call me before. We were still several minutes' walk away from my home, in a very rural area, when Matthew pushed me to the ground and raped me in front of his friends, who shouted obscene words at me. I was completely frozen and so shocked that I was unable to shout or defend myself in any way.

I felt totally numb when I eventually found my way home. Although I love my parents, they are elderly and a little old-fashioned in their views and I felt I could not confide in them. I also feared that nobody would believe me anyway if I accused Matthew, who was well respected in the community, of having raped me in front of his friends. I felt that people might either laugh at me and not take me seriously or accuse me of having led Matthew on at the party. I felt ashamed and dirty at that thought and I blamed myself and felt guilty for not having been stronger and stood up to Matthew and his friends.

I kept my secret for eight years, until therapy finally enabled me to work things through. Over these years, I changed completely. I broke off all contact with my previous friends and apart from going to work I was spending all my evenings at home. I never went to a party again or any other social events after the rape. When people invited me I would make up excuses about being too busy with other things. Eventually, all invitations stopped. I was unable to use any public transport and only felt safe going out during the light hours. In the winter months, when I had to return from work in the dark, I would park my car right outside the office block and at the other end drive up almost to my front door. I was dutiful at work but withdrew whenever any of my colleagues tried to get close to me. Emotionally I felt completely empty and I couldn't experience any loving feelings any longer, not even really towards my parents. They were worried *about the change in my personality but couldn't help, as they did not understand my reasons for behaving in the way I did. Regularly, if my sleeping was very badly affected by intrusive memories I would use alcohol to help me relax and settle to sleep more easily. Eventually I started drinking a bit too much and it became a habit isolating me even more. Although my world felt fairly safe and under my control, I was very isolated, cut-off and lonely.*

Cathy

DISSOCIATION

Dissociation is a survival reaction that helps separate the distressing memories or experiences of the traumatic events and stores them in memory systems away from everyday conscious awareness. Our brain uses dissociative processes all the time, because otherwise our active, conscious mind would be so overloaded by all the information and stimuli impacting on us that we would not be able to focus on the tasks we want to master as part of daily life. Dissociative reactions during trauma are very common and they can be understood to have been helpful at the time as it enabled the focus on survival.

There are different types of dissociative reactions, which can range from mild to quite severe. Dissociation is an area of trauma research not yet sufficiently understood. It seems that the extent of dissociation in response to trauma varies between people and is linked to a great number of factors, including the trauma severity, how long it went on, a person's developmental age, the external and internal resources available at the time, previously acquired innate coping responses and others. Dissociative responses can be so diverse that a whole psychiatric classification category is dedicated to this[5] and books written specifically.

This book can only focus on some of the dissociative responses that it might be helpful for you to be aware of. Some of these were already briefly mentioned earlier as part of the descriptions of the various reactions to trauma. It is so important for people to recognise these responses and understand that they are part of survival-driven dissociation that they will be detailed again here.

Trauma leads to fragmentation of memory and quite a common dissociative response might be that you struggle in remembering aspects of your trauma, even though you know they must have happened. This might be part of what is called **Dissociative Amnesia** and can be quite frustrating. It may help you to understand that this is a survival response shielding you from experiences that might have been too overwhelming at the time had you remained conscious of them. Now when you are in safety and can be sure the trauma lies behind you they may still be inaccessible to you. You may feel that important parts of your life are missing and this can be quite disorienting, especially if your memory before the trauma was very sharp. Your healing process, which may involve specialist trauma therapy (see also Chapter 17 in the Addendum on Useful guidance), may enable those memories to be recovered where they can then be worked through.

People frequently experience a sense of not being fully in their body during and also following a trauma. It can feel as if they are watching themselves from outside, such as for example, a sense of observing themselves from above. This is refered to as **Depersonalisation (DP for short)**. Depersonalisation might be very mild and transient, but for some people, it can be there most or all of the time. This can feel as if life is taking place and you are watching it from the outside and feel not really part of it. This can be intensely disturbing as it might feel so different to how you experienced yourself before the trauma.

Another quite common dissociative response is **Derealisation (DR for short)**. This can feel as if the world around you, familiar places or people you know seem alien, bizarre or surreal. It can feel as if you are experiencing your surroundings through a veil of sensory fog, somehow they lack vividness and familiar things feel very different and unreal compared to how they felt to you before the trauma. These feelings could also affect your senses of hearing, smell, taste, touch, speech and co-ordination. Things no longer taste or feel the way in which you remember them and everything seems unreal. You may not feel properly co-ordinated in your body, your speech might be slurred and your movements strange. This is a feeling that can be very transient or short lived, but for some people can last for significant amounts of time, sometimes hours or even days if very severe. It can feel extremely disturbing to experience yourself drifting in and out of these different states of consciousness. It may even feel to you or others around you as if you are under the spell of alcohol or some mind-altering substance even though you know this not to be the case.

Sometimes, when people have experienced very severe trauma, they can find themselves ending up in locations and places with no recollection of how they got there. This could be places you know, such as the house of a relative, or places you cannot remember ever having been at. This is called **Dissociative Fugue** and can be extremely disturbing to those who are affected by this. It may also be quite dangerous because you have no conscious awareness of the journey of getting there. A milder form of a similar dissociative response is finding items in your house that you have no conscious recollection of ever buying and yet there is evidence that you must have done so. You may also experience episodes of milder forms of temporary absences or disorientation, such as driving on the motorway and not focusing on the road or only noticing that you have taken a wrong turning when you become aware of features in your surroundings that you do not recognise. You may have absences during conversations with others and when you tune in again, you have no idea how the new subject was arrived at. In their more severe form these dissociative symptoms can pose a significant risk to your own or other's safety and you are advised to share this with your GP and seek professional help (refer to Chapter 17 in Addendum – Useful guidance). You are also advised not to drive unless you can be sure you will be safe to do so. This book is not a replacement for specialist trauma therapy where needed and if you are suffering from strong dissociative symptoms you need therapeutic help.

Other dissociative responses can include feeling as if you are at times switching into different feeling states or parts that you might experience as separate from yourself and from each other as they seem so distinctly different. Sometimes when trauma was very severe, ongoing, and often when it happened in early childhood, different parts of you might have been created in order to enable your survival. These parts usually have different personalities, ages and hold memories of different parts of the traumatic experiences and differing survival behaviour, which may not be part of your day-to-day awareness. This could be what is known as **Dissociative Identity Disorder (DID for short).** If you feel that this describes your problems this book is not comprehensive enough to be of significant help to you. You are advised to contact your GP and request a referral for therapeutic help to a service or professional that specialises in helping people with such severe dissociative responses.

I was discharged from my battalion because of enduring chronic pain problems. I had never told them about my mental-health problems which had started after witnessing my best friend being killed in front of me during active service. I had numerous problems which I tried to cover up as I knew how they would treat me if I couldn't cope. The most difficult had been to hide my problems with dissociation. I had long periods of absences during which I would lose all track of time, couldn't focus on the conversations of others and would even find myself in places that I couldn't recall having gotten there. Everything around me seemed unreal and often I couldn't even feel myself in my body and it seemed as if I was watching myself from outside. This wasn't there all the time, but much of the time. I'd pretend nothing was wrong to the others, but I thought that I was going mad or maybe had some terrible illness like a brain tumour or Alzheimer's.

Ron

Important summary checkpoints:

- Trauma triggers complex neurochemical processes in the brain and body systems activating necessary survival responses.
- There are five human survival responses:
  - Fight, Flight, Freeze, Flop, (Be-)Friend or Fawn
- Trauma can cause a wide range of diverse reactions and most people have some responses.
- Each person responds differently and there is no clear pattern that applies to all.
- Reactions are categorised into four clusters:
  - Intrusive Reactions
  - Avoidance Reactions
  - Negative Changes in Mood and Thought Processes
  - Heightened Arousal Reactions
- Additional reactions to trauma can be:
  - Dissociative Symptoms
  - Depression and Traumatic Grief

- Alcohol, Substance Abuse or Comfort Eating
- Low Self-esteem and Loss of Confidence
- Others are often puzzled and can't make sense of the changes in mood and behaviour of a traumatised person.
- Symptoms are more severe in trauma involving intentional harm, sexual violation, crimes against children, crimes against humanity, mass trauma, terrorism.
- Developmental trauma, childhood abuse and prolonged, enduring and repeated trauma cause the most severe and complex effects. This book is not comprehensive enough to help such Complex Trauma.

3

Understanding the reactions of families and loved ones

The effects of trauma often leak out to partners, family members and supportive others, even though you may try to shield them. This chapter is written with those others in mind. It is written to help the trauma survivor understand how others might be affected and for those close others to understand that they are not alone. Sometimes it can be helpful to read parts of it together in the context of a safe relationship with a trusted relation or friend and use this as an opportunity to talk things through. This needs to be done in a manner that feels respectful and safe for the trauma survivor.

There are situations when this may not at all be appropriate or safe, for example, if there is ongoing domestic violence, emotional abuse, such as scorn or mockery, or a general lack of support or understanding in a relationship. In these situations trauma survivors may need to keep their recovery work secret. Trauma survivors are advised to determine whether it could be helpful and with whom it would feel safe and supportive for them to share this chapter. In situations where their recovery process might be damaged or undermined by others they may need to safeguard themselves. They may need to keep this book, any journal or other activities related to their recovery in a safe location.

Sharing this book will only be helpful if it enhances the recovery process and this chapter is written with this in mind. If in doubt about the safety and support of close others around you, you are advised to either do the work privately by yourself or seek professional help to support you with this.

Carrying the emotional scars of trauma

The trauma seems to have changed him! He is no longer the person I used to love.

This statement was made by Lucy, the wife of Phil, survivor of a commuter train crash.

Phil used to be so loving and caring. When he came home from work he would cuddle me and ask me if I had had a good day. We would typically sit and have a drink together and share each other's experiences from the day. We would often go out, meet friends, entertain at home. We would laugh and joke together and there was a lot of intimacy, closeness and a very warm atmosphere between the two of us. This has now completely changed! Phil hardly greets me now when he gets home from work. Usually he goes straight upstairs into his study, where he will just sit in his chair, sometimes just staring into space. At other times he reads the newspaper, but I have the feeling that he doesn't actually take in what he reads, because it seems to take him hours to turn a few pages. I no longer look forward to Phil coming home – the worst is his temper. He gets so angry and shouts about such unimportant, petty things. The other day, I hadn't completely turned off a tap in the bathroom, so that it was still dripping a little. Rather than going to turn it off, which Phil would have done in the past, he really had a go at me. He ranted and raved, I was so frightened that I thought he might even hit me. We also hardly ever go out now. Friends have given up calling on us. On the few occasions that they do come round, Phil is not really entertaining any more. It is as if he has lost all his sense of fun – he takes everything that others say so seriously. He has also become so controlling; he has to check on every little thing to ensure it's safe. He doesn't seem to trust me any more and will check on things, for example, that the gas is turned off, even when I have assured him that I have done it already. Sometimes he really gets on my nerves with his behaviour.

Lucy

Lucy is not alone in feeling this way. Many partners of trauma survivors and other family members or close friends find it difficult to cope with the emotional scars left by the trauma on their loved ones. After an initial period of relief, partners and family often feel increasingly puzzled, confused and helpless as they begin to witness the emotional and psychological changes incurred by the trauma, often long after the physical wounds have healed. Most partners or family members try to help the trauma survivors as best as they can, but it is often very difficult for the recipients to receive this help and for it to have any effect.

The ripple effect or how trauma affects family and loved ones

The effects of trauma are felt in families, partnerships and in other relationships trauma survivors may have. Unfortunately, the ripple effect of the trauma on close relationships is often ignored and not addressed by professionals, whose main concern is to aid the trauma survivors.

Trauma can have devastating long-term consequences on relationships. It is not uncommon for previously well-functioning marriages or partnerships to break up and for family members to become increasingly alienated from each other. The resulting effects of these break-ups or breakdowns can then lead to further, so-called secondary traumatisation. The trauma survivor can thus end up in a downward spiral that seems to make the prospect of recovery even more challenging.

In order to lessen the destructive impact of this ripple effect it is important to understand the nature of the emotional scarring that the trauma survivor bears and the effect that this can have on previously normal, well-functioning relationships. This can make it easier to find constructive ways of talking about the changes and work out together how you could support each other during this life-changing time.

The need for closeness and intimacy

As Lucy described in the example above, one of the positive features of her marriage with Phil was the degree of intimacy and warmth between them. Closeness and intimacy are key requirements for a well-functioning human relationship. *Unfortunately, survivors of trauma often lose their capacity for such closeness after a life-threatening experience.* This is because they are in the grip of their survival system's automatic responses, which regards closeness or intimacy as a threat. In order to be intimate and feel close to another person, a person has to be able to relax, but relaxing requires the body to soften and ease, which is really difficult when the survival system just wants to tense up and protect itself, because it still feels under threat from the trauma.

> I had been so happy with my wife Paula, before the trauma.
> Afterwards, there were no real reasons at all why I shouldn't
> still be as happy, or maybe even happier than before - because
> I had actually survived the trauma. I knew in my head that
> in many ways I should appreciate my relationship with Paula
> even more now. She was so good to me, trying to help me as
> best as she could, trying to be supportive. However, it was as
> if something inside me had been switched off by the trauma.

This was my capacity to feel. I felt completely dead inside, even though there was absolutely no external reason for me to be this way. I felt so out of control and so helpless. I wanted to find this internal switch, but nothing that I tried seemed to be able to help me to get back my feelings. I noticed how Paula suffered from the distance between us and the internal loneliness that she felt as a result, but I myself felt frozen like a stone, unable to move closer towards her.

Mark

Mark's description captures very well how many people feel after a trauma: an internal deadness, a feeling of helplessness to change or do anything about it. The feeling of emotional deadness often interferes with the need for closeness in a relationship and can also have a profound effect on a couple's ability to have intimate sexual contact. There can be both a loss of capacity for emotional closeness as well as for physical intimacy. Sometimes it is hard for a traumatised person to tolerate touch. Partners can jump to the conclusion that their loved ones don't love them any more and members of the family can also feel rejected. The result is often further distancing, as partners and family members tend to give up after a period of being locked out of their loved one's internal, emotional world. Nevertheless, as Mark's example illustrates, this is usually the last thing that a trauma survivor actually wants, nor is it helpful for the process of recovery.

Remember these are feelings that a trauma survivor can't avoid; they are the direct result of the emotionally scarring effects of trauma and the fact that they are still in the grip of their survival system. It is usually not the case that trauma survivors cease to love the people who were close to them before the trauma, but rather that, for the present, they can't respond to those people normally, because they have lost access to their capacity to love while they are still affected by the trauma.

The need for openness and communication

Well-functioning relationships need openness and good communication to thrive. In order to feel connected to another person it is essential to talk openly. Again, such a facility is frequently blocked as a result of the trauma.

Before the trauma I used to share everything with Kim. We would sit for hours in the evening and chat away about things. We used to plan together and shared most of our responsibilities in life - we were a great team. Since the trauma something has changed. Kim doesn't really understand how I feel. I have talked to her about the trauma in a general way, but I couldn't describe to her all the ghastly details that keep haunting me day after day. I feel embarrassed and ashamed about feeling so out of control internally, and often I feel physically sick when reminders of scenes that I witnessed during the trauma keep intruding into my mind throughout the day (and night). Any person who hasn't been through this couldn't really understand how it feels and I wouldn't want to burden Kim with the internal turmoil that I am going

*through. It would only worry her. As a consequence, we don't
really talk as we used to. Kim still tries, but I also find it very
difficult to concentrate on her chatter - it even gets on my
nerves sometimes. Kim says that I am often silent whereas in
the past I would have had my say. She feels that I am not as
open with her as I used to be. But how can I be?*

Steven

It is often very hard for trauma survivors to share their
internal distress and their experiences with others, however
close. One reason for this may be, as in Steven's example,
the wish to protect the loved one and not to burden them.
Another reason for Steven is that he feels embarrassed and
ashamed of his feelings. People often fear that they are
'going mad' or 'losing complete control' after a trauma and
they may feel that others would not really understand them,
or may indeed confirm these fears.

In addition, opening up and talking about aspects of
the trauma can reawaken painful memories and distressing emotions. This can be a source of worry, particularly
if they don't understand their feelings and see them as a
sign of personal weakness, rather than as a natural part of
the healing process. A further reason can be the spoken or
unspoken expectation 'that they ought to have got over
things by now' which trauma survivors can pick up from
others around them. Being aware of this can definitely
make a person keep things to themselves. Difficulties
with concentration and the ability to absorb only limited
amounts of information at a time, as described by Steven

above, are also common reasons for not engaging in communication. Remember that opening up and talking often isn't easy for people who have been involved in trauma. In order to reduce the impact of the emotional scarring, it is important for the trauma survivor to allow themselves to open up to those close others in their life and for close others to listen openly without judgement or pressure. This is only advised if close others are genuinely supportive and the relationship is essentially a safe one. Sometimes there are valid reasons for not opening up, for example, if it puts the trauma survivor at risk, might jeopardise recovery or invite scorn, mockery or punishment. If the effects of the trauma have been very overwhelming or the relationship is not safe, trauma survivors might benefit from seeking professional help which might enable them to learn how to open up safely and determine with whom it could be beneficial to do so.

The need for trust, a sense of predictability and safety

Trust, a sense of predictability and security are all very important factors in healthy human relationships and social interactions. Unfortunately, it is often the very nature of trauma that shatters the capacity for trust in a traumatised person.

> My sense of trust and safety has completely gone. The world around me has become completely unpredictable and I can never relax enough to feel safe now. I notice that people in

my family have become very cautious around me. They seem to avoid certain topics of conversation and seem to talk about me behind my back. I know that I often blow up at them over completely stupid things, which in the past I would only have laughed about. I hate myself for it, but don't seem to be able to control it or stop it. It is as if, suddenly, a really black cloud completely grips hold of me and installs in me this capacity to destroy everything around me. I sometimes even get a perverse sense of pleasure from this wish to destroy and dismantle. I find myself being sarcastic with people, who before the trauma I cared about very much. Also I don't trust anyone any more. I sense danger everywhere and I find myself checking what others have done to make sure that they have done it properly.

Will

Frequently, a traumatised person's loss of trust, and a sense of safety and predictability, is mirrored in their behaviour towards those around them.

Remember *that a traumatised person doesn't want to act in this way, but often can't help it. Their behaviour reflects their magnified fears about the world after their trauma. They will need to re-learn how to trust and feel safe, and the more predictable and reassuring you can be the more helpful it will be for the process of their recovery.*

The need for fun, leisure and relaxation

Relationships also need to be fun and to contain space for leisure and relaxation. The impact of trauma often makes this very difficult to achieve naturally.

> Tom and I used to have great fun together. We shared similar interests and most of our evenings and weekends were spent doing things that we both enjoyed. We were very active sports people, used to play squash, tennis and go riding together. We also used to dance and liked going to the theatre, cinema and had a lot of friends. Doing these things together created a great sense of unity and closeness in our relationship. All this is gone now. Tom doesn't really understand. He feels I ought to be happy that I survived. I could have been far worse off, my physical injuries weren't even that bad. He is right and I still can't help myself from feeling the way I do. It is as if all my motivation and interest in any activity has gone. I just can't be bothered with anything. Everything seems such an effort and I just prefer to stay at home and don't want to see anyone or do anything. Tom wants to include me in his plans for our next holiday. I used to love holidays, but even my sense of pleasure for those is now gone. I don't really feel like planning anything at the moment. All I can think about is how I can get through tomorrow - I have no sense of a future for myself.
>
> Jennifer

Both interest and motivation in previously enjoyable activities can be severely impaired in people who have suffered a trauma. This can be especially difficult in families where one of the parents has been traumatised and no longer feels able to play with the children or do all the fun things that they used to do together. The lack of a sense of a future, as Jennifer described, can also be very disabling to the affected person and to others around them. It can feel as if life has completely stopped at the time of the trauma and this is often exactly how it feels to the traumatised person.

> *It is important to help the traumatised person slowly to find ways of re-engaging with their present life. Their lack of interest is not a reflection of how they feel about their partner or others who are close to them, but rather another outcome of the trauma and the fact that they are still affected by this.*

How to survive the trauma together

The emotional scars of trauma can really get in the way of previously well-functioning relationships, whether they are with partners, family, friends or even colleagues at work. It is important to recognise that the traumatised person doesn't do these things deliberately to hurt or destroy, but that they are a true reflection of how badly they have been affected by the trauma. True healing and recovery does take time and may require professional help.

Here are some tips for surviving the trauma together:

- Don't pressure the traumatised person to get better but acknowledge that they probably don't like what they are going through themselves. Allow them to heal in their own time. This may take some time and it is important that they can work through things at their own pace either on their own or with professional help. It will greatly support them if you can help create this time for healing together with them.
- Recognise that each person is different and accept that *the path to recovery is unique for everyone*. There is no right or wrong way of responding and traumas affect people in different ways.
- Whenever appropriate, indicate gently to the traumatised person that you are prepared to listen to their story, only if you truly feel able to do so. Try not to exert any pressure. If you feel that you may not be able to bear hearing the story yourself, or your loved one doesn't want to open up to you at all, it may be helpful to explore the possibility of some professional help with them or for yourself on your own. Chapter 17 in the Addendum – Useful guidance may be helpful for you to read.
- Try to appreciate that people may experience strong emotions when they think or talk about their trauma. It may feel to them as if they are being transported back in time to the trauma and their emotions and physical responses might be almost as strong as at

the time they initially experienced them. While it is important for these feelings to be expressed as part of a natural healing process, this must be done in a way that doesn't overwhelm either you or the one you care for. It is important that you allow the traumatised person to pace themselves gently. This might involve them only talking about a little part of what they experienced at a time. If it feels to the traumatised person that their emotions are too overwhelming to be able to pace themselves, they are advised to seek professional help before talking to you. If you feel that you wouldn't be able to cope seeing the person you care for so upset or strongly emotional, don't offer your help with this. Instead either point them in the direction of professional help or another close person who could cope better with this.

- Maintain as much stability and routine as you can at this time. It is important that the traumatised person learns to regain a sense of safety; some anchoring might need to take place before any new life changes can be initiated. For instance, this would not be the right time to make major life decisions, such as moving house, changing jobs, etc. to make 'a fresh start'. It is advisable to wait until the one you care for has recovered from the trauma and settled back into a more balanced inner state.

- Treat each other as equals. Just because a person might be suffering from disabling responses doesn't mean that they are in any way inferior to you. The more you can establish an empowering healing partnership, the better. Ask the traumatised person for feedback on what feels helpful and what is not helpful to them when you are together. Move towards doing more of those things together that feel helpful.

• Sometimes a traumatised person's reactions might be so strong that you could feel overwhelmed and might need to withdraw. In these situations, it is vital to ensure that you keep yourself safe. Afterwards, the person will be grateful that you have protected yourself. It is easier for both of you to agree beforehand what you will do to keep yourself safe in such situations so that your withdrawal is not interpreted as rejection by the traumatised person.

• Be mindful of your boundaries with each other. It is not okay for the one you care for to hurt you either emotionally or physically even if this happens as a result of a trauma-related response. It is important for both of you to stay safe and respectful towards each other, even if closeness and intimacy is difficult at this time and your relationship is compromised by the trauma.

§ You have to keep yourself safe and if the one you care for seems unable to control their emotions or reactions and poses a risk to you, you must leave the situation. If you are being hurt or abused by the one you care for, you must tell them to stop. If they don't respect your safe boundary you may encourage them to seek professional help for their problems. You may need to seek help yourself and contact your medical practitioner or a support service (some resources are listed at the end of the book).

- Read this book together only if it might be helpful for both of you. If the one you care for feels too traumatised to be able to take in the content of this book, it may not be the right time, although it may be possible to read it in small sections. You could also introduce an even easier to read book on trauma first[1] before moving on to this one. Try to establish with your partner what kind of a role you could usefully play in order to give the maximum help in the recovery process.

- Work out a contract for healing together. Write down what is blocking you in your relationship at the moment. Agree what you would like to be able to change in due course so that your relationship will be happier and more rewarding again. Set down what you will do for each other and how you will work together to achieve these changes over time. Some of these may not be possible until the one you care for has more fully recovered from their trauma. If the one you care for is receiving therapeutic help, they and their therapist might be open for you to join them for part of a session to explore some of the areas that could improve for both of you in your relationship.

- Partners and close others need support, too. It is

helpful if you find a person outside your immediate family to confide in and share your feelings with. Do not give up living your life, because the one you care for can't presently live life as fully as they did in the past. It is important that one of you stays connected to a healthy, non-traumatised way of life. This makes it more likely for the one you care for to join you again when they are ready and it keeps up your own resilience and sense of well being. Support services and information sessions might be available through professional agencies. They might be able to help you understand more about trauma-related reactions and support you during this difficult time so that you can stay strong enough for both of you until the one you care for is able to join you more fully again.

Important summary checkpoints:

- Trauma can have a significant effect also on partners, family members or other close ones who may find it hard to comprehend the changes that seem to have taken place in the trauma survivor.
- Close others usually want to help but might feel rejected in their efforts because their traumatised loved one might find it difficult to receive this help.
- The traumatised person may have lost their capacity to experience love or engage in closeness

or intimacy even if they were very affectionate before.

- They may find it difficult to communicate their feelings, as this may connect them to their traumatic experiences and they might fear losing control.
- They may no longer trust others and become very controlling, hypersensitive and watchful.
- They may have lost all interest in activities or hobbies that used to be a source of pleasure and joint exchange before.
- They may withdraw from life and no longer take part in social gatherings or outings.
- Relationships can really suffer and may even break up when these responses are not understood within the context of the trauma.
- There are many ways in which those caring can support a traumatised person during their healing and recovery process.
- It is important that those caring also know how to care for and look after their own needs.

PART TWO

MANAGING TRAUMATIC STRESS

4

Moving towards your path of recovery

A framework for healing

If you have been distressed for a long time, or if your reactions following a recent traumatic experience have been particularly intense, or again, if your symptoms did improve but then recently returned with a disturbing intensity, you may have turned directly to this section of the book and not bothered to read the chapters in the first part.

The temptation to seek the practical strategies first is very understandable; your world has probably felt so out of control that you want to fix it as quickly as possible. Nevertheless, you need a framework from which to apply these practical strategies in order to manage your symptoms. At the very least you should have read Chapter 2 'Understanding your reactions' and in the Addendum – Useful guidance also Chapter 17 'Seeking professional help'. Chapter 2 will make you are aware of the 'why' as well as the 'how to' in symptom management. Chapter 17 as part of the Addendum – Useful guidance will enable you to determine whether you should seek professional help for a specialist trauma assessment and trauma-focused psychological therapy. You could still work with this book while you are waiting for your appointments and also alongside your trauma therapy. Please let your therapist know if you are doing this.

This book is not designed to offer a 'quick fix' (although some of the techniques offered here may make a considerable difference for you right away, the first or second time you try them). Rather, this book is aimed at providing a lasting improvement, and that can only be achieved by acting on the techniques and strategies which this book proposes. This chapter is very important as it prepares the foundations for your trauma recovery work.

Preparing the foundations for your path to recovery

Rather than starting with your direct trauma work it is necessary to take time to prepare yourself for the changes you are about to make. This chapter takes you through some important aspects to consider, take care of and organise in preparation for your journey of recovery. These lay the foundation for your trauma recovery work. **Building a solid foundation is extremely important and without it your recovery will be compromised. It is therefore necessary that you work on this first before starting with any of the deeper level trauma recovery work.**

Ensuring that you are safe now

The very first step is to ensure that you are safe now. Although you may not feel safe at the moment, because you are still in the grip of your trauma memories, it is important that your actual trauma is over now. This means that there is no threat of it recurring at the moment; that the people that might have been harmful or hurtful to you are no longer in your direct life; that your living and working environment is free from harm or threat to you and that those close to you are also no longer under threat or danger. Safety means that you are now reasonably invulnerable to harm inflicted by yourself or others[1].

There are four different types of safety[2]. The one that we most commonly think of is our **physical safety**, which means that our body is safe from danger. To ensure your physical safety now, you must be able to notice when it is threatened or compromised and take the necessary steps to remove or protect yourself from the source of the danger. Another type is your **mental safety**, which means that you are able to choose belief systems, thought or awareness patterns that enable you to follow those things that are important to you and give meaning to your life. There is also the concept of **emotional safety**. This refers to your ability to identify what you feel in a given situation, recognise and then act on what your intuition or feelings tell you, especially when they signal danger. Sometimes this ability is very impaired after trauma, because you may either have numbed yourself to your feelings or they give you constant signals of alarm even when there is no actual danger now.

Your emotional safety guidance system may have become very disrupted and it may take time, conscious awareness and effort to re-build this again. The fourth type is your **spiritual safety**, which refers to your belief and trust in a Higher Consciousness, God or Supreme Being and your ability to draw on those beliefs as a means of protection for yourself or others. Trauma can destroy some or even all of those types of safety, leaving a feeling of total inner desolation. This is especially the case if it disconnects people from their sense of spiritual safety, and is at its most damaging if the trauma was committed by others who claim to have acted in the name of a Higher Power.

The reason why it is very important that you bring yourself into safety now is that you cannot work through and recover from a trauma while you or your loved ones are still under actual threat of danger or harm. The survival mechanisms in your body (controlled by your autonomic nervous system, which is not under your conscious control) will quite rightly stay activated and alert in this case. They still need to protect you! Therefore, even if you tried, this would override any attempt for you to overcome and recover from your trauma.

Allow yourself to evaluate if there are still any factors in your life that compromise your sense of safety.

- Is there still anything that puts you under pressure or threat of harm?
- Is there anything in your home or immediate physical environment now that doesn't feel safe to you?

- Are you able to protect yourself from people you don't know or those who feel unsafe to you?
- Are there people in your life that make you feel unsafe?
- Are you able to mostly act on things you wish to do for yourself and follow your interests without being put under pressure, threat or intimidation?
- Are you able to express your beliefs and thoughts without being put under pressure, threatened or intimidated?
- Are you able to put safe boundaries in place now with people who may have harmed you in the past?
- Are you able to say: 'No' to anything that unduly compromises your safety?

Write down a list of any factors that might still stand in the way of you being reasonably safe from harm. This includes anything that threatens your emotional safety. Examine your list and change any factors in your life that are still compromising your safety. This has to be done before you can start with any of the trauma recovery work.

If there are too many reminders of the trauma in your house or working environment that trigger strong feelings, you might have to make changes so that your environment feels safe enough now for you to start your recovery work. Later, when you are stronger and more stabilised, you can introduce some of these back into your environment if you want.

Sometimes even a litigation process to compensate for your injuries, although it should be helpful, can be harmful and threatening. The problem is that even though you have been a victim of injury or crime such process can be very adversarial. Rather than protecting you, you may find yourself in a position of having to justify and account for everything in minute detail, making you feel uncomfortably scrutinised; having the reactions to your experiences questioned, undermined and minimised by the defendant's experts; and having to fight for your claim to be recognised. This can feel very injurious and harmful especially if the trauma seems to have totally destroyed the secure base of your life and you now fear that your existence is threatened financially. When you are in the midst of a litigation process it may not be the right time to work on your recovery journey. Your levels of stress might be too high to properly engage in this process. Some of the grounding, relaxation, nurturing and mindfulness techniques may, however, be helpful to you.

Sometimes you may need to greatly reorganise your life, such as moving into safer housing, leaving a harmful and destructive relationship, or changing jobs, for example, if your boss is your abuser. You may need professional support to help you make these changes, especially if you are in a vulnerable position and still the target of potential abuse. This is not the time for you to do trauma recovery work. Your first priority must be to get yourself into a safe and stable position.

If you are now safe, but still feel reminded a lot of the trauma, then another strategy might be to introduce little changes in your home to make this feel safer. This could even just be to change the position of the furniture in your room or decorating your home with a new colour paint or changing the curtains or carpets. This might help you see things a bit differently and signal that you are safe now in making a new start.

Creating a special Place of Safety

Trauma shatters most people's sense of safety. It is therefore necessary for your healing process to find ways to reconnect and re-build a sense of safety, both in your external as well as your internal world.

Creating an External Safe Space[2]

When your external environment is safe and you can be sure that there is no threat in your home, you could select a special area in your home that you designate as your safe space. This might be a room that you can retreat to with a comfortable sofa or seat you can cuddle into, or it can be a particular area or space in the house which can be yours to claim during this recovery process. It is very important that the space you choose does feel very calming, soothing and safe to you. This will be very different for each person and needs to be whatever works for you in this regard. Some people find it helpful to put comforting things into their safe space, for example a cosy blanket, a comfy armchair, an aromatherapy diffuser with their special favoured scents (spicy, floral or herbal), a sachet or cushion filled with dried herbs, for example lavender, soft materials to touch, a special painting, beautiful candles, the warm glow of a salt lamp, pebbles, shells, touch stones or crystals, calming pictures, a wind chime, or anything else that has a soothing, calming effect on you and can help connect you to a sense of safety. You are encouraged to experiment and try things out that work well for you. If you are sharing your home with others try and negotiate with them that they respect your safe space as being used only by you as part of your trauma recovery process.

You can use this safe space as an external anchor, for when you feel agitated or restless and want to comfort yourself, or after having worked on some of the more challenging aspects of your trauma recovery. It is better not to do the trauma processing work in your safe space, but keep it as a resource that you can use for anchoring and soothing yourself after you have done this work. When you have to go out to work or other places, you could take one special small item from your safe space with you as an anchor to connect you to your safe space at home and the comforting feelings that go with this. You can also connect to your safe space and the feelings of safety, comfort and calm before you go to bed, last thing in the evening. This might help you get to sleep more easily.

Make a note here of what your external safe space is:

_____

_____

Creating an Inner Sanctuary[3, 4]

It can be very helpful also to create an inner, imaginary safe place for yourself. You can imagine this to be your inner sanctuary. This can serve as an internal anchor point for you to connect with a sense of inner calm and security whenever you might need it.

When you create your inner sanctuary it is quite important that you don't choose a place that currently exists in your life (as this could be spoilt for you by others) and that you don't introduce other people, not even your loved ones, into this space with you. You might like to create an imaginary place that you have not been to or somewhere that has been a very secure place to you in the past by following the instructions on page 101.

- It works best if the instructions to help you find and create your inner sanctuary are read out to you while you close your eyes. If closing your eyes is difficult for you, you can keep them open and focus softly on a neutral spot.
- You can do this yourself by creating a voice recording reading the instructions aloud beforehand. At this stage, read them out as if you are reading this for someone else and please don't try to apply the instructions to you, yet. If you have particular physical disabilities which prevent you from being able to carry out all the steps in the script please adjust those aspects that might present difficulties for you. It is helpful to do this beforehand so that when you read

the script and apply the instructions they will be just right for you.

- Please allow enough time after each instruction so that you can really focus inward on what you are asked to do.

- You can play this back to yourself when you are in a comfortable place and sufficiently calm to follow the instructions. This is something you could do in your external safe place if you have already created this.

- You will need to allow at least 40 minutes for this exercise, during which you should not be disturbed.

- You should feel reasonably calm when you do this exercise. You will be asked before you start with the sequence to give yourself a rating of your level of calm between 0–10 (0 – totally calm and 10 – totally tense). If your score to start with is above 5, then now is not the right time to do this Safe Place installation as it is unlikely to work for you.

- If you feel uncomfortable doing this for yourself, you can ask a close other to read the instructions out to you, while you close your eyes and follow them.

- You could also ask your trauma therapist to read this to you and they could help you install your inner sanctuary. This protocol was originally developed for trauma therapists to use with their clients[3, 4].

- You can sit or lie down while you are listening to this, whatever feels most comfortable to you.

- There is no 'right' or 'wrong' inner place, as long as it feels comfortable and positive to you.

- If someone else reads this out please make sure that they give you sufficient time in between each step for you to connect with the sensations you are asked to feel into.

  § Agree with them a signal (e.g. lifting a finger, or nodding) that will indicate to them that you are ready to move on to the next step.

  § Also agree with them beforehand that they will not ask you afterwards how it went and what inner sanctuary you chose. It is important that your chosen place is unique to you. If you share it with another person it can lose some of its uniqueness and may no longer feel this safe.

EXERCISE 1: CREATING YOUR INNER SANCTUARY

(SAFE PLACE PROTOCOL[3, 4])

- Get yourself into a very comfortable position, make sure that you are warm enough and that you will be undisturbed. If you like, you can close your eyes now.
- Once you are comfortable, check on how you are feeling now. Give yourself a rating of between 0 and 10 in terms of how calm you feel at this stage (0 – totally calm and 10 – totally tense). (If your score is above 5 come back to the exercise when you feel a bit calmer (below 5).

- First you are starting with a relaxed breathing sequence:
  - Feel the temperature of your out-breath and then your in-breath; notice the difference between the two . . . (pause)
  - Now allow yourself to feel the pace of your breathing. Just notice if your breathing is slow or fast . . . (pause) . . . Now allow yourself to breathe as slowly as is comfortable for you . . . (pause)
  - Now allow yourself to notice the balance between your in- and your out-breath . . . (pause) Just notice the time it takes you to breathe in and the amount of air you breathe in and the time it takes you to breathe out and the amount of air you breathe out, just notice . . . (pause) and now gently balance your in- and your out-breath, just balancing the two . . . (pause)
  - Now gently focus on the depth of your breathing. Just notice whether your breathing is more 'shallow', stopping somewhere in your chest cavity, or whether it is 'deeper', going right down into your abdominal area . . . (pause). Now allow yourself to gently take a few really deep breaths, breathing as deeply as you comfortably can . . . (pause)

- Now focus your attention into the connection between your body (regardless of whether you are lying or sitting) and the surface that you are in contact with right now and allow yourself to feel comfortably supported by this . . . (pause). Feel yourself securely supported by this connection . . . (pause). Notice your whole body making a secure and comfortable contact with the seating (bed or the floor) . . . (pause). Feel yourself comfortably grounded and held by this. . . . (pause)

- Now focus your attention inward again and this time imagine a palette of colour (in any medium you like, e.g. pastel, oil, watercolour, etc.) . . . (pause) . . . (For reader: 'When you have got a good inner sense of this, let me know by giving me the pre-arranged signal and we can then move on).

- Now out of these many colours, allow yourself to choose a few only, may be three or four colours that have an especially calming and soothing effect on you . . . (pause). (For reader: Let me know when you've got this and want to move on).

- Now that you have identified those colours, allow yourself to get an inner sense of if there were to be a place that could feel safe to you (use: 'secure', 'comforting', 'soothing', etc. as alternative words if the word 'safe' doesn't work for you) what colours would this need to have? . . . You may like to use some of the colours you have just identified or it could be totally different colours: whatever feels most suitable for you . . . (pause) (For reader: Let me know when you've got this and want to move on).

– Now that you have got a sense of colour, allow yourself to notice if there would need to be any sound in this special sanctuary of yours in order for it to feel safe ('secure', 'comforting', 'soothing', etc.) for you. You may also choose that there would be no sound. . . . (pause). (For reader: Let me know when you've got this and want to move on).

– Now that you know about the sound, allow yourself to notice whether there would need to be special scents or fragrances in your inner sanctuary to make it feel safe ('secure', 'comforting', 'soothing', etc.) for you. You may also choose that there would be no scent at all . . . (pause). (For reader: Let me know when you've got this and want to move on).

– Now that you have an idea about the scents or fragrances in your sanctuary, allow yourself to get an inner feeling of what the temperature would need to be like in order for it to feel really comfortable for you . . . (pause). (For reader: Let me know when you've got this and want to move on).

- Now that you know about the colours, the sound, the scents or fragrances and the temperature . . . allow yourself to notice if there would be any elements of nature, such as specific aspects of weather, plants, trees or landscape, in your inner sanctuary for it to feel really safe ('secure', 'comforting', 'soothing', etc.) and unique to you . . . (pause). (For reader: Let me know when you've got this and want to move on).

- Now that you have created your inner sanctuary allow yourself to look around it and get a sense as to whether there are any special objects (no people!) or animals or spirit guides you wish to add to make your place feel even more unique for you. Again just choose what feels most comfortable for you . . . this is your own inner sanctuary . . . (pause). (For reader: Let me know when you've got this and want to move on).

- Now allow yourself to explore if there is anything else that you would still like to change or need to be different to make your sanctuary even safer and more containing for you . . . (pause). (For reader: Let me know when you've got this and want to move on).

- When you feel that your sanctuary is just how you like it, focus on what it feels like in your body when you are in that space. Allow yourself to really enjoy those feelings and notice how it feels when your body is in a place that has these safe qualities ('secure', 'comforting', 'soothing', etc.) . . . (pause). (For reader: Let me know when you've got this and want to move on).

- Notice now if there are any thoughts in your mind that would go with this sanctuary and say them inside yourself now . . . (pause). (For reader: Let me know when you've got this and want to move on).

- From now on you can use this inner sanctuary as an inner anchor point for whenever you want to access those calming feelings and thoughts inside you. You can visit this place anytime, as often as you like. It is unique to you and only you have control and ownership over it.

- You can now build yourself an imaginary inner pathway that carries you from your inner sanctuary to the here-and-now, and from the here-and-now back to your sanctuary. This could be anything: an actual path, or a mode of transport or anything of your liking that is unique to you and that enables you to travel back and forth . . . (pause). (For reader: Let me know when you've got this and want to move on).

- When you have found your inner pathway, allow yourself to practise going back and forth to find out if it works. If it doesn't yet, then explore what changes you might need to make until you can use it comfortably . . . (pause). (For reader: Let me know when you've got this and want to move on).

- When your pathway is nicely established, you can stay in your special place a little while longer until you are ready to gently, via your inner pathway, bring yourself back to the here-and-now.

- Spend a few moments just resting, keeping your eyes still closed. Check into your body to give yourself another rating of your level of calm (0–10). If you remember, notice if there is now a change to the rating you had when you first started this.

• You can use your sanctuary any time when you want to access those feelings. Sometimes people use this sanctuary as a safe anchor point just before they need to do something important that they are nervous about, such as attending for a job interview, or other challenging situations.

- If you feel at a later time that you need to make changes to your sanctuary, you can go through these instructions again. People sometimes find that they need to change or update their safe place after a while.

- Remember that you can't do anything wrong with your imaginary inner sanctuary. Just follow what comes up for you and appreciate that this is uniquely yours.

- If you can't connect with all the elements that were introduced (e.g. colour, sound, scents or fragrances, temperature, elements of nature, objects, animals or spirit guides) just focus on those that work for you. Sometimes people just have a very special colour that they surround themselves with and that makes them feel safe. Or just a particular sound. Choose whatever feels right to you.

- It is not uncommon as your recovery progresses that your inner sanctuary might change. There may be other elements that want to be included or the place may change altogether. This is perfectly fine. You can use this protocol again whenever you feel it might be needed to update your inner sanctuary. For some people this is not necessary as their inner sanctuary remains the same and this is fine too.

Lastly, some words of caution:

- If you notice that you dissociate or feel strange or dizzy during this exercise, open your eyes immediately and connect yourself back to the here-and-now.
- Stop this exercise immediately, but take your time getting up, and do something completely different to distract yourself.
- Only try this protocol again when you feel better.
- Sometimes people experience bad memories or flashbacks while they are trying to create an inner safe place. If this is the case for you, do bring yourself out and gently focus on a here-and now object, reminding yourself that you are safe now. You may need to address what's come up for you first and it may not be the right time to install this safe place protocol for you yet. You might benefit from professional help, from someone who may enable you to build your inner sanctuary whenever you are ready.

Frequently, we take our safety for granted. It is only when it has been compromised, such as during a trauma, that we notice how precious and vital it is for us to feel safe.

Reclaiming your sense of external and internal safety is a paramount step on your journey to recovery.

Even if you can only partially achieve this at the moment in relation to the above exercises, every step in this direction is progress and moves you further out of the grip of your trauma. It is helpful to re-evaluate your sense of external and internal safety again and again and come back to this section in the book throughout the course of your recovery.

Journaling, record-keeping and creative expression

Here are some useful tools that will really support you on your journey of recovery and that you will probably never miss again once you have introduced them into your life.

Working actively will mean writing things down, not just keeping them in your head. This process is also called journaling. It will enable you to get to know yourself and your inner world better. After you have experienced a traumatic or stressful life event, your mind tries to process and understand what happened. However, if your memory system hasn't been able to update yet, it still registers danger and alerts you by keeping the same disturbing thoughts circling inside your head in repetitive, negative patterns. The process of journaling engages your analytical left brain: structures that are different to the parts engaged by your traumatised brain, which are usually an amalgamation of strong emotions and body sensations.

Journaling may enable you to gain greater emotional and mental clarity and there is scientific evidence that regular journaling helps increase your immune system functioning[5] and has a direct impact on your body's capacity to withstand stress and fight off infection and disease[5]. This is especially beneficial, as the chronic effects of trauma can weaken immune system functioning. For some people, writing things down may be difficult or not possible. An alternative method might be to voice record your troubling experiences, confusing thoughts or feelings. The idea here is to externalise what goes on in your inner world of thoughts, feelings and sensations by giving this verbal expression. There may be situations where it is not safe for you to write things down or voice record your very inner thoughts or feelings. If this describes your situation please ensure that you give your own safety first priority. Journaling or voice recording is only helpful under conditions which are safe for you and you are encouraged to protect yourself by making sure your journal is completely private.

For most people, change takes place in gradual stages that build on each other. As progress is made, it is quite common to forget where you started and therefore how far you have already advanced and changed along the way. Look back to the example of Harry in Chapter 1 (page 14). Harry described his process of recovery as like climbing out of a deep, waterless well. While he was climbing up the well, he sometimes thought it would be safer for him to go back right to the bottom where he started. This seemed an easier option at times than continuing his climb upwards. This was partly because he could not recognise at the time how far he had already managed to climb. All he could see was the potential danger that might lie ahead, but not the danger he had already successfully mastered and left behind at the bottom. To avoid falling into the same pattern as Harry, you can also use your journal as a record to remind you of the progress you are making over time.

Get yourself a special notebook and a special pen that you only use for making notes about your personal recovery process. This will be your personal journal for keeping to yourself. It's a good idea, too, to date all your entries in the journal.

If writing is difficult for you, get yourself a voice recorder or voice app or use your iPad or computer to set something up that enables you to log your inner experiences and the progress made along your healing journey.

Sometimes drawing pictures, cartoons or diagrams, or creating a collage, producing a clay model, using other craft material (if you like doing art); or creating music (if you can play an instrument) or using your voice through singing, chanting or sounding; or making your own movie can all be therapeutic ways of expressing what you have been feeling and going through. Here, the idea is not to produce an artistic masterpiece. You are encouraged to use these creative methods as an expression of what goes on in your inner world and to develop your own story. It is important that you don't worry about the outcome. You are doing this only for yourself and do not need to worry about sharing the outcome with anybody else. Research has found that developing a story or narrative may be a core component of understanding a trauma and helps you to process the traumatic or stressful life event[5]. This has been shown to predict recovery from trauma[6, 7]. These more creative techniques can be especially helpful if you tend to ruminate a lot. They can help to re-focus your attention and give you relief from your thinking processes.

> *Get some material that you could use for creative expression of how you feel along the way of your recovery path. Choose something that might be fun for you and you could potentially enjoy (even if you might not be able to feel any joy at the moment). Allow yourself to try something that you may have never used before, but that seems interesting. Remember you can't go wrong . . . you are only trying!*

Switching your mind into gear for healing

Trauma frequently narrows our outlook on life and it can feel as if you are stuck in this restrictive tunnel where there is little space for anything else. This will be explained more in Chapter 5 on Your life before the trauma. Preparing yourself for the journey out of this tunnel requires a change of outlook. Even though you might currently still feel stuck as you are reading this, it is helpful for you to start contemplating what you might need to change so that your internal mindset can come on board and support you on your way forward.

It might be helpful to think of your journey of recovery as an opportunity for positive growth. It might enable you to develop a deeper connection to and understanding of yourself. You may discover aspects about yourself that will surprise you and you hadn't known existed. These may open the way to new possibilities in your life, which you would have never thought about before the trauma. You may also be able to use this journey to re-evaluate your priorities in life and find out what is truly meaningful to you now. This may turn out to be quite different from what you had previously placed importance on.

One of the first changes therefore to switch your mind into gear for healing is *to develop an open curiosity towards yourself.* You may currently carry a lot of negative and judging thoughts about yourself in connection with the trauma. Like many other people after trauma you may also think some of the ones below:

- 'I am to blame'
- 'This was my fault'
- 'I have let myself down'
- 'I deserve this'
- 'I am a bad person'
- 'This is my punishment'

- 'I am not worthy'
- 'I should have seen this coming'
- 'I am weak'
- 'I should just be able to snap out of this'
- or any other similarly undermining thoughts.

You may also be aware of carrying very negative feelings about yourself, such as feeling gloomy and low, sadness, grief, guilt, self-blame, shame, anger, irritability or other similarly negative feelings. If you do carry any of the above thoughts or feelings, allow yourself to identify them and write them down in your journal under today's date. Be truthful with yourself and identify as many of these thoughts as you can and record them under: 'My thoughts about myself at the beginning of my recovery journey'. Now do exactly the same with your feelings and record them under: 'My feelings at the beginning of my recovery journey' under today's date. Do it right now!

It is helpful to acknowledge these on paper. Once you have written these down, don't judge yourself for them, just accept them for what they are, namely your thoughts and feelings right now. It does allow you to know where you are at this stage. We call this establishing a baseline. Just leave them for now where they are in your journal – you can come back to them at other times throughout your work with this book.

Well done for doing the above exercise. You have just put into action what was described earlier as developing an open curiosity towards yourself. You have looked at yourself with an honest and open mind and even though you may have found this quite uncomfortable, you did it. Well done! This is exactly the attitude that your healing process needs of you: the willingness to look at yourself openly, even if it is a bit uncomfortable. Then straight away to allow yourself to note and record what you found out. This is an enormously valuable starting step, because it connects you closer with yourself, and in time it increases your power to make choices and changes. You can't change anything that you are not even aware of.

Allow yourself to be openly curious about as many of your thoughts, feelings and behaviours as you can. Use your journal to record whatever you observe. Allow yourself to accept what is there with open curiosity. Notice also with open curiosity those times when you find yourself going into self-judgement. Just notice and write this down. You may even notice yourself thinking: '*I shouldn't judge myself!*' That is your self-judgement of your self-judgement. While this might seem strange, also notice that and write it down. This will help you in time to get to know yourself better and become more and more open, curious and accepting towards yourself. It might in time even make you smile at yourself.

Another change that helps your mind switch into gear for healing is **to commit to giving yourself another chance of life now.** Whatever the severity of your trauma, whatever the damage, destruction and consequences to your life, you could now decide to give yourself another chance. This will be entirely up to you, but it would be like contracting with yourself to make a new beginning, however awful you feel or devastating your experience has been. This will involve you sorting through the 'rubble' and aftermath of the trauma to salvage those things that still might have some use to you. At the same time it means letting go of those things that are broken, destroyed and you no longer can now return to. You may need to allow yourself time to grieve appropriately for all the losses you have had, and yet there is the chance of creating something entirely new, something that is different to how it had been before the trauma. It might be very scary at this stage to embrace this change because you don't know yet what it will be like. You may also lack courage and fear that if you build up something new, it could again be destroyed. There is indeed always that possibility. However, not re-building your life means that you will have to stay living in the rubble and destruction that surrounds you now.

In order to switch your mind into gear for healing, ask yourself internally now if you are ready to give yourself another chance of life? Whatever this takes . . . Take a moment to pause and listen in . . . are you ready for this? . . . If your inner voice (however quiet it might be) is curious and there is even just the slightest interest and agreement in giving yourself another chance of life, notice this and write it down. Well done! You have already made another step on the way to switching your mind into gear for healing. Allow yourself to listen to this inner voice more often and it might get louder and louder until you forget one day that there was ever any doubt.

The third aspect that will help switch your mind into gear for healing relates to your inner attitude towards yourself. We have already explored different types of safety earlier in this chapter, but there is one last type not mentioned yet and this is the question of **how safe you are with yourself?** This is very important because your autonomic nervous system and associated brain systems (which register and respond to danger) do not distinguish between external and internal threats.

Listen to your own inner dialogue. Are you giving yourself messages that put you under pressure, undermine, intimidate or threaten you? Are you possibly even destructive or damaging to yourself in some way? If you are doing any of this as part of the way in which you communicate internally with yourself (your inner commentator, which we all have) or in which you behave towards yourself, then your autonomic nervous system will respond in the same way as it would if there was an external threat, such as another person abusing you. It will activate your survival system and pump your body full of stress hormones and neurochemicals designed to help you under emergency situations. Except that there is no outside emergency now. The emergency is caused solely by yourself and the way in which you treat yourself. It is nevertheless as harmful to you as if there were an external danger trigger.

You have probably already guessed that these are not conducive conditions for your own recovery and healing process. You cannot heal while you still feel under constant threat. Constant threat from yourself. The change that is required here to help shift your mind into healing gear is *a different, more compassionate and kinder language with yourself.* Whatever you currently think or feel about yourself, in order to heal you need to allow yourself to soften towards yourself and develop a gentler, more patient and kinder inner dialogue. This does not mean that you are not responsible for the decisions that you have made in the past, even if some of these have been hurtful or harmful to yourself or others. It does however mean that now that you have decided to give yourself another chance at life, you also will have to learn to use a different inner language towards yourself. The language of loving kindness and compassion. It may take some time to learn this and may feel quite difficult at first. Trying to be kinder to yourself may even trigger emotions that you had not been expecting. Just notice these and write them down in your journal. In order to give yourself a chance at healing now, whatever may have happened and whatever your part in this may have been, it is necessary that you commit to learning to use a kinder and more compassionate internal language with yourself.

- Make a start now and observe and then note down in your journal under today's date how you speak to yourself.
- Then look at what you have written down. Now notice if this makes you feel good and open about yourself or if it feels hurtful and harsh.
- If it feels good and open, see if you can make it even kinder and more compassionate towards yourself and notice how this difference feels to you.

- If it feels hurtful and harsh, notice the effect of these feelings on your body. Does it make you feel hard and closed down? Then try and moderate your words towards yourself. Notice if you can soften them and speak to yourself in a more nurturing and a little kinder way.
- Practise this regularly for as long as you need until it becomes automatic that your inner dialogue with yourself is compassionate and kind.

You have now committed yourself to three changes that will enable you to switch your mind into gear for healing:

- **To develop an open curiosity towards yourself**
- **To give yourself another chance of life now**
- **To develop a language of loving kindness and compassion towards yourself**

Well done! This is a very big step and will lay an important foundation for your healing. Give yourself time to practise the above commitments. Be patient with yourself as you will find that it is easier on some days than others. Use your journal for record-keeping and check in regularly on all three aspects and see how you are doing.

Devising a schedule of positive self-care

Now that you have committed to making the above changes you are ready to build other support mechanisms for yourself. Recovery does not happen by magic. It involves aspects that can be quite challenging at times. For example, when you are ready for this in time, facing unpleasant memories instead of avoiding them. It is very important that you have put in place helpful support mechanisms for yourself before you can start this more challenging work. One of these involves committing yourself to a schedule of positive self-care throughout your recovery process and beyond. Trauma has made you feel under threat and out of control and positive self-care is necessary to be successful with your healing. This should include:

- Allowing yourself space and time for your recovery work
- Setting aside sufficient time for relaxation, grounding and nurturing activities
- Keeping a journal or some other form of record throughout your journey of recovery
- Sticking to the contract that you make with yourself (see page 128)
- Taking responsibility for ensuring your own safety
- Recognising your limits and pacing yourself appropriately – working only at what feels manageable and does not overwhelm you
- Controlling destructive impulses, such as risk-taking or self-destructive behaviours or suicidal

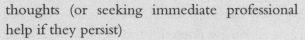

thoughts (or seeking immediate professional help if they persist)

- Removing anything dangerous or potentially harmful from your home
- Not abusing alcohol, drugs or any other addictive substances
- Seeking professional help if your symptoms get worse or if you feel out of your depth
- Being willing to try things out and being patient with yourself if they don't immediately work
- Being kind to yourself and agreeing to develop a compassionate approach towards yourself
- Here is space for some more of your own self-care ideas:

_____

_____

_____

_____

Identify which obstacles you need to remove or which things in your life you must change so that you will be ready to commit to your schedule of positive self-care. If you use alcohol or other addictive substances or recognise other unhealthy behaviours, then focus first on minimising these before starting any deeper trauma recovery work. Replace them with healthier strategies, such as physical exercise, yoga, walking, swimming, cycling or regular body work, such as massage, to help you self-regulate. (Chapter 10 on Managing your avoidance and numbing reactions may also be helpful for you). If you can't trust yourself to remove dangerous or harmful things from your home, explore if you can ask a close other to help you with this. If you can't manage this, commit to seeking professional help (refer to Chapter 17 in the Addendum on Useful guidance).

Positive self-care is an important pre-requisite for engaging in your recovery process. It helps you to re-create further conditions of safety, including your bodily wellbeing.

Some practical aspects for your trauma recovery

You need to be able to set aside time for yourself to work through this book. It is important that you tailor this to your individual circumstances and conditions and this will be different for each person. For some people it may be easy to find time to do this every day and work at it quite systematically. Some people commit to spend between 30–60 minutes on this every day. For others this might be totally unrealistic given their other responsibilities in life. It may also be that concentration is very difficult for you at this stage. It may take you a long time to work through a chapter and you may have to work in short bursts and come back again and again to it. That is okay. Just work at your own pace and at what is possible for you. It is important that you make a realistic commitment that is achievable and in itself consistent, but does not put you under pressure or overwhelm you. Any form of pressure or overwhelm is counterproductive and will keep you in the stress loop. What is important, however, is that you make a genuine commitment towards this process, and keep working at it. Some of the considerations highlighted in 'Make a contract with yourself' (below), will be of further help to you.

Initially it is helpful to work through the chapters in some form of order, or at least familiarise yourself with their content. The early chapters help you build a safe and secure foundation and groundwork. The later chapters take you into the deeper trauma recovery work. Without the early foundation you will struggle to do the deeper work and it is not helpful to skip it. Like the foundation of a house, you may not see it, but if it is not laid properly the most beautiful house is in danger of collapse or subsidence. It has been shown in clinical practice that the more initial time is spent on establishing safe foundations, including the building of inner resources, the better the deeper recovery work will flow. It is therefore important for you to understand that it is a necessity for you to spend time to create safe foundations.

Make a contract with yourself

The next step for you is now to set down in your new journal book a contract with yourself. This will help you start off with the best recovery conditions for yourself.

Read and work through these steps to assist you in making this contract with yourself:

1. Take some time to think about what your life is like at the moment. Think about all those things that might make it difficult for you to commit yourself to your own process of recovery. List them under 'Obstacles to Recovery' in your journal:

    a. First, think about all the *external* obstacles that might stand in your way of recovery. These might include: too little time in the day; too many conflicting pressures due to other commitments, like work, children or hospital appointments; other people or partners are not supportive; physically you can't get about very well at the moment; you use alcohol or drugs to help you cope with your pain, etc. Write all of these down.

    b. Second, think about all the *internal* obstacles that might be hindering you in your process of recovery. These might be: being too fearful of change; lacking in motivation and energy; being too critical and undermining of yourself; never giving yourself praise for any of your achievements, etc. You could also include what you have already observed about yourself when you did the work on shifting your mind into gear for healing. Write all the internal obstacles down.

2. Now look at all the obstacles that you have identified and ask yourself how you could reorganise or change aspects of your life to reduce some of these obstacles.

a. For example, if you have too little time in your day. While it is important not to put yourself under pressure in relation to your healing process, it could be important to take time to think about your real priorities at the moment. You may find that your own process of recovery is rather more important than some of those other things that are occupying so much time and are part of your routine. Remind yourself of having committed to giving yourself another chance of life. This would include also allowing yourself to work on restructuring your time and reorganising some of your current activities. Also notice if you give others more priority than yourself. If this is the case, again allow yourself a shift in balance.

b. If other people or your partner are not supportive, think of ways in which they might become *more* supportive of you. For example, do they really understand what you are going through at the moment? Would it help to show them this book to see if that changes their approach? They might like to become more actively involved in supporting your healing process. Even if you find that they remain unsupportive, you can still think about ways in which you could succeed without their help. It is important that you allow yourself to put your needs first at this time.

c. If you have observed that you are too critical and undermining of yourself, make a commitment to monitor the times when you tell yourself off or think badly about yourself. Now allow yourself to notice if there are times when this inner language you use with yourself is also presenting an obstacle to your healing process. Ask yourself if saying these things makes it more likely that you will succeed with your recovery or less likely? You have already made a commitment towards treating yourself with more kindness.

d. Explore if you could say something to yourself instead that gives you a better chance of success. For example, you might say, 'I can only try and do my best under the circumstances'.

You may not be able to lift every obstacle that stands in your way at this time. Remember that already you made a commitment to give yourself another chance of life. As part of that commitment, allow yourself to remove as many as you can at the outset of your recovery process. Write down *what* changes you want to make to remove as many obstacles as possible, and how and when you intend to make these changes. At the same time allow yourself to be realistic, so that you can succeed in what you set out to do.

Now make a list of promises to yourself that will aid in your process of recovery. This is your contract with yourself. These may well be things that you are not doing at the moment.

Your contract with yourself might look like this:

a. I promise to commit myself to my own process of recovery. I will try to make those changes that feel helpful to me and set aside time to do so.

b. I promise to be honest with myself, even if this means facing things that require more effort from me or feelings that are a little uncomfortable. I will allow myself to develop an open and curious attitude towards myself.

c. I will give myself a chance and persevere in my efforts. I understand that the process of recovery will take time and I will allow myself as much time as I need for this.

d. I will not expect techniques to work the first time I use them, but I will stick with them and try them out over a longer period of time. I will tailor them to fit my own needs and situation.

e. I will listen to myself and recognise my limits. I will not push myself unduly and will pace myself in my efforts. I know that it is better to work at things in a steady and planned way rather than try to solve everything at once.

f. I will give myself regular breaks and time off for relaxation or nurturing activities. I will aim to achieve a healthy balance in my life, where I take regular breaks and pursue activities that are nurturing and relaxing for myself. These will help me in my process of recovery.

g. I promise to do those things that are helpful to me and not those that could put me or other people in danger. This includes a promise to myself that I will not use alcohol or drugs to block out my feelings of pain or discomfort.

h. I am committed to speaking to myself more kindly and to noticing the times when I am struggling with this. I will be patient with myself as I am practising this.

i. I have read the Cautions at the end of Chapter 1 (page 24) of this book and I will stop if any of the exercises cause me unbearable distress. I will seek professional help (refer to Chapter 17 in the Addendum – Useful guidance) if I can't progress on my own or if I am a risk or danger to others or myself.

(Your signature, dated)

The preceding list is not exhaustive and you may want to include other promises that will help you in your recovery. Write this contract in your journal so that you can come back to it whenever you need to remind yourself of these promises towards yourself. Well done! You have already taken a lot of positive steps in this chapter to build a strong foundation to start you on your path to recovery!

Summary checkpoints:

- Before starting with your direct trauma work it is necessary to take time to prepare yourself for your trauma recovery process. This will lay the foundations.

- The very first step is to ensure that you are safe now and that you and your loved ones are no longer under direct threat of harm.

- There are four different types of safety[2]: physical, mental, emotional and spiritual.

- Change any factors in your life that are still compromising your safety. This has to be done before you can start with any of the trauma recovery work.

- Once you are safe in the here-and-now, you can create a safe place both in your external environment and in your inner mind, such as your own inner sanctuary[4].

- Regular journaling benefits greater mental clarity, monitoring of progress and the body's capacity to withstand stress and fight off infection and disease[5].

- Getting yourself a journal or other recording device is an important tool in your healing journey. Other creative processes can further support you with this.

- Your journey of recovery could be an opportunity for positive growth and for re-defining your priorities in life.
- To switch your mind into gear for healing, three changes in outlook are helpful:
  - To develop an open mind and curiosity towards yourself
  - To give yourself another chance of life
  - To develop a language of loving kindness and compassion towards yourself
- The first step is to make a commitment to and a contract with yourself. Now you can commence with your healing journey, moving at your very own pace, gently step-by-step.

5

Your life before the trauma

Stuck at the time of your trauma

Too often, when people have lived through a catastrophic experience, their sense of the past and vision of the future stops – all that they can see in front of them are continuing pictures of the terrible tragedy that has befallen them. They begin to think and speak in extremes, such as 'I'll always feel like this!', 'I'll never get over this!' or 'I'm permanently damaged!'

The diagram[1] on page 134 demonstrates how trauma can affect a person's whole outlook on present and future life. Think of the middle arrow line in the diagram as a person's lifeline. It starts at birth and for many people then moves on through a period of relative safety. During this time it would be normal for a person to have both positive and negative life experiences. In the diagram, imagine these taking place anywhere in the lighter shaded area above the middle arrow or in the darker shaded area below the middle arrow. Most people have to cope with some negative or difficult experiences in their life. However, if these are non-traumatic and there are enough resources, such as a good family network, friends or other support systems, then most people can deal with adverse experiences reasonably well and adjust to them. The more positive experiences may also counteract and balance some of the more difficult times. This person's sense of safety, therefore, feels relatively intact.

However, at the time of a trauma (illustrated here by a rectangular box in the negative life experiences area) it is as if most of the person's energy gets stuck in that one place and continues to stay there from then on. In other words, from the time of the trauma onwards all of this person's subsequent experiences, whether positive or negative, are overshadowed by the trauma. This is demonstrated by the shadow that emerges out of the trauma rectangle, casting an ever-larger influence on this person's present and future life. People often describe this experience in words like: 'I feel stuck at the time of the trauma', 'It is as if most of my energy stayed in that place', 'Everything in my life is clouded by the memory of the trauma'.

Even worse, the trauma seems to have blocked access to this person's previous sense of relative safety in their life. This is illustrated by the vertical black broken line that runs through the trauma rectangle, indicating the shut-off from previous feelings. It feels almost as if the period before the trauma never existed.

If this represents how you have been feeling, or what you have been saying, to yourself or to others, it probably seems as if the trauma now defines the way you are, rather than

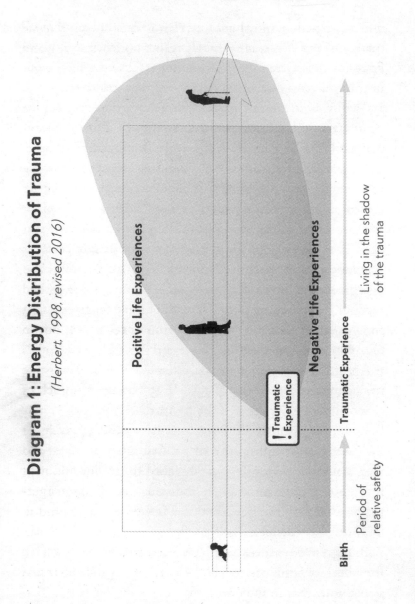

Diagram 1: Energy Distribution of Trauma
(Herbert, 1998, revised 2016)

Positive Life Experiences

Negative Life Experiences

Traumatic Experience

! Traumatic
• Experience

Birth

Period of
relative safety

Living in the shadow
of the trauma

you having any control over it. This is linked to an *internal trauma imprint in your memory system* that keeps repeating and does not allow you to see beyond the trauma, which is right in front of your face, all, or almost all, of the time.

This trauma imprint creates 'tunnel vision' – all you see now is interpreted through the lens of your traumatic experience. The accompanying feelings of guilt, panic, shame, and/or depression, lead to a questioning 'Why me?' – a sense of being singled out by fate. You may wonder if you are cursed or jinxed. You expect that things will never get better.

Until it is possible to feel connected with life again, your choices and your coping strategies will be very limited. This is common after a trauma. Your problem-solving skills and your ability to make decisions are likely to be diminished too. So, what can be done? It is important to believe that things *can* get better. The trauma cannot be erased, but in time this experience can be integrated so that it can become part of your life, rather than your sole focus. It is possible to contain your reactions and begin to claim back much of your functional life, even though your life after trauma may be quite different to life before. This is understandable, as the trauma has confronted you with aspects of yourself and your life that previously you probably weren't aware of. It may help to think of it as shifting your focus – not forgetting the trauma, but starting to see beyond it, or around it. The traumatic experience, and your reactions to it, can, with time and perseverance, move to a place on a 'shelf' in the memory bank of your life, where you decide how and when you want to look at it.

Reclaiming your functional life

Trauma therapists, both in Britain and North America, have found that drawing a chart of the stages or significant events in an individual's life *before* the trauma, is useful in helping people to reclaim a sense of meaning and purpose. This type of diagramming method has been called the Eriksonian 'Lifeline' exercise and originated in the 1960s in the writings of Dr Erik H. Erikson, a professor at Harvard University, and a leading figure in the field of psychoanalysis and human development. Erikson proposed[2] that there were eight stages in the development of the human personality, and that an individual's movement or progression from one stage to the next could be charted by means of a diagram. He suggested that all development could be considered 'a series of crises', and that the critical steps in development, the turning points, were 'moments of decision between progress and regression'. He believed that people could move a bit forward and backward, and could repeat a stage if something happened to block their progress at that time in their lives.

Erikson's concept of growth over the span of life events implies that the human spirit will rise to new challenges and that traumatic experiences can be overcome. The next exercise is offered to help you view your life span as a whole, a total picture. By moving beyond the boundaries or tunnels in your vision that were created by your experience of the trauma, you can begin to recognise your strengths again. You will be able to rebuild a functional life that reflects who you are now, despite and because of what you have been through. Although it may take time and conscious effort, your trauma can lead to a path of positive growth, however harmful and disruptive it may have been at the time and continues to be so.

Introduction to the climbing chart exercise

One of the aims of this exercise is to remind you that you have coped in the past and you are still coping with a lot now. Gently, cautiously, 'take a look' at the *whole* of your lifespan, beginning as far back as you can remember, and carrying forward *beyond your trauma* to the time now. It is important to recognise your achievements and strengths, and decide how to transfer them to the present. Try to ensure that you are not clouded in your views by a type of 'negative filter' (the opposite of 'rose-tinted glasses') that becomes a way of looking for the worst in things or picking out all the bad things that have happened in your life and using them as evidence that somehow you 'deserved' the trauma. That would be doing this exercise from within the shadow of the trauma. Instead, give yourself a fair chance and be as objective and loving as you can be. Look at your life as if you were an understanding and compassionate friend looking at it. You want it to be fair and non-judgmental.

Although it may seem that time has been standing still since your trauma, or that you are 'stuck' at this point in time, it is very important *to realise that this is an illusion!* Time has passed, and you have survived and, somehow, your life has kept moving. Therefore the point of this exercise is to take stock, to look back at the events that have shaped your life significantly, both positive and negative, and to see the patterns that emerged before the trauma took place. After completing your chart, let it 'rest' for a while. Come back to it another time, when you have a private, uninterrupted hour or two to carry on with the interpretation part of the exercise.

EXERCISE 2: PART 1 - GETTING STARTED ON YOUR CLIMBING CHART

You should allow yourself at least two hours of private, uninterrupted time to do this exercise (to complete it in one go). You can also do it in several smaller steps coming back to it as often as you want, and take longer over it. If you have photographs from childhood years or other mementoes, it may be helpful to look through them to help you remember. Do not be too concerned about remembering things in order, or very clearly. There may be long gaps in your chart, where you remember very little at all. While you continue the process of making the chart, however, you will probably find that other bits and pieces of memories will pop back into your mind and you can add new dots to mark these remembered events at any point. Try not to edit or make judgements, just write them down as you remember them. Just report.

On a large piece of paper (or with several sheets pasted end to end), draw a vertical line from bottom to top. (You can also use a piece of string instead of drawing the line if you would like to use your craft materials.) Use this line as the centre. On either side of it – the right side for positive, or growth, experiences, and the left side for negative, or 'held back', experiences – plot the events of your life. Position the dots relative to how you remember experiencing an event at the time. The more positive you remember it feeling to you, then the more to the right-hand side, and the more negative the more to the left-hand side. Start at the bottom, with your earliest recollections, and work your way to the top, where you see yourself now. With each dot or memory that you mark along the way, indicate: What happened? How old were you? How did you feel about it at the time? Any memory or event that was significant to you should be noted, for example, if you had a pet that died, or a favourite pair of red shoes that made you feel special when you were very young, etc. It does not matter if it was significant to (or even noticed by) anyone else.

You may feel some emotions when you do this exercise and this is okay. Just allow them. However, if you become overly distressed, stop! Put the material aside for a while, and use your journal as an outlet to write down your feelings. When you are feeling calmer, you can go back to the exercise, or complete it at another time. Take as long as you need. You may want to stretch this exercise over several days or even weeks. It is very common for people after trauma to struggle with their concentration and memory. You may find that you can't work persistently on this in one go. That is fine and please don't worry. Just do a bit at a time as and when you can. It might be hard for you to remember some things about your life and again it is important that you don't stress yourself about this. Just write down what you can at this stage and you can always come back to adding more information if it occurs to you another time.

The intention here is to help you make sense of your life experiences and put events in some sort of order. You will find 'clues' from your past that will help you to contain your feelings now and strengthen your coping skills. You will notice that when you start to connect to your memories, they all connect back to the centre, which acts as a kind of stabilising pole. That is a very good image to keep in mind. Remember, all your life, things have happened to you, both good and bad, and you are like the stabilising pole in the middle and still here and alive!

Traumatic experiences may have blocked you from accessing your inner strength. It is still there, or you wouldn't have survived. By reading this book and doing these exercises, you are trying to reconnect to your strength again. Don't despair if it seems to be taking a long time. If it was easy, you would have done it already, right at the start. One of the most important things to remember right now is to be patient with yourself!

The following example may help get you started

Diagram 2: The Climbing Chart

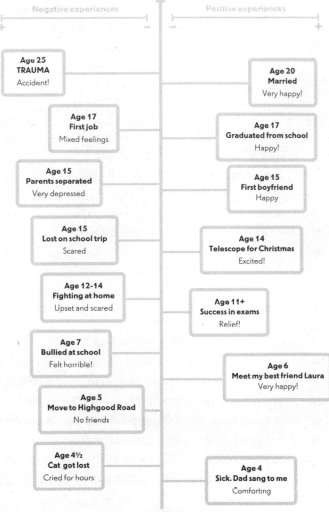

WHERE I AM NOW

Negative experiences — Positive experiences

Age 25
TRAUMA
Accident!

Age 20
Married
Very happy!

Age 17
First job
Mixed feelings

Age 17
Graduated from school
Happy!

Age 15
Parents separated
Very depressed

Age 15
First boyfriend
Happy

Age 15
Lost on school trip
Scared

Age 14
Telescope for Christmas
Excited!

Age 12-14
Fighting at home
Upset and scared

Age 11+
Success in exams
Relief!

Age 7
Bullied at school
Felt horrible!

Age 6
Meet my best friend Laura
Very happy!

Age 5
Move to Highgood Road
No friends

Age 4½
Cat got lost
Cried for hours

Age 4
Sick. Dad sang to me
Comforting

MY BIRTH

CAUTIONS:

- *If, while you were compiling your chart, you remembered and recorded other traumatic incidents from your past — particularly from childhood — such as physical abuse or sexual violation, it may be too difficult or upsetting for you to complete this exercise by yourself.*
- *Do not put yourself in harm's way if you sense that you are in any danger of hurting yourself or that you could be a danger to others!*
- *Stop working on this section, re-read the Cautions section on page 24, and find a health professional you can talk to (refer to Chapter 17 in the Addendum — Useful guidance).*
- *Your first priority is to keep yourself safe!*

Interpreting your climbing chart

When you look over your chart, you may be quite surprised to find that your stabilising pole has so many events attached to it. You may also start to realise that you are not your life events. Your life events have shaped and influenced you, but you are more than what happened to you[3]. You are the centre pole that has been responding to, holding and coping with all those life events. *You have really managed to carry and cope with a lot over the course of your lifetime so far.* Regardless of how bothered you may still be by the memories of the trauma that you experienced, somehow you found the strength to live through it, even though there may have been moments when you didn't believe you would.

Frequently the coping strategies we use quite appropriately to help us through very stressful times become habits that are inappropriate or excessive at times of normal, everyday stress. For example, it's appropriate to run out of a large burning building, but not appropriate to run out of *every* large building! Rationally you will probably agree to this, as it makes sense. However, when you have survived potentially life-threatening events, your coping responses at the time were controlled by your autonomic nervous system in conjunction with specific structures in your upper brain stem which take over automatically in such times (not in your conscious rational control!), as part of an evolutionary very adaptive process[4], as it can respond much faster than your rational thinking system. These helped you to survive and this is truly amazing. The problem with this is that once switched on, your survival system may not have switched off again. It may even now, although you are safe, still trigger coping responses in slightly stressful (not at all threatening) or even just normal life situations which are the same that you used when you were in real danger. This is because your survival system hasn't been updated. It still acts and behaves as if you are in danger. It is stuck at the time of the trauma as the energy distribution diagram on page 134. This is why you might cope in ways that aren't necessarily helpful for you now, such as for example, running out of a large building when there is no danger, or letting yourself cower down to the floor when you hear an exhaust backfiring, or many others.

The purpose of this section is to help you to take a look at your life and identify the methods you have used to cope with important events. These will not all have been stressful life events and you may notice that there is a difference between the coping responses you used in response to positive and those in response to stressful events. Some of the coping strategies may have been really useful to you and you may notice that you are not using them any longer even though they could be really helpful. Equally, you may find on examination that some of the ways of coping used in the past may not actually serve you well now (for example, alcohol may be an old coping strategy that you now use too much, before you have given any other ways of coping a chance). You may decide that you would like to replace them as part of your journey of recovery. It may become obvious to you that now you could use better ways of coping than you did in the past.

The next exercise of interpreting your climbing chart will help you bring into consciousness processes that so far may have happened largely out of your awareness. Bringing these into your conscious awareness will give you greater choice. You may need to help your survival system to update by reminding yourself that you are safe now and that you don't need to use the danger-triggered coping responses any longer. It helps not to 'fight' your survival system, but to appreciate it for how much it has been trying to help you in times when you were under threat and in danger. To appreciate it for having done its job so well. Yet, at the same time letting it know that now all is safe and your conscious rational system in alignment with your bodily needs can now choose again what strategies may be the healthiest and most helpful to bring into your life now. Use the interpretation of the climbing chart below to help you see clearly how you have been coping in life so far and what strategies you may like to use more in the future as you are setting your path for your recovery now.

EXERCISE 2: PART 2 – INTERPRETING YOUR CLIMBING CHART

A *Ask yourself the following questions, as you look over your 'climbing chart' drawing. As you write down your answers (in your journal), you will begin to recognise some repeated patterns of coping. You can then explore and choose whether you want to continue to behave in the same way or change.*

1. How have I reacted to important events in my life? List the important events and examine each one until a pattern emerges.
2. How did I cope with positive events? And with negative events? (Examples of possible reactions:

---

talking to others; getting angry or violent; tears; walking away; avoiding it; solving it)

3. Do I give myself credit for my accomplishments? How often? Do I appreciate my achievements or do I take them for granted?

4. When I am under stress, do I use a 'flight, freeze or fight' or be-'friend' (or 'fawn' – see Chapter 12) response? That is, do I either run away, freeze into inactivity, become very aggressive or placate and please the other? Is this a pattern for the way I cope with everyday events? Is it successful?

5. Which ways of coping have been the most useful and successful for me in the past? How often do I use those now?

6. Has my coping pattern changed since the trauma? In what ways?

7. Are there some coping strategies that I know would be helpful that I haven't tried or don't use any more?

8. How do I cope with people a) who are close to me? b) who are strangers? c) who are in some official capacity?

9. How do I cope when I am alone? Do I allow myself to be alone?

10. Do I take better care of others than I do of myself? In what ways?

11. Add any additional questions, that you think might be helpful, to the end of this list.

B *Look at the answers you have written in your journal and then see if you can make two lists:*

1. Your helpful or positive coping strategies
2. Your unhelpful, outdated or negative coping strategies.

Now use this information to help yourself identify your common patterns of thinking and reacting:

- Record these in your journal
- Start to explore what you might like to change for your path of recovery.
- Write in your journal a plan of what you may have to notice in your everyday life to support you with these changes.
- To start off with, concentrate on only one or two of the ones that you think you can manage now.
- Do the easier ones first and then progress to the more difficult changes.
- Give yourself time with implementing these changes and at the same time be sure you don't lose sight of your goal of change – make sure to praise yourself for achievements.
- Use your journal to help you with this process.

When you work through the Climbing Chart Interpretation, follow these guidelines:

- Concentrate on shifting to the positive, and reducing the negative.
- Be totally honest with yourself, even if this might feel a little uncomfortable.
- Allow yourself realistic time to change long-established and now unhelpful coping strategies.
- Be patient with yourself. Recognise your achievements even if change doesn't initially work every time.
- Don't try to predict the future.
- This is an exercise to help connect you to the present by looking at what has come before.
- Just because things have always been a certain way, doesn't mean they have to stay that way.
- Do not minimise your strengths or achievements, or maximise your faults or shortcomings!
- Allow yourself to be kind and compassionate and don't judge yourself if you have used coping strategies that may have been unhelpful or hurtful to you.
- The kinder you can be with yourself now, the safer you will feel. The safer you feel in yourself, the easier it will be for your survival system to

reset to the fact that you are safe now and release its automatic control.

- This will enable <u>you</u> to feel in control rather than you being controlled by your trauma.
- There is always scope for change! Remind yourself that you have committed to giving yourself another chance of life. Changing your unhelpful coping patterns forms part of this.

Summary checkpoints:

- Your energy and focus may still be 'stuck' at the time of the trauma, with the traumatic events feeling as if they are 'right in your face'.
- Even though you felt relatively safe in your life before, it is as if at the time of your trauma a shutter came down, now blocking access to any previous feelings of safety. You sense danger or adversity much or all of the time.
- Shifting your focus means not forgetting the trauma, but starting to see beyond it or around it.
- Reviewing your life events, both negative and positive, helps you recognise the rich tapestry of the life that you have had so far.

- It helps you realise that you are more than your life events or the trauma – you are the carrier ('stabilising pole') around which life happens.
- Bringing into conscious awareness the coping strategies that you are using now helps you take stock of which of these are helpful or unhelpful in your life now.
- It allows you to set into place those changes that are most helpful and healthy for your path of recovery now.
- The more helpful and kind you can be with yourself now, the safer you will feel. The safer you feel in yourself, the easier it will be for your autonomic nervous system to reset to the fact that you are safe now.

6

Methods to soothe your disturbed nervous system

Taking stock

When you have worked through the previous two chapters, you will have already done some very useful preparatory work to take you along on your journey of recovery. You may have started to feel a little more in control of your trauma through starting to understand more about it and sense that there is a way forward. Before moving on with this chapter, set aside a little time on your own. Take your journal into your safe place and take stock. Reflect on how you are feeling now, compared to when you first picked up this book.

- Notice what has changed and write this down.
- Reflect on what you have understood already about trauma and what you have observed and learned about yourself.

- Note down what has been difficult for you to do.
- Write down the areas you are still struggling with.
- Write down what has been helpful and worked well for you.
- Give yourself credit for having come this far already and showing so much engagement with this process.
- Notice how you are gradually taking more and more conscious control.

Understanding your autonomic nervous system!

Chapter 5 explained that coping responses during stressful events are activated by our autonomic nervous system in conjunction with other specific brain structures to ensure our best chances of survival at the time. This part of our nervous system is not under our conscious control. It may help you to understand how this works and its relevance to you now. Our nervous system is quite a complex system and not easy to explain. In this next part, to help you while reading it, the technical terms are put in brackets, which you can just ignore if this is easier for you. If this section feels too technical for you or if it doesn't interest you, you can just skip the text below and go straight to the part on 'Soothing your disturbed nervous system'.

Our autonomic nervous system is organised into three different subsystems. These respond in a hierarchical order to environmental challenges[1]. They are organised so that the most evolved response is engaged first, but when this fails, more primitive responses are activated.

The social engagement system (linked to the *parasympathetic ventral vagal system*) is the most evolved. This enables us to communicate and socially engage with others in a helpful and constructive manner. It allows us to feel secure and safe with others, reach out for help when needed and promotes a secure sense of self. When this subsystem is activated (*together with other brain structures and neurochemical processes*) we feel resilient and can cope even with challenging situations. When social engagement during traumatic or stressful situations is not possible, our autonomic nervous system will activate its next available subsystem.

This is the subsystem (*sympathetic nervous system*) that, in conjunction with specific arousal structures in the upper brain stem (*such as the Recticular Thalamic Activating System, including the mesencephalic periaqueductal gray – PAG, a structure in your midbrain*[2,3]), activates either a fight or a flight response. Fight does not necessarily mean actual physical fight, but also includes being able to stand up to a challenge or confront it. Flight relates to any behaviour that enables escape or avoidance of the threatening situation. When either fight or flight is not possible in a stressful situation then our third and most primitive subsystem will be activated.

This subsystem (*parasympathetic dorsal vagal system*) together with specific other brain structures (such as the

PAG[2,3,4]) initiates immobilisation, shutdown, freeze or dissociative responses, such as a flop response, to try to ensure the best chances of survival in a traumatic situation.

When the social engagement system can no longer be utilised during trauma we move out of the emotional comfort zone[5] and leave our window of tolerance[6,7] (this will be explained in the section 'Recognising the state of your nervous system', below). It moves us into an internal 'danger' zone, where we are literally taken over and controlled by our highly activated autonomic nervous system. Mostly, once the trauma is over and we are safe again, within a few days or weeks the overactive autonomic nervous system settles down and people move back into their resilient zone. This is why a good social system, such as a supportive partner, family, friends or colleagues, can play an important role. It encourages us back into our resilient zone as it re-engages our social engagement system.

If there are factors preventing you from feeling safe after the trauma is over, your nervous system may not be able to settle down and might remain disturbed. Examples of this could be:

- When the medical system that you may have needed to rely on after a trauma was not sufficiently supportive.
- If the nature of your trauma was such that human contact no longer feels safe.
- If the consequences of your trauma led to complications that meant that you couldn't know if you were safe for a long time after.

If you are still suffering from stress-related symptoms or PTSD this is an indication that your autonomic nervous system probably has not been able to stabilise enough to enable you to move back into your resilient zone. Before you can start with any of the direct trauma processing work, it is important that you learn techniques that will help your autonomic nervous system be calmed and soothed. This chapter provides you with methods that you can use to try to do this.

It may be helpful for you to think gently about your own trauma and explore which survival responses your nervous system had to mobilise. You could write these down in your journal. You are then ready to move to the next part of this chapter, below.

Soothing your disturbed nervous system

It is very common for people to think after a trauma that they should have done things differently at the time. Frequently this type of thinking generates guilt, shame or self-blame. It is very important for you to understand that whatever responses were activated and whatever the consequences of this are now, at the time this seemed the most adaptive response your autonomic nervous system could master. The situation you were in was urgent and your nervous system had to take over and respond as fast as it could under those circumstances. It is always easier with hindsight, because you now know the whole situation that at the time was just starting to emerge.

The more you have these thoughts of *'wanting it to have been different'* or for you to *'have acted in a different way'* the harder it is for your disturbed nervous system to reset. Essentially, your thoughts are signalling that you haven't accepted and come to terms with how things were and how you responded at the time of the trauma. This means that your focus is still very much in the past wanting to change the way things were. This makes it difficult for your nervous system to update to the fact that in the present you are safe again. Your thoughts about how you would like it to have been different have become an additional source of disturbance to your nervous system. This makes it difficult for your nervous system to settle and feel calmer again.

There are things you can do which can restore your nervous system to a more settled state. This will also help you heal from potential symptoms of hyperventilation which are outlined and explained in Chapter 10. The following methods help you to befriend, to update and to soothe your dysregulated nervous system.

Befriending your disturbed nervous system

The first step is to start to befriend your nervous system. After all, it is a vitally important part of you that you need to be on good terms with. Try out the following exercise which helps you note some of the thoughts that may make it difficult for your system to settle. Set aside sufficient time and work in a safe place where you will be undisturbed. If you feel some emotions while you are doing this exercise, just allow them to be. If your emotions are too strong or overwhelming to handle, please stop. Follow the guidelines that you have agreed to in your contract.

EXERCISE 3: APPRECIATING YOUR NERVOUS SYSTEM

Use your journal or write a letter. Note down thoughts that still disturb and aggravate your nervous system, making it difficult for you to calm down.

- Note any thoughts that you may hold about how you feel it should have been different. Do this without connecting to the specific details of your trauma experience. (You will be guided on how to work on your trauma safely in Chapter 7).
- Focus on those thoughts. Allow yourself to acknowledge that even though with hindsight things are not how you would have wanted them to have been at the time, because of the responses activated by your nervous system you managed to survive a very difficult life situation.
- Even though this may have meant that some damage or injury occurred to you or others as

---

part of this process, at the time this was all that you could do to get through this.

- If there are feelings coming up for you, for example sadness, loss, anger or resentment, just acknowledge these, stay with them gently and allow them to pass. If they are too overwhelming, stop and come back to this exercise another time. If this is the case for you, work in little chunks, one thought at a time.

- Rather than being resentful about what didn't happen or couldn't be done, allow yourself to express some appreciation to your amazing nervous system. It did kick in and helped you get through this experience.

- Speak to yourself like you would to a trusted friend who did everything they could in a very difficult life situation to survive.

- Recognise the costs involved to you doing all the things that you did in this emergency situation. Appreciate what you, with the help of the survival responses generated by your nervous system, managed to do.

- Whatever happened and whatever the costs, it did ensure you are still here!

- In your own words find a way to articulate your appreciation and thank your nervous system, like you would a trusted friend, for having protected you in the best way they could.

- After this exercise, allow yourself some more time and notice what you are feeling.
- Write down your observations. Do not attempt any other exercises for today.
- Give this book a break for at least a day.
- After that, before moving on to the next section and exercise in this book, check in again and notice if there is a change in how you feel now compared to before you did this exercise.

Updating your disturbed nervous system

Were you surprised by your reactions when you looked at the thoughts that still agitated your nervous system? Did you notice a change in how you felt afterwards when you had found a way of appreciating your nervous system? Many people report feeling calmer and more peaceful in themselves after this. If you don't feel any change, allow yourself to check if you did really engage with the last exercise. If you find you didn't really take it seriously or couldn't do it properly when you tried, you could go back and try it again before moving on further in this book. If you found it too difficult to do just move on to the next step, below.

The next step is to update your nervous system to the safety of your here-and-now reality. This will only work if things are indeed relatively safe for you now and this is the precondition for working on your recovery anyway. If it is not safe, please go back to Chapter 4 and work on your safety issues first.

For the next period of time, this could be over several days or even weeks, start to remind yourself of the relative safety of your present here–and–now. This may seem strange initially, but will make sense once you try it.

EXERCISE 4: UPDATING TO THE SAFETY OF YOUR HERE-AND-NOW

Start noticing as often as you can during the day if you are really in the here-and-now or whether your mind or thoughts have wandered to a different space in time, such as the past or your future:

- When you notice that you are not in the present, focus on where your attention has gone. Acknowledge that you are not in the here and now. Then bring your attention to your body. Notice any sensations, feelings and thoughts. If you can, write them down.
- Then bring yourself back to the present by using a reminder in your environment. This could include reminding yourself of the time, the day or the date it is or focusing on or touching a particular object that connects you to the here-and-now. More grounding techniques are also

outlined in Chapter 9 – Managing your arousal reactions.

- Once you are in the present, say to yourself (internally): 'Wherever I've just been and whatever I was dwelling on, I am just noticing that I am safe now.' Say this as soothingly and gently as you can.

- As you say this allow yourself to breathe in and out deeply, balanced and slowly. Notice your breath in the here-and-now.

- You may want to expand this inner message to yourself by listing evidence that confirms that you are safe now.

- You may also remind your nervous system that it has known how to feel safe in the past and although something difficult happened, this doesn't mean that it will always be unsafe.

- Remind it that it is safe now and that it can re-set to the relative safety in the present. This will help it recover and regulate so that it can be strong again should it ever be needed. Use your own words for this and tailor them to your specific circumstances.

- Make sure that your focus remains on the present moment in time and if it wanders off again, gently bring it back using the same steps.

- This exercise needs your practice and patience. It is important for you to remind yourself to do it as often as you can. You can build it as a regular feature into your day, checking in as often as you can. Nobody needs to notice what you are doing.

- It can take some time for your nervous system to update. The likelihood is that quite often you are still stuck somewhere in the past. It may take some time until your nervous system feels confident enough that things are indeed safe enough now. Just give yourself the time you need and remain patient. You can continue with this exercise even when you have already moved on to other parts of this book.

- Ensure that you stay with your focus in the present. Stop at any time if this exercise feels too difficult or overwhelming to you right now. Give yourself a break and come back to it another time. This exercise will only work if it is relatively safe for you in the present now.

- Connecting regularly to your inner sanctuary or external safe place that you created as part of your preparatory work in Chapter 4 can also help your nervous system regulate. This reminds your nervous system and associated brain structures what it feels like when you are in your emotional comfort zone. Some other exercises in this chapter and in forthcoming ones will help you further strengthen this process.

Recognising the state of your nervous system

Living with a dysregulated nervous system is not only very unsettling but can also be extremely exhausting, as it costs you so much extra energy. 'Dysregulated' is a term that is used to indicate that your feelings are outside your resilient zone and you find it hard to control them. Your nervous system may still be quite shut down and there may be times when you feel frozen and numb. You may feel tired a lot of the time even though you may not have done much during the day. Equally, your nervous system may keep you overactive and you may be on constant alert and even though you are tired you may not be able to settle and go to sleep. Both of these problems indicate that your nervous system is still dysregulated. This section helps you to recognise the state of your autonomic nervous system and to notice when it is dysregulated. In this context the window of tolerance[5,6] is a useful model to be familiar with (see page 164).

Diagram 3 illustrates that when we are in our emotional comfort zone, which is referred to as the window of tolerance, we can cope with life's challenges constructively. This is because we can think and feel at the same time and adapt our reactions to fit each situation appropriately. Life will always bring new challenges and demands, but when we can operate from within our window of tolerance our feelings are tolerable and our reactions feel within our control. This is your emotional comfort zone. The two dark, dotted lines either side of the window of tolerance indicate the boundary beyond which we move out of our emotional comfort zone into either hyperarousal or hypoarousal

Diagram 3: Window of Tolerance Model

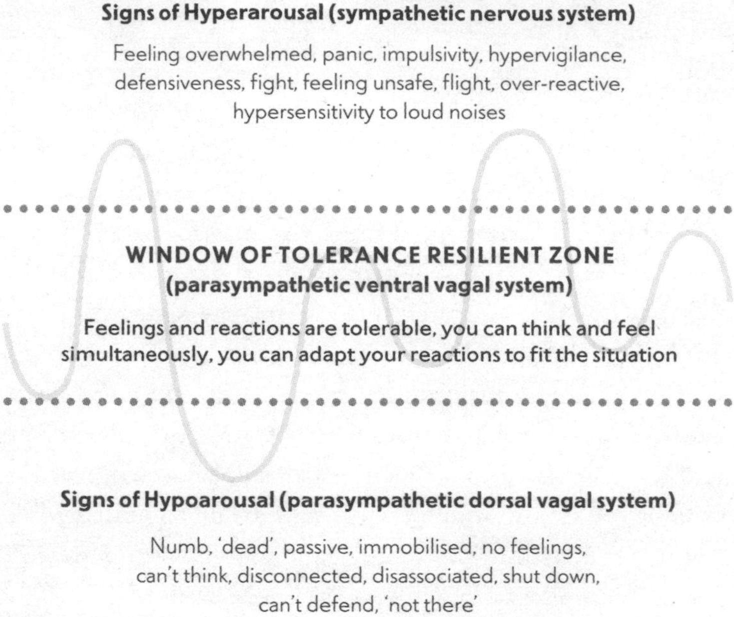

Signs of Hyperarousal (sympathetic nervous system)

Feeling overwhelmed, panic, impulsivity, hypervigilance, defensiveness, fight, feeling unsafe, flight, over-reactive, hypersensitivity to loud noises

WINDOW OF TOLERANCE RESILIENT ZONE
(parasympathetic ventral vagal system)

Feelings and reactions are tolerable, you can think and feel simultaneously, you can adapt your reactions to fit the situation

Signs of Hypoarousal (parasympathetic dorsal vagal system)

Numb, 'dead', passive, immobilised, no feelings, can't think, disconnected, disassociated, shut down, can't defend, 'not there'

responses. These are linked to the different subsystems of our autonomic nervous system explained at the beginning of this chapter. The model shows you the different responses that are part of either a hyperarousal state (e.g. feeling overwhelmed, panic, hypervigilance, etc.) or a hypoarousal state (e.g. numb, 'dead inside', passive, immobilised, frozen, etc). Both of these states feel very uncomfortable and mean that we are no longer properly in control of our responses in a given situation. We are dysregulated. This diagram may help you to recognise when you are feeling or reacting in ways that indicate that you are out of your window of tolerance or emotional comfort zone. It is common after a traumatic experience for this window of tolerance to become quite narrow. This means that situations which before the trauma would have been easy for you to deal with may now pose a real challenge and take you out of your emotional comfort zone. It is perfectly possible for some people to experience both hyper- and hypoarousal reactions which fluctuate (as the diagram indicates with the curvy line crossing over the upper and lower boundary lines) at different times during the day. Part of your trauma recovery work is to:

1. Recognise when you are operating from outside your emotional comfort zone (and are dysregulated).
2. Develop a range of resources to stabilise your nervous system and more easily bring you back into your window of tolerance.
3. Over time, be able to expand your window of tolerance and alongside experience an increase in your resilience.

Before the trauma you may not have paid much attention as to whether you responded from within or outside your window of tolerance or emotional comfort zone. In order to build awareness of this, it is important that you start to focus on the sensations, feelings and thoughts you notice in response to events that arise in your day-to-day life. When your nervous system is dysregulated it is especially the sensations and feelings that you will need to learn to pay attention to. This will help you in time to notice when you are dysregulated and once you can do this you can start to use strategies to regulate and soothe your nervous system.

The following exercise will help you with this.

- Set aside some time (about 30 minutes) and find a place where you can be undisturbed for this time. You can do this in your external safe place.
- Make sure that you are very comfortable and make a conscious connection with the here-and-now (as in the earlier exercise on page 160).
- You will be asked to use a rating scale. You could make yourself several copies beforehand, so that you have them to hand whenever you want to do this exercise. You may not want to open your eyes and write things down during this exercise, but you could internalise the score you give yourself, especially once you are more familiar with the scale, and then write it down after you have opened your eyes again. Make sure you have the rating scale to hand before you start.
- Stop at any time if this exercise feels too difficult or overwhelming to do right now.

EXERCISE 5: GETTING TO KNOW YOUR EMOTIONAL COMFORT ZONE

Focus into your body. For most people this works best with their eyes closed. Do this, if you can. Then focus on the space between your eyes and from this turn your attention inwards into your body. If you don't feel safe closing your eyes or can't because of a physical injury or disability, adjust this exercise to suit your particular circumstances and needs. You could keep them slightly open and, if you can, gaze downwards, selecting a neutral point on the floor. Try to become aware of the point between your eyes and, from there, focus your attention inwards. Use the following guidelines (you could pre-record them) to help you focus:

- Notice what you are feeling inside your body right now. Does your body feel:
  - Calm and at ease
  - Agitated and on edge
  - Numb or shut-down
- Now identify whether these feelings fall inside your emotional comfort zone or outside it. If outside, note if they are part of a hyper- or hypoarousal response.
- Once you have identified the state of your body right now, notice where you can sense these

particular feelings in your body. What sensations do you notice? Do you feel these all over your body or only in certain parts? Describe to yourself where you can feel them and make a mental note of this in your inner mind.

- Next try and determine how strong these feelings are for you right now. Give yourself an internal rating score for the particular state you are in right now. You can use the scale below. It ranges from 0 to 10 for both the hyper- and the hypoarousal response.

Rating Scale:

10--Hyperarousal--0 **| Window-of-tolerance |** 0--Hypoarousal--10

10-9-8-7-6-5-4-3-2-1-0 **| Emotional Comfort Zone |** 0-1-2-3-4-5-6-7-8-9-10

| For Hyperarousal mark 10 – 0 here | **no mark here – observe how it feels** | For Hypoarousal mark 0 – 10 here |

- If you are in your emotional comfort zone you don't have to give yourself a score, but you could notice how your window of tolerance feels right now. Does it feel wide and expansive or rather narrow and confined? You could note internally how close you feel to the boundaries on either side of it right now.
- Now allow yourself again to notice what it feels like in your body when your nervous system is in the state you have just identified. At this

stage, just notice what it feels like. This is part of observing yourself. Do not judge this feeling or try to change it at this stage. Just note, understand and accept what it feels like, even if it does not feel very comfortable.

- When you are ready, open your eyes very slowly, and take some time to ensure that you are safely back in the here-and-now time. Remember the mental rating score you took internally and note this down now on the rating scale with today's date. Record your observations in your journal.

Well done for trying this exercise. Even if it wasn't easy for you it is good that you tried it out. The more often you practise sensing in, the easier it will be for you to notice the internal signals for when you are operating outside your window of tolerance and when your nervous system is dysregulated. This is very important information because it can help you, once you are familiar with this, to notice even during normal day-to-day challenges how they affect you and how you are coping with them. Triggers that lead to dysregulation can either relate to events in your outside environment or to particular thoughts you may be having. Try and identify what might have been triggering you. This will give you greater self-knowledge and you could also gain awareness of how you might come across to others in particular situations. This may help to increase your sense of control.

Building resources to stabilise your nervous system

When you are able to recognise that you are dysregulated you can start to establish resources which will help you to soothe and stabilise your nervous system. Resources are anything that makes you feel stronger internally, safer, more positive and alive in yourself. This is very important because the experience of trauma sensitises those brain structures responsible for ensuring our survival to look out more for bad things[8] rather than good in our life. Therefore you may be highly sensitised to triggers alerting you to potential threats rather than noticing all those signals that indicate that life is safe and good at the moment. Obviously our internal alarm system is very important, but it can make life quite miserable when it has become too sensitised and over-focused on potential danger. It is important that on a regular basis you include and focus on positive resources in your life. Resources can counteract that internal imbalance, rebuild your resiliency and stabilise your nervous system[9].

Positive resources fall into three broad areas:

- External resources
- Internal resources
- Imaginary resources

External resources are those that have given you support and nurture throughout your life. This could include supportive partners, friends, family members, colleagues, neighbours; special places you have visited or lived at; beautiful holidays you have had; skills or hobbies that hold meaning to you and give you joy; activities that are strengthening and uplifting; special community activities that you value; particular sports or exercises that are uplifting and calming to you; appreciation of aspects of nature or landscape that give you pleasure; pets that provide comfort and company. Even if some of those aspects are no longer in your life now, the memory of the positive or good associated with this can in itself act as a resource to you.

EXERCISE 6: REPLENISHING YOUR EXTERNAL RESOURCES

- Take out your journal and list down all those things (the above will give you some guidance) that have given you nurturance, support, pleasure or joy in your life so far.
- Write down the actual resource and also the positive aspects that you associate with it, for example:

My dog Orwell – unconditional love and companionship, fun walks on a regular basis, reassurance and security.

- While you write down each resource, spend time focusing on the positive qualities that are associated with it for you and really notice how this makes you feel.
- When you have finished with your list, appreciate all the positive qualities you have already been able to experience in your life.
- Focus on those that gave you the most pleasure and joy and mark them out.
- Then notice how many positive resources are still in your life and give those a tick.
- Evaluate if you are still making full use of those positive resources that are in your life now or if that has changed.
- If it has changed then examine how it has changed. Explore if you could reconnect to those positive resources that are still in your life in a way that would feel nurturing and supportive to you. Write this down.
- If you find that your positive resources have really fallen away and there are very few left, start to explore what new resources you could build into your life now. Tailor this to your current ability and needs.
- Make yourself a list of at least five positive external resources, which you can start with. This could include very simple things, such as:

- Watching a movie that makes me laugh – once a week.
- Starting to greet and speak a few positive words with my neighbour and her dog, whenever we meet.
- Connecting to one positive aspect of nature in whatever way possible for me, e.g. appreciating the sun as it lights up my room, watching a beautiful sunset – once a day.
- Listening to uplifting music that makes me happy – several times a day.
- Taking up painting again for the fun of it, just experimenting at this stage – once or twice a week.

• Regularly review, revise and expand your list as you get better at enjoying the benefits of your positive external resources.

Other positive external resources include, for example, the use of simple soothing techniques for when your nervous system becomes dysregulated and you feel overwhelmed. Although you may not be used to treating yourself in this way and you may think that some of the suggestions, below, are rather strange or weird, they are based on what has been found to be very soothing for most human nervous systems. These could include:

- Hugging yourself and stroking very gently down your forearms with both hands in a soothing manner (this is a therapeutic method called butterfly hug and used as part of EMDR therapy – explained in more detail in Chapter 17 in the Addendum - Useful guidance).
- Making yourself a hot water bottle and curling up in a safe corner or in bed.
- Breathing slowly, balanced and deeply and feeling your feet connecting safely with the floor.
- Wrapping yourself up in a cosy blanket (or if you are dissociating regularly, a fairly heavy, weighted blanket, which you can order online, might be more soothing).
- Making a hot drink or warm soup for yourself and focusing on enjoying the comforting feeling that this gives you.
- Cooking for yourself nutritiously healthy and regular meals and focusing on the beneficial effect of this for your body while you eat it (also keeps blood sugar level stable).
- Listening to some uplifting, inspiring music.
- Running a fragrant, warm bath for yourself.
- Putting on an aromatherapy burner with your favourite essential oil fragrance.
- Looking at photos or pictures that connect you to happy times.
- Touching and stroking objects with a sensual structure, such as a textured cushion or a cold pebble or a wooden massage roller.
- Doing some gentle physical exercise, such as tai chi, qi gong or yoga.

- Using simple body postures to help you rebalance and calm your nervous system (some of these come from yoga).

Body postures to calm your overactive nervous system

There are a number of body postures you can use. Please do not use these if you have specific physical limitations, disabilities or injuries that mean that this exercise could worsen matters. Be very gentle with yourself. If you have specific limitations please adjust the postures accordingly keeping yourself safe. Below are some simple postures you could try out for yourself:

Reclined goddess pose

Legs on chair

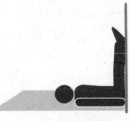

Legs against a wall

Leaning against a wall

Inner resources relate to your belief and value systems, including your spiritual beliefs, qualities that you have, such as your character traits and body strength, aspects about you that make you unique and that give meaning to your life. Trauma can shadow the way in which you feel about yourself and the meaning and value you assign to life. In order to regain control, increase your emotional comfort zone and help stabilise your nervous system, it is important for you to rebuild your inner resources.

EXERCISE 7: REBUILDING YOUR INNER RESOURCES

Wait at least a day before attempting this exercise if you have just done the external resource building exercise.

- Find a quiet space where you will be undisturbed for about 30 minutes and take out your journal.
- Think back to a time before your trauma when life still felt relatively safe for you. If a good friend or colleague would have been asked to describe five of your most positive qualities, then what might they have said about you? Write this down.
- When you think back to that time, which of your inner beliefs or values gave your life meaning? Write this down.

- If you look back in your inner mind now, what particular qualities, character traits or body strengths were unique to you? What were you especially good at? Write these down.
- Now look over what you have written and explore if anything has changed? What is different now? Write this down.
- Explore what has led to these changes. Did these happen just as a result of the trauma or had these started before? What was it that moved you away from your inner beliefs and values, losing touch with what gave you meaning?
- Now allow yourself to gently connect to your past self, that part of you who still held these values. What would that part say to you if they looked at you as you are now? Could they give you some advice as to what might be missing in your life? What might need to change for you to reconnect with who you really are and what you stand for?
- Spend some time listening to this inner advice. If you notice yourself feeling some emotions, just gently allow these (only stop if this feels too overwhelming). Thank your younger self for assisting you.
- After a while, write down which of your values or inner beliefs you would like to be able to reconnect to. What would you need to start to

shift in order to be able to get closer to your true values again? For example,

- You find that your true values are clouded by focusing too much on the bad things that have happened rather than appreciating some of the good things that are still here in your life, now. You could then decide that you want to start becoming more aware of when you do this and always focus also on one positive, good thing at the time when this happens.

• Write yourself an intention of what you will focus on shifting first. Give yourself plenty of time to practise and be patient with yourself. Regularly review and revise this to fit your changing circumstances.

Imaginary resources refer to an inner picture you build for yourself to give you courage, hope, confidence, strength or other positive, helpful qualities. This then becomes an inner power source for you that you can draw on. The inner sanctuary or safe place that you created in Chapter 4 would be an example of this. You could choose the image of an animal that you associate with particular qualities, such as strength, wisdom, loyalty, etc. This can also include inner places of worship or power that hold meaning for you or power heroes symbolising particular qualities for you. Some people choose angelic helpers or connection to spiritual powers as their inner imaginary resource.

EXERCISE 8: FINDING YOUR IMAGINARY POSITIVE RESOURCE

- Find a quiet, safe place where you can be undisturbed for 30 minutes. Make yourself very comfortable. You may want to pre-record these instructions so that you can follow them undisturbed.
- Focus into your inner mind, by bringing your awareness on this space behind your eyes, and if comfortable close your eyes.
- Take a few slow and deep breaths to settle yourself.
- Then ask yourself internally what positive quality would help you at this particular stage in your recovery process? This could for example be: hope, strength, determination, courage, safety, trust or any others.
- Now staying connected to your inner mind, allow yourself to sense into the particular quality you just identified. Can you already feel this inside yourself somewhere? If so, allow yourself to feel this and notice where this sits in your

---

body. If you can't, ask yourself if there is an imaginary positive resource that symbolises this particular quality for you.

- Allow yourself to bring up a picture of this imaginary resource in your inner mind as vividly as you can. Make eye contact with it and then ask this resource if it would assist you in holding the quality that you desire on your behalf and gradually show you how you could hold this in you, too. Thank the resource if it agrees to do so.

- You can now reconnect to this imaginary resource whenever you want to connect to the felt sense of that particular quality. You can do this as often as you wish until more and more of this quality becomes part of your felt experience.

- If you could already feel this particular quality in yourself earlier, you can think about ways in which you could strengthen this quality in yourself. What might you want to do differently now to hold even more of this particular quality in yourself?

- You can do this exercise as often as you like each time you become aware that you desire other qualities to help you with your recovery. Concentrate on embedding one quality at a time, even though the imaginary resource that you have chosen may be able to symbolise several of the qualities you desire.

Every person is different and what works for one person may not work for another. Try out which positive resources work for you and fit with your particular circumstances. In order to override your threat system and rebalance your nervous system, you need to focus on the positive resources and the qualities that you associate with each, about three times longer than you would focus on the negative, fearful things[8]. It takes your brain longer to encode and embed positive stimuli than negative ones[9]. It is important for you to bear this in mind when you are practising the methods introduced in this chapter. Give yourself time, practise consistently and repeatedly and be patient with yourself.

As a general rule when you notice that you are dysregulating, if at all possible, either:

- Take yourself out of the situation you are in
- Take a break from the activity you are engaged in
- Find a way in which you can withdraw for a little while until you are more regulated again
- Try and reduce sensory input if you can (for example turning the radio or television off), because whatever you are doing or wherever you are, it is too much for your autonomic nervous system.

Once you are out of the triggering situation try connecting to your resources and the feelings and qualities that these represent to you. When you have practised and mastered the steps in this chapter you are well on your way to recovery. Well done! You are now ready to progress to the more direct trauma processing work.

If despite engaging with the practice in this chapter and giving it a good go over some time (at least three to four weeks) you notice no change and still feel totally unable to regulate your nervous system this is not a sign of failure. This may be a sign that you need to see a mental health professional for more specialist help. If this is the case, you are advised not to move on to the trauma processing exercise in Chapter 7, but to seek therapeutic help first. Chapter 17 in the Addendum – Useful guidance gives you advice on how to do this. You may come back to this book as part of your therapy if your specialist feels this could be helpful.

Summary checkpoints:

- Coping responses during stressful events are activated by the autonomic nervous system in conjunction with specific brain structures, outside our conscious control. This ensures our best chances of survival at the time.
- Our autonomic nervous system is organised into three different, hierarchical subsystems:
  - The social engagement system
  - The fight and flight system
  - The immobilisation system

- These are organised that the most evolved response is engaged first, but when this fails more primitive responses are activated.
- If there are factors preventing you from feeling safe after the trauma is over, your nervous system may not be able to settle down and might remain dysregulated.
- Living with a dysregulated nervous system is not only very unsettling but can also be extremely exhausting, as it costs you so much extra energy.
- Before you start with any of the direct trauma processing work, it is important that you learn techniques that will help you soothe and stabilise your autonomic nervous system.
- The first step is to start to befriend your nervous system.
- The next step is to update your nervous system to the safety of your here–and–now reality.
- You can then move towards learning to:
  - recognise when you are operating from outside your emotional comfort zone or window of tolerance
  - develop a range of positive resources to stabilise your nervous system and more easily bring you back into your emotional comfort zone
  - expand your window of tolerance and alongside experience increased resiliency

7

On the path to recovery

Processing your experience – telling the story!

If you have followed the preparations in the previous chapters, you are now ready to take your next step towards healing and to unlock some of those aspects of your trauma that you may have kept secret from yourself or others, or that you have simply avoided confronting. This chapter can help you with this process in a practical way. The exercises should only be undertaken if you have made the necessary preparations suggested in Chapters 4–6 and if your trauma is no longer present as a daily reality in your life. If your trauma is still ongoing or recurring, please go back to the section on 'Ensuring that you are safe now' in Chapter 4.

Keeping secrets

Most people have to face a barrage of questions during the time immediately after their trauma. These questions can come from relatives and friends as well as from emergency and rescue workers, such as police, firemen, ambulance personnel, nurses or doctors at the hospital, your own medical practitioner and even sometimes the press. At the same time, most people feel very shocked and stunned in this initial period after their trauma and find it difficult to cope with questions.

Such questions may be experienced as very intrusive, overwhelming and inappropriate, and it is only natural for trauma sufferers to want to keep their responses brief.

There might also have been some other reasons that prevented you from sharing your true feelings with others:

- A feeling that although people asked you questions, they didn't really want to know the full details, perhaps because they felt uncomfortable being confronted by the horror of your experiences.
- You may have felt ashamed about some aspects of your trauma and this felt so uncomfortable that you didn't want to talk about this.
- Some people said very tactless and completely inappropriate things, which upset you. You didn't feel strong enough to let them know that the things they were saying hurt you or may even have made the trauma worse, and instead you just closed down and refused to share things with them altogether.
- Some only talked about the physical aspects, about your injuries or wounds, but completely

discounted how the trauma affected you emotionally.

- Other people may have asked you about your feelings, but you felt uncomfortable opening up to them. You may have felt you should be brave or that it was a sign of weakness if you allowed yourself to share with them what you really felt. Another possibility is that you felt you shouldn't upset or burden them with some of the distressing experiences you had.

- It could also be that people really cared and asked you lots of helpful questions about your feelings, but that at the time you just felt completely numb, and couldn't respond. You may have still been too shocked to feel anything or to verbalise your feelings.

- People were too preoccupied caring for others, who were also involved in the trauma, or suffered as a result of it, and completely ignored you because they thought you were all right. Maybe your injuries weren't as serious as other people's; maybe others died and you didn't.

- Either you or other people felt you were to blame or were responsible for the trauma because of some action you took or didn't take. As a result nobody showed any sympathy for the physical or emotional effects on you. If you blamed yourself this might have led you also to avoid answering questions.

The following example illustrates one aspect of why people are reluctant to share their true feelings:

I had been in a fire caused by a gas explosion at my work in a biscuit factory. I was one of the few survivors to sustain only minor physical injuries and, immediately following the explosion, I was responsible for rescuing others, who were trapped by collapsed parts of the building and needed pulling out before the fire could reach them. When emergency personnel arrived they took over from me, concentrating all their efforts on those that seemed worse off. Although very badly shocked and exhausted from my rescue attempts, I was put in a safe corner of a nearby building that served as a rescue shelter and given little attention. After a physical examination and some minor wound care at my local hospital I was discharged. Members of my family were very pleased that I hadn't been hurt more seriously and they kept saying to me how lucky I was to have got away with it so lightly. My family seemed more concerned about my other colleagues, some of whom were also personal friends, who were still in hospital with severe physical injuries. Even the fire investigation officer, the police, my boss and the owner of the factory, who later came to talk to me to take a statement of my account of events, thanked me for my rescue attempts but disregarded my feelings during or after the trauma. They repeatedly emphasised how lucky I could count myself not to have been one of the people whom the trauma had hit more seriously. I secretly felt guilty about 'having got away with it so lightly' and ashamed about the continuous upsetting thoughts and feelings about the trauma that kept intruding into my mind day and night completely out of the blue. Even four weeks later I hadn't had a single night's peaceful sleep, was suffering from terrible nightmares and felt emotionally extremely distressed. I felt very bad about these feelings as I thought I should be grateful that I was one of the lucky ones. Secretly I thought that I was going mad and I hated myself for my weakness. I kept completely silent about my feelings because I felt I had no right to seek anybody else's support, when most of my colleagues were so much worse off.

Pete

Opening up

In order to work through, come to terms with and resolve a trauma, it is really important that all aspects of it are processed. This enables the successful integration of the trauma. This means that you need to make sense of:

- What exactly happened
- How you reacted
- What it meant to you.

The above example illustrates how people can be affected by a trauma in very different ways. There is no prescribed way of reacting to a trauma and, while for some people their physical injuries are the most painful, for others their emotional wounds are far greater. Your experience of the trauma is unique to you and a recognition of this helps you to re-establish control and positively change the deeply unsettling and disruptive effect the trauma may have had on you.

There are many ways in which you can make sense of your trauma and often it can be enough to talk about it in detail to a person or friend whom you can trust. When you do this it is normal that you should experience quite strong emotions and even some of the physical reactions that you felt during the time of the trauma. If this happens, allow these feelings their space – they are an important part of the normal healing process. To keep feelings from becoming too overwhelming, ensure that you keep yourself safe and that you stay within your window of tolerance. Use some of the strategies and resources that you have learned in the previous chapters while going through your experiences to help you with this.

How to process and make sense of your experience

Frequently it is difficult to share your experiences in such depth with others and you can find other ways of processing your experience. Some alternatives are suggested below.

1. WRITE AN ACCOUNT OF YOUR OWN PERSONAL TRAUMA

You could think of this account like a personal 'testimony' to the world, so that others could witness it and understand the terrible experience you have gone through. It might help to think of it as being similar to the way in which the people in this book have shared their experiences in order to help you better understand and recover from your own trauma.

Here's how to prepare your account (please read all of the preparatory steps, a–g, before starting to write):

a. *Only work on your trauma if it is actually over,* so, for example, a road traffic accident that took place six weeks ago or a bank robbery four months ago. If your trauma is still with you, for example, if a person who has hurt you is still around and continues to hurt you or could hurt you, then do not attempt to work through your experience at the moment, as it will not be beneficial. Go back to Chapter 4 and explore if there is anything you can do to stop the trauma from continuing.

b. *Set aside a limited amount of time each day, at a specific time, and arrange to do a pleasurable and nurturing activity afterwards, for example, some of the resource strategies you learnt in Chapter 6.* This should be a time when you are not disrupted by others and when you can feel safe expressing some of the emotions that come up. Do not write your account of the trauma last thing at night. Set yourself a time limit of about 45 minutes to one hour. If you haven't finished writing your account at the end of the time for that day, jot down a few notes and resume the next day. It is important that you stop after the time limit that you have set for yourself. Finish each session by connecting yourself with your inner sanctuary or safe place. Afterwards you should have arranged to do a personally pleasurable and stabilising activity, such as meeting with a friend, taking the dog for a walk, listening to some music, going to church or your specific place of spiritual worship, taking a relaxing bath, arranging for an aromatherapy massage – or whatever else is likely to be a helpful resource to you.

c. *Allow yourself as much time for recounting the whole of your trauma as you need.* You may need several days or possibly several weeks until you have completely accounted for all aspects of your experience. It is important that you don't rush things and that you always stop after the time limit you have set yourself for the day. Don't be impatient with yourself – there is no standard guideline about how long it should take you to work through your trauma. It is a good idea, though, to work on this for a set period of time each day. If you need longer than a week you might like to give yourself a day off from it at the weekend, before starting on it again the following week. If you have to miss a day because of other commitments, just carry on the following day.

d. *Include as much information and detail about the trauma as possible.* It is important that you think about everything that you saw, smelled, heard, touched and sensed around you at the time. Remember that this experience was unique to you, no other person would have experienced the trauma in exactly the way in which you did. Even if at first you think that you don't recall very much, when you allow yourself to revisit the experience, it is often surprising how many things your mind and body *have* registered, often over a very short period of time. If your trauma experience has been quite extensive involving many aspects, work through little chunks of experience one at a time. This also works if parts of your experience have been extremely distressing. Break these down into manageable, distinct chunks. If 45 minutes or an hour is too long and feels overwhelming to you, tailor your processing time to a period you can manage and build up to longer as it gets easier working through your trauma.

e. *Write in the present tense, using the first person.* Start your account at a time from just before the trauma happened and continue to a point afterwards when you were safe. Work through all aspects, including the aftermath, rescue attempts, your experiences at hospital, how others reacted, etc. Write your account in the *first person* as if you were really revisiting your trauma, for example: 'As I see . . . I go to . . . and I feel . . . ' This will help to make your account more vivid. If accounting in the first person feels too overwhelming for you to start off with, work through your whole experience first from a third-person or slightly removed perspective, such as watching it happening like a film on a cinema screen. When you have completed this safely, progress to reliving your whole experience again in the *first person*. You may need several days or weeks until you feel safe progressing to a *first person* account. Take your time and pace yourself in a way that is manageable for you. The aim is for you to stay within your own window of tolerance and present while you work on your account. If you notice that you are dysregulating and dissociating, stop immediately. Use some of the resource strategies that you explored in Chapter 6 to soothe yourself and regulate your nervous system again. Only go back to your account when you are regulated and in your window of tolerance again.

f.   *In your account, work through:*

- What exactly happened, i.e. start with the facts: what were you doing and thinking just before the event? Go through the entire sequence of events until the aftermath and to the stage when you were safe again.
- How you reacted, i.e. what were your feelings? What did you do? What physical sensations did you notice? What was running through your mind at the time?
- What did it mean to you? What was the worst part for you? How have you changed? What is your life like now? What can't or won't you do

now that you used to do before? What things or people aren't there any more because of the trauma? What is the hardest part for you to get used to? Where are you stuck at the moment? What needs to happen for this stuckness to be resolved?

g. *Allow yourself to experience the feelings and sensations that may arise.* Traumatic experiences wouldn't affect us if we didn't have feelings. It is very important that you acknowledge the presence of these feelings and bodily sensations, for example, feeling hot or cold, etc. To do so is an essential part of processing the experience. It is important not to be frightened, even if these feelings surprise you by their strength. Remind yourself that you are revisiting the time of the trauma and this is how you felt then but that is past. These strong reactions were part of your survival system's coping responses and were aimed to help you survive the trauma as best you could. You are reliving now what you felt then, but under the circumstances most likely couldn't work through at that time. It is totally understandable that you would have had very strong and often confusing reactions both during and after your trauma. It is also entirely understandable that you may have felt, said or done things during the trauma that you would never have done under ordinary circumstances. Some people feel that the trauma has brought out characteristics in them that they didn't know they had. If you feel ashamed, angry or guilty about having reacted in a particular way during the trauma, remember that you reacted in the only way you could at the time. With hindsight, what you did may not seem right to you now. You feel you should have acted differently or done more. This is a very common reaction. You already explored this briefly in Chapter 6 as part of Exercise 3. Remind yourself that you were under the control of your autonomic nervous system that took over at that time as explained in Chapters 5 and 6. At the time of your trauma and under those specific conditions those were the only things that you *could* do. This doesn't necessarily make those decisions that you took morally or legally right, but it puts them into a realistic perspective.

Caution: *Stop writing if any of your feelings become too overwhelming and you move out of your window of tolerance. Take a break and use one of the resourcing strategies that you know works for you from Chapter 6. Only go back to processing when you feel stable and regulated again. If your overwhelming reactions continue and you find it very difficult to soothe and regulate yourself then this technique may not be helpful for you at the moment. Stop using it. If your symptoms still don't improve you are advised to seek professional help.*

2. OTHER WAYS OF PROCESSING YOUR EXPERIENCE

There are other ways of processing your experiences if you find writing difficult. Follow the same guidelines as above (a–g), but instead of writing, choose one of the alternative methods, outlined below:

- Make an audio recording dictating your experiences in it. Then listen to it being played back to you.
- Paint or draw. You don't have to be very artistic, but sometimes it can help to express all your experiences in the form of a drawing or painting. It doesn't have to be an accurate representation of what went on, but it should capture the personal meaning for you and reflect all the feelings and sensations that you experienced. Allow yourself to express all the imagery and associated feelings that come up for you when you revisit your trauma.
- Make a collage. Use anything you can find, such as old magazines, old clothing material, wood, threads, colours, etc. to build up a representation of what happened to you. Again, the aim is not to create a fantastic piece of art, but rather to capture the meaning of the trauma for you in the collage.
- Write a poem or a song. If you have a bit of literary talent or if you are musical you might

find it healing to express and process your experience in this way. Try to come up with a series of verses in your poem or your song as you process your experience over several days.

- Make a sculpture, using modelling clay or other bits of material.
- Use any other artistic or creative way of expressing what you've been through and the meaning it held for you. These creative trauma processing methods can help you bypass your active 'thinking mind' and 'language systems' and tap more easily into the felt sense and emotions connected to your traumatic experience. These methods are also useful alternatives if you can't find a language for the trauma you have experienced. Sometimes people find that they remember and know what has happened to them but can't put it into words. It is literally as if the trauma is frozen into a sense of speechless terror. In this case creative or artistic expression can be a really helpful first step to processing your experience. Later you may additionally want to produce a written account or audio record it.
- Whatever method you may choose, only work in a way that is tolerable for you and pace yourself. Follow the principles outlined on pages 190–95 (a–g) and make sure you have a clear beginning and an end to this process. Allow all

the feelings or sensations that might be coming up for you. During the process stay within your window of tolerance and stop if you dysregulate. Use resourcing strategies and only resume the processing work when you have brought yourself fully back. If this is not possible and your symptoms continue, give this work a break.

- You might consider seeking professional help with this. Trauma processing is an important part of NICE recommended psychological treatments for PTSD, such as TF–CBT and EMDR. Depending on the services available in your locality you might be able to self-refer to these. Chapter 17 in the addendum gives you further guidance.

Trauma processing is quite an advanced step on your healing journey and may not come easily to you. Most people initially feel some resistance to connecting to their traumatic experience this closely and it is entirely understandable that you may want to avoid this step.

It is therefore very important that you have prepared yourself for it and you have mastered some of the self-regulation techniques explored in Chapter 6. When you understand about your window of tolerance, can recognise when you dysregulate and move out of your emotional comfort zone and can bring yourself gently back, you should be ready for tackling the trauma processing. It is very important that you follow your very own pace and that you tailor the processing to your unique circumstances. Allow yourself as much time as you need and start with baby steps and then slowly build up. It is better to go easy on this rather than being too ambitious. Later, when you feel you have advanced in your healing process and nearly recovered, you may want to mark your journey in a similarly creative way by trying some of the suggestions made in Chapter 16.

When you have completed this step in your recovery and healing journey, reward yourself for your achievement!

Summary checkpoints:

- There are many reasons why you may not have been able to talk or face the full details of your traumatic experience yet.
- To come to terms with and resolve a trauma it is really important that all aspects of it are processed. This enables the successful integration of the trauma. This means making sense of:
  - What exactly happened
  - How you reacted
  - What it meant to you
- There are many ways in which you can make sense of a trauma and it can be enough to talk in detail about it to a person or a friend whom you can trust.

- It can be difficult to share your experiences in depth with others and then other ways of processing your experience will be important:
  - Write an account of your personal trauma
  - Audio-record the details of your trauma
  - Use creative or artistic means to express your trauma, its effect on you and what it meant to you
  - Write a poem or a song about what happened and how it affected you emotionally and mentally
- Whatever method or methods you choose it is important to allow yourself to process your experience in as much detail and as fully as you can.
- Follow the guidelines outlined in this chapter to keep yourself safe and within your emotional comfort zone so that your processing is helpful to you.
- It is entirely normal for you to feel some reluctance about exploring your trauma in greater depth.
- It is therefore important that you have prepared yourself for it and mastered some of the self-regulation and resourcing techniques explored in Chapter 6, as well as, your connection to your inner sanctuary or safe place (Chapter 4).
- You should then be ready to advance to the trauma processing. Work at your own pace and

tailor this to your own unique circumstances. Start with baby steps and then slowly build up. Reward yourself when you have completed this very important step on your healing journey.

- If you dysregulate or have adverse effects, stop and go back to the self-regulation techniques in Chapter 6. If your symptoms continue you are advised to seek therapeutic help, Chapter 17 provides some guidance on this.

8

Managing your intrusive, re-experiencing reactions

What seems right is not necessarily the most helpful

As most of us know from everyday life, when something is on our minds so much that we can't stop thinking about it, feel taken over by it or find ourselves ruminating about it at inappropriate moments, it is usually ineffective just to tell ourselves to forget about it. Trying to suppress a worry or an obsessive idea often causes it to rebound even more strongly and persistently.

Most of us have had the experience of being dumped by a boy- or a girlfriend at some stage in our lives. Do you remember the very first time this happened to you? It would probably have been in one of your early relationships. Do you still remember why the person dumped you at the time? Can you recall how you coped with this then? Like most people, you may have wanted to put this experience behind you as quickly as possible in order to get on with other things in your life. You may have gone to school or work as usual, trying to push it out of your mind and not to think about it any more. If you used that strategy, can you remember if it actually worked for you at the time? Could you successfully push the feelings and thoughts about that experience out of your mind – or did you find that trying not to think about it made it harder for you and thoughts kept intruding anyway, distracting you from what you wanted to get on with?

Most people find that trying not to think about something makes them think even more about it – it makes the thought stronger. It is the same with traumatic thoughts and memories. A scientist called Wegner[1] found that thoughts that have been deliberately pushed away occur about twice as often as thoughts that haven't been suppressed. Nevertheless, this is precisely what many people try to do after a trauma. A very common strategy used by those suffering from post-trauma reactions is to 'try not to think about it', 'try to put it out of my mind', 'try to avoid reminders of it that would make me think about it'.

The Post-traumatic Stress Disorder Checklist[2] (PCL-5[3]) is a questionnaire that is used to measure post-traumatic stress reactions. It asks how people cope with thoughts about their trauma. It looks at how often people tend to use the 'not thinking about it' or 'avoiding' strategy. It uses this as a way of measuring the severity of a person's distress. The more often these strategies need to be used, the more severe the intrusive reactions are likely to be.

Getting to know your intrusive (re-experiencing) reactions

In order to be able to manage these intrusive and re-experiencing reactions, you need to be aware how much they are bothering you. Measuring how much they bother you will enable you to establish what is called a *baseline*. This is the measure of your reactions *before* you start to make any changes and has several advantages:

1. When you have made changes you then take another measure to assess whether the changes you have made have helped to lessen your reactions.
2. As you advance in your healing you will see that the gap between your baseline score and subsequent scores will get wider. This is a recognition of the improvements that you have made.
3. You will also become aware if certain strategies are not helping – by an increase in your score compared to your score at the baseline. *If that is the case you must stop the strategies that you have been using and seek professional help.*

Copy these questions into your journal, date the entry and try to answer them as best as you can. The scales 0–4 are explained below:

- To rate how much you have been bothered by each of the experiences in the past week, use the following 0-4 scale:

0	1	2	3	4
Not at all	A little bit	Moderately	Quite a bit	Extremely

Please answer the following questions by circling the number on each scale that best applies to you:

1. In the past seven days how much were you bothered by thoughts, images or sensations (including smells or sounds) about the stressful experience intruded into your mind at times when you did not want them to?

0	1	2	3	4

2. In the past seven days how much were you bothered by repeated, disturbing dreams or nightmares about the stressful experience?

0	1	2	3	4

3. In the past seven days how much were you bothered by suddenly feeling or acting as if the stressful experience was actually happening again (as if you were actually back there reliving it)?

     0   1   2   3   4

4. In the past seven days how much were you bothered by feeling very upset when something reminded you of the stressful experience (very sad, tearful, angry, fearful, anxious, etc.)?

     0   1   2   3   4

5. In the past seven days how much have you been bothered by strong physical reactions (for example, heart pounding, trouble breathing, sweating, headaches) when something reminded you of the stressful experience?

     0   1   2   3   4

Once you have circled the number that best applies to you on each question on how much you are bothered ratings, add the scores from all the questions (1–5). Record the total score in your journal.

TOTAL SCORE FOR INTRUSIVE, RE-EXPERIENCING REACTIONS ON...................... (date)

Your total score is:...

If your total score is:

5 or below = they are low

6–10 = they fall into the mid-range

11 or more = they are high

Lastly, give an overall rating for how disabling these intrusive, re-experiencing reactions have been to you in the past week by circling the number that applies to you on the scale below (you could also copy this into your journal):

0	1	2	3	4	5	6	7	8

Not at all disabling	Slightly disabling	Definitely disabling	Markedly disabling	Severely disabling

Now that you have established your baseline for intrusive (re-experiencing) reactions, you can begin to try to reduce these responses. It is important for you to regularly monitor your intrusive re-experiencing reactions to notice any changes. If you have scored in the mid- to high range, you might find that specialist trauma therapy would really be useful to you, in addition to working through this book.

The difference between a flashback and an intrusive memory

Intrusive memories and flashbacks are the most prominent index symptoms of PTSD. Intrusive memories are vivid pictures, smells, sounds, etc. that are experienced as being very real, while the person affected remains aware that these are actually recollections (often very disturbing ones) of what happened before, during and in the aftermath of the traumatic event. Intrusive memories can often entail intense physical sensations and it is very common for people to try and block these memories out or push them away when they occur.

During a flashback, the trauma, or some aspect of it, are experienced *as if it were happening all over again*. You might re-experience images, sounds, the presence of others, smells, tastes, things touching or hitting you. Flashbacks are sensory fragments of the trauma stored in your memory system, being played back to you. They can be triggered by a whole array of reminders in your everyday life and are usually experienced as very overwhelming and vivid. This is because parts of your brain have not been able to update to the fact that the trauma is now in the past and your survival system still responds to triggers as if there is immediate threat. Reactions like these tend to make people feel like they are 'losing their minds', or that their minds are playing tricks on them: they know logically the event can't be happening again, yet it seems to be. Flashbacks can be truly terrifying, because of their unpredictability and the accompanying feeling of being out of control.

Both intrusive memories and flashbacks can be triggered by very subtle reminders in the everyday environment, such as a brief sound, a smell, or just a feeling or a thought. The experience both of intrusive memories and flashbacks can make you feel very much out of control, especially because they seem to come totally out of the blue and can elicit such strong physical reactions. What follows are some strategies for managing these intrusive memories and flashbacks. The aim is to help you learn how to gain more and more control over them. The first step, as always, is for you to find out and understand what is happening. Second, we will introduce you to techniques to help you master some of these distressing intrusive reactions. Although examining and confronting intrusive reactions can make you feel uncomfortable, it is usually not harmful or dangerous, so please allow yourself to be as open as possible as you begin these exercises. There is also specific advice if you have experienced trauma relating to sexual violation.

First, a couple of ground rules:

- Work at your own pace and don't push yourself too hard. This is not a race!
- *Caution*: Stop the exercises and distract yourself if you are unable to tolerate the strength of the physical sensations that are called up. Draw on your resourcing strategies to calm, soothe and regulate yourself. Try the exercise again another day and focus on reducing these physical sensations to a tolerable level. If your reactions persist or get worse, seek professional help.

Managing intrusive memories

You may already be aware that trying to block out your intrusive memories is not necessarily the most helpful approach. It would be more constructive for you to learn strategies to enable you to integrate them into your life in a gradual way. Work through the following exercise to help you to ascertain just how often you try to dismiss your traumatic memories.

EXERCISE 9: RECOGNISING YOUR AVOIDANCE STRATEGIES

1. Do this exercise when you have an hour to concentrate on yourself.
2. Take your journal and draw a table, similar to the one in the Example Record below (blank copies are provided in the Appendix and online).
3. Look at your watch and note down the time.
4. Then get on with your activities as you normally would. For the next hour observe whenever a thought or feeling about your traumatic experience pops into your mind. Each time it does, notice how you react. Try and rate the strength of your distress on a scale 0–8 (see below).
5. Note how you are trying to cope with the memory. If you find yourself automatically trying to push it from your mind, make a tick in that column of your table.
6. Note also if your intrusive thoughts or feelings trigger ruminations which make you go over events again and again in your mind.
7. Stop yourself after an hour.
8. At the end of this hour check to see how often you tried not to think about it when an intrusive memory about the trauma popped into your mind.

Rate your strength of distress on the following scale:

0	1	2	3	4	5	6	7	8
No distress		A little distress		Definite distress		Marked distress		Severe distress

Here is an Example Record:

Date: 21.12.2016   Time: 11.15am.

Time	Intrusive Memory	Sensations in your body	Strength of Distress (0–10)	Able to tolerate it	Push it away
11.20	Thought about the ice on the road before the car slipped	Tightening of chest, faster breathing	4 Definite distress	✓	
11.35	Smell of burnt rubber (know it's from the accident)	Headache, nausea	7 Severe distress		✓
11.40	Image of other car	Feeling sick	6 Marked distress	started rumi-nating	✓

What did you observe from your own record? Was the result as you had expected? Or were you surprised at how often you push memories away? Did you notice if you started to ruminate? Note down your findings in your journal, being aware also of bodily sensations and the level of distress the intrusions caused. At what level of distress did you find it hard to tolerate the intrusions?

You will probably have noticed from the exercise that different memories can cause different levels of distress. Not all of them are equally strong in terms of how they affect you.

You are probably also aware that the less distressing a memory the better you are able to tolerate it and the less you want to suppress it. The next exercise offers some strategies for integrating and tolerating intrusive memories rather than suppressing them.

EXERCISE 10: INCREASING YOUR TOLERANCE LEVELS

This exercise helps you learn, at a gradual pace, how to accept more and more of the intrusive memories into your life. This will only work if you are safe now. You need to allow about half an hour a day on a regular basis for this exercise.

From your observations in the last exercise note at what rate of distress you feel unable to tolerate your intrusive memories and start pushing them away. In the example in Exercise 9, the person could still tolerate her intrusive memories at a strength rating of 4. However, 6 was too high for her to tolerate the distress. She started ruminating and then noticed herself pushing the memories away. Her physical sensation at that level was feeling sick.

1. Write down in your notebook what physical

---

sensations you notice at the level where you start to push your memories away.

2. Now focus on your body and see whether you can make your body feel those sensations. Although this might be a little uncomfortable, it is not dangerous! Just allow yourself to stay with those sensations as long as you can. Just notice them and feel them. Try to stay as calm and relaxed as you can. Say to yourself that this is how your body feels when it experiences that strength of distress. Allow yourself to breathe gently and slowly into this distress and use some of the soothing techniques if you find yourself moving out of your emotional comfort zone. Make sure that you stay connected to the here-and-now all throughout doing this.

3. Some people also find it helpful to think of these bodily feelings as a shape or a specific colour. Try to do that: if you can feel them as a coloured shape. Explore if that shape changes as you stay with it and breathe into it. Does it get bigger or smaller or change its form or colour? Just gently breathe into it and stay with it if you can. Observe this and notice how it changes. Write this down in your journal as you go along.

4. The longer you can allow yourself to feel your physical sensations, the more you will realise that tolerating them is possible for you, even if it feels a little uncomfortable.

5. Perform this exercise for several days, for half an hour at a time. After you have learned to tolerate your bodily sensations at that level of strength, repeat Exercise 9 to measure your distress levels.

6. After a while, if you notice that you no longer need to push away the intrusive memories that cause you this level of distress, try Exercise 10 again, moving onto the next higher level of strength of distress.

7. If you find that you still need to push those intrusive memories away, go back to Exercise 10 and stay with it for a bit longer until you can move onto step 7. Use some of the resources you learned about in Chapter 6 – Methods to soothe your disturbed nervous system, to help you stay in your emotional comfort zone, if this feels quite overwhelming or difficult for you.

Managing flashbacks

One of the most distressing aspects of a flashback is its unpredictability and its potentially overwhelming strength. Your flashbacks may feel to you as uncontrollable as a nightmare and indeed, flashbacks have been described as 'waking nightmares'[4].

Rather than letting them control you, you can find ways of controlling your flashbacks, as you did with the intrusive memories.

Step 1: Getting to know your flashbacks and listening to your body's responses

EXERCISE 11: GETTING TO KNOW YOUR FLASHBACKS

The first step is for you to notice and understand what happens to you while you experience a flashback. Think back to the last time you had a flashback or alternatively, wait until you experience the next one. Copy the questions from the boxes below into your journal and answer them (additional copies are provided in the Appendix or online). Exercise 11 consists of 3 parts: 11A. Recognise the triggers; 11B. Identify the traumatic memory; and 11C. Get to know your body's responses.

A. Recognise the triggers	Record your observations:
1. When did it happen?	
2. What were you doing at the time?	

3. What else was going on when it started?

4. Was anybody else with you?

5. What are the similarities between your current situation and the situation that you were transported to in your flashback?

6. What was going on for you when you felt this way before?

7. What is similar to and what is different from the previous situation/s?

8. What do you think triggered it? (For example, a particular thought, smell, sound, picture, feeling, taste, sensation in your body – or reminder such as a conversation, media or a special event, such as an anniversary.)

B. Identify the traumatic memory	**Record your observations:**
1. What do you remember about your flashback?	
2. Even if it feels a little distressing, describe in as much detail as you can what went through your mind.	
3. Can you describe or draw the images that you saw during your flashback?	
4. How long did it last?	
5. Were you noticing what was going on around you or did the flashback block everything else out?	

0	1	2	3	4	5	6	7	8
No distress		A little distress		Definite distress		Marked distress		Severe distress

C. Get to know your body's responses	Record your observations:
1. What sensations or feelings did you notice in your body during the flashback?	
2. Try to describe them in as much detail as you can.	
3. How strong were these sensations? Can you give them a rating between 0 to 8 (using the above scale)?	
4. What were your thoughts about these feelings or sensations?	
5. How did you react and respond to those feelings or sensations in your body?	
6. What actions did you take to make yourself feel better?	
7. What other ways may you have used in the past to control your flashbacks?	

Having answered these questions in your journal, start a diary to monitor your flashbacks. The more thoroughly you understand them, the more likely it is for you to learn to control them.

Understanding flashbacks

Every flashback has three stages[4]. The first is the trigger stage. This tells you what started it in the first place. Triggers are different for each person and therefore it is important that you try and work out what the special triggers might be for you. (This could also be useful for controlling your intrusive memories, as these also are caused by triggers.) Triggers can be thoughts, feelings in your body, images, sounds, smells, something someone does or says, tastes, special events, currently stressful situations, financial or medical problems, and many more. Make a list of what you believe to be your most common triggers below.

EXERCISE 12: IDENTIFYING COMMON FLASHBACK TRIGGERS

I have identified the following, most common triggers for my flashbacks:

_____

_____

_____

_____

_____

_____

The second stage consists of the 'surfacing of memories' during the flashback. These are the upsetting memories that make you feel as if you are reliving aspects of the trauma. They can seem so real and their images can be so sharp and acute, that you may feel that you are right back in the actual trauma. You may literally feel as if you are 'taken over' by these memories and that you stop all other activities while you are experiencing the flashback. Traumatic memories take the form of visual images but can be accompanied by sounds, smells, tastes and other physical sensations. You may even engage in behavioural actions that are related to the flashback, such as diving to the floor or hitting out, even though there is no actual danger now. Flashbacks usually last between a few seconds and a few minutes, but when they are severe they can last much longer, sometimes several hours.

The third stage is the 'aftermath' of the flashback. At this stage the person will often still feel very strong physical sensations. Some people find that their breathing rate increases, others notice that they are feeling cold and shivery or very hot or that their heartbeat is rapid. Often people can have very strong emotional responses to the flashback itself, getting very angry, for example, or feeling very sad and distressed. The feelings can be disorientating: if you have stopped all other activities during the flashback it can then be hard to remember what was said or went on during the current episode of your flashback. Others may have noticed certain behaviour in you during your flashback that you are not aware of. This is more likely to happen if a flashback lasts longer than a few minutes.

It is important to remember that flashbacks are an indication that your body-mind system is still pre-occupied with the trauma. It has not yet been able to re-set and update to your current reality, which is that you are safe and you did survive whatever frightened you. Whatever was threatening or dangerous at the time of your trauma is no longer present in the here-and-now for you. (If it is, then please go back to Chapter 4 – ensuring that you are safe now before doing these exercises.) However, the information that was encoded (through neurochemical processes in your brain system) during the trauma is still there and gets reactivated by the triggers causing your flashbacks. Noticing your triggers can help you make sense of your flashbacks and the reactions that they might provoke in you. Flashbacks are common and it may help you to understand that like other PTSD symptoms, they are an indication of 'unfinished' business, suggesting that further healing needs to occur before the impact of the trauma is resolved. Although what happened to you at the time of the trauma really was threatening, your present-day reality is no longer threatening. Healing from the trauma requires your brain systems to re-orient and update to the present day reality of it being safe for you now. It could therefore be very helpful if, while you are reading this chapter and doing the exercises, you regularly use the methods that you have found helpful to soothe your disturbed nervous system in Chapter 6. This will indicate to your mind–body system that you are safe now. Exercise 13 demonstrates what you can do to increase understanding of your flashbacks:

EXERCISE 13: RECORDING YOUR FLASHBACKS

Below is an example of a simple flashback record chart. Copy the chart into your journal and then use it to monitor your own flashbacks over a longer period of time. The longer you monitor your flashbacks the better the understanding you are likely to gain of them. You might also like to refer to the questions you asked yourself in Exercise 11 when you are using this chart (blank copies are provided in the Appendix or online).

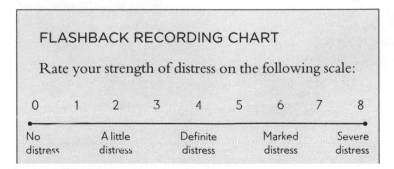

FLASHBACK RECORDING CHART

Rate your strength of distress on the following scale:

0	1	2	3	4	5	6	7	8
No distress		A little distress		Definite distress		Marked distress		Severe distress

Date/ Time	Trigger (external and internal)	Traumatic memory (content)	Your reactions (physical & emotional responses), Rate their strength (0–8)	Duration of flashback and nature of aftermath
12.3.16 6.30pm	Electricity goes off. Lights go off due to a short power cut in this area	Takes me back to the time when the lights went off during my solitary confinement after being taken a prisoner	Fear. Feeling of out of control. Feeling of coldness. Shivering all over my body. Severe distress = 7	30 min – lost touch with surroundings
14.3.16 11.15am	Backdoor was open. Tom walks in without ringing bell	People would just come in and I never had any control over it	Shouted at Tom. Increased heartbeat. Definite distress = 4	1 min acute – lingered in my system for some time afterwards
14.3.16 1.00pm	Maggie cooked lunch – smell of onions in the house.	Can see person who interrogated me. His breath smelt of onions	Feeling of nausea and sickness, had to walk out of house. Marked distress = 6	5 min – took time to shake off his face
15.3.16 2.30pm	Went to visit mum. Toby (dog) moved out from under the sofa (one of his favourite places)	Set off a flashback to the time in combat when someone shot at me from under a car	Terrified, nearly killed Toby. Had a real go at mum. Took me ages to calm down. Severe distress = 8	3 min – took long time to calm down after
17.3.16 9.00pm	Invited to party. Fireworks display	The sound brought me right back to my experiences under combat fire.	Terrified, nearly wet myself, heart pounding, lost it with friends – shouted. Severe distress = 8	15 min – friends had to stop fireworks. Took a long time to calm down after

Step 2: Learning to manage and control your flashbacks

The more you are able to monitor when your flashbacks happen, and what they are like, the more familiar you will become with them. Once you can recognise a flashback and notice your reaction you are ready to try to gain more control over them. This is the next step and it is not an easy process. Most people find that learning to manage and control their flashbacks takes time. It is important that you give yourself a chance and do this gradually. It is normal for this not to work immediately and important that you give yourself time to persevere. Here are some exercises that should help you control your flashbacks.

EXERCISE 14: CONTROLLING YOUR FLASHBACKS

The eventual aim is for you to manage all triggers to flashbacks. This can take time and needs to be done gradually. One way of temporarily controlling flashbacks is to avoid certain situations or thoughts that are known triggers for your flashbacks. This can be helpful for any triggers that at the moment cause such strong responses in you that you, or others around you, do not feel safe when they occur. Go back over your notes from Exercise 12 and Exercise 13 and highlight those triggers it would be helpful for you to avoid at this stage of your recovery.

Make a new list in your journal like the one below and plan what you might do to avoid those triggers you have identified:

Example record:

List of Triggers to avoid:	My plan of what I can do to avoid them:
Firework displays	*I will avoid public firework displays when I know about them*
	I will check with friends beforehand if there is going to be a firework display at their party. I will explain my problems to them and ask them to excuse me if I have to leave a little earlier, before the display starts.

Remember: *The use of avoidance strategies can be helpful temporarily under certain circumstances because you have to protect yourself from the strong reactions that a flashback can trigger (including behaviour that could be unpleasant or dangerous to others). However, generally it is not helpful to use avoidance strategies, especially if, in order to avoid a potential trigger, you have to forego situations that under other circumstances would be pleasurable for you. The aim is for you to gradually learn to manage all trigger situations and enable your mind-body system to re-set to the safety of the here-and-now.*

EXERCISE 15: CATEGORISING YOUR TRIGGERS

Look again at your notes from Exercises 12 and 13. Now divide the triggers that you have identified into the four groups outlined below.

Example record:

●━━━━━━━━━━━━━━━━━━━━━━━━━━━━━━━━━━━●

Least difficult   *Most difficult*

1 Triggers that I might be able to handle now	2 Triggers that I can't cope with yet, but I may be able to handle soon (may be in a few weeks' or months' time)	3 Triggers that seem really hard to gain control over at the moment, but that I would eventually like to manage	4 Triggers that I currently want to avoid (for my own and others' safety) – as I heal from my trauma I will re-visit these and explore how these may become more manageable
Leaving backdoor open when I am around and allowing family to walk in without shouting at them	*Smell of onions during cooking*	*Things jumping out from underneath objects (e.g. Mum's dog or in other situations)*	*Firework displays*

Now that you have classed your triggers into easy and hard ones, choose one target trigger that you think you might be able to handle now and try out some of the strategies in Exercises 16 and 17. Allow yourself sufficient practice time for your one, identified, trigger: 30–40 minutes. Ensure that you are safe now, maybe carrying this out in your external safe place. Look around to notice everything in your environment that makes you feel safe and secure now. Connect to your inner sanctuary or use one of the methods that help you soothe your nervous system. Start with these strategies only when you feel within your window of tolerance. If you notice that you are coming out of your window of tolerance during this practice, stop. Bring yourself back before continuing. Take your time. This will only work if you stay regulated and within your window of tolerance while trying out the different management strategies.

EXERCISE 16: WORKING WITH A TARGET TRIGGER

Different management strategies

1. Rescript your memory
    a. Write down in as much detail as possible the flashback memory that normally occurs in response to this particular trigger.
    b. Ask yourself what the most distressing aspect of this flashback memory is. Write down why this affects you so much.

   c. Describe the sensations that this flashback memory sets off in you.

   d. Now think of a way in which you could rescript the flashback to make it less distressing to you now. Is there is anything in this imagery that you could change so that you would feel more in control?

   e. Rewrite the flashback memory including this changed image.

   f. Imagine yourself experiencing the flashback in this changed form.

   g. Once you are comfortable doing this, you can then rescript this flashback each time it is set off by your identified target trigger.

2. Resize your memory and watch it like a film

   a. Follow steps a to c as above.

   b. Now try and imagine watching your flashback memory like a film. See if you can reduce its image in size so that it would fit onto a small television screen.

   c. Practise watching this as often as possible. Slow down the speed of the film, or 'freeze' frames if you wish. 'Grey' down the colour.

   d. Once you are comfortable using this strategy, you can practise watching your flashback in this way, whenever your identified trigger sets it off.

Once you have mastered more control over this identified target trigger and feel fairly comfortable about tolerating it, you can then select a different target trigger to work on. It is very important during this practice that you feel safe in the here-and-now and stay regulated and present. Exercise 17 offers you some grounding techniques to try out when you feel very disconnected during a flashback. In addition, to the soothing techniques explored in Chapter 6, these will help to connect you to the present and enable you to feel more in control. You can use these during your practice and once you know those that are helpful to you, you can use these whenever you experience a flashback.

EXERCISE 17: GROUNDING TECHNIQUES

Grounding techniques can help bring you back into the present if you have become disconnected from reality during a flashback. They shift your focus away from the flashback and reduce its intensity.

1. Grounding to the here-and-now
As soon as you notice the first signs of a flashback, focus on any object in your environment around you. Look at the chosen object and describe to yourself:
- its colour
- its shape and size

- its texture (go over to it if you can and really feel it)
- its age and what it might be used for
- what do you like about it?

2. Grounding smell
   a. Identify a scent you really like that is not connected to your trauma.
   b. Obtain a small item that carries this scent, for example, a tissue impregnated with an aromatherapy oil that you like, such as the smell of cedar, cinnamon or cooking vanilla, a small bottle of your favourite perfume or aftershave, or anything else that carries the scent.
   c. Each time you notice the first signs of a flashback breathe in some of this scent and feel its soothing effect. Allow yourself to be calmed by it.

3. Grounding object
   a. Instead of using scent, find an object, like a stone, pebble or crystal, a piece of smooth wood, a conker or an acorn or other nut, a worry stone or worry beads, or a small cuddly cushion or a special piece of cloth or anything similar.
   b. Carry this with you and feel, touch and look at it each time you notice the first signs of a flashback.

4. Grounding position

    a. Identify a bodily position that is especially comforting to you. Choose a position that is different to the one you may have used during your trauma and that does not connect you to an aspect of your trauma. This could be curling up, leaning against a wall, squatting down, or using one of the yoga poses introduced to you in Chapter 8, etc.

    b. Use this at times when you notice the first signs of a flashback. As these positions can be very personal, you may find they work best when you are on your own. You could also find another position or gesture that is quite subtle so that you could use it also in public.

5. Grounding breath

Lisa Schwarz[5] has described the 'Earthbreath' as a method to help people ground. Here are the instructions for this:

Sit down comfortably on a chair. Now ask your body (not your mind!) which side of your body you should receive energy from: left or right? Take the first answer that springs up (without thinking). Then imagine feeling the energy from deep, deep down within the earth coming up as breath into the sole of the foot of your receiving side (if you chose 'left' then this would be through the sole of your left foot and if you chose 'right' then this would be through the sole of your right foot). Imagine receiving breath energy through all the layers of the earth, from the lava and the magma, through the crystalline cave structures, through the layers of earth minerals, through the water passages and through the boulders, rocks and stones, right into the sole of your receiving foot (left or right), then spiralling up your receiving leg (same left or right) into the base of your spine (for men) or your womb space (for women – if the womb space carries trauma for you, imagine breathing into your tummy area). Now hold your breath there for a count of four or five. Then breathe out through the other leg and foot through the sole deep, deep down back into the earth. Continue this breath creating a cycle between the earth, the base of your spine/womb space (or tummy area) and back into the earth again. Continue this for some time, allowing yourself to let go of blockages that you might feel and allowing this breath to comfortably connect you to the earth and ground you.

You can use this breath as often as you like. You may find that the receiving side of your body varies with different practice times.

6. Other techniques that might help ground you during a flashback are simply walking about, telling yourself (silently) your name, the date and time of the day, or reciting a poem or singing a song, or simply squeezing thumb and third finger together. Anything that safely connects you to the here-and-now present.

7. Information about other breathing, mindfulness and relaxation techniques, which are very helpful in combination with the exercises suggested here, can be found in Chapters 6, 9 and 11.

Step 3: Flashbacks in sexual relationships

For people whose trauma has included abuse of a sexual nature it is common to suffer flashbacks during acts of sexual intimacy. Here are some suggested ways of dealing with these[6,7]:

1. As soon as you start to become aware of a flashback, open your eyes (if closed) and focus on the immediate environment around you. Bring yourself as fully into the present moment as you can. Notice where you are.

2. Recognise the differences between your present

partner and the perpetrator, between your present environment and that recalled in your flashback.

3. Focus on an object of safety, security or comfort, for example, cuddle the pillow, touch a stone nearby, imagine a pleasant image, use relaxation or any of the grounding techniques suggested on pages 230–34 or one of the soothing techniques that you know work for you.

4. If the image persists, imagine putting it on a television screen. You have the remote control, you can darken the picture, you can turn off the sound, you can freeze the picture, or you can switch off the TV.

5. Let your partner know what has happened and allow him/her to comfort you if he/she can.

6. Agree beforehand on reassuring things your partner can do or say if this happens. Hearing your partner's voice might enable you to connect to the safety of the present moment more quickly.

7. Ask your partner to be patient with you when this happens and give you plenty of time and space, if necessary. It could be helpful for your partner to have read some of this book to understand how you might be affected and what he/she can do to help.

8. Stop any form of sexual contact until the flashback is completely over.

9. Ensure that you are oriented in the here-and-now present and feel safe again, before resuming any sexual contact.

Once you are grounded again, feel safe and can create some time on your own, you could use the journal to note what exactly it was that triggered you during sexual contact. You and your partner could then work on gradually managing the trigger by following some of the steps suggested above in Exercises 14, 15 and 16. Ensure that sexual contact is tender, respectful and loving towards you. Ask your partner to pace any form of sexual or physical contact to your window of tolerance. Avoid doing anything that takes you outside your window of tolerance, even if this means that when you are starting to practice this, you start off with quite limited physical contact and very few body zones (only those that feel safe to you).

Please be mindful that in order for you to recover from past sexual abuse trauma, it is important that your current relationship is secure and safe. If there are aspects that do not feel safe in your current relationship try and address these first before attempting to work with your partner on your sexual flashback triggers. It could be that some of the triggers relate to you not feeling safe at the moment and this needs to be tackled first. You may like to consider doing some therapeutic couples work together to see if you can address aspects in your relationship that do not feel safe and that might be an obstacle to your recovery.

Recognising your achievements

Congratulations on tackling your intrusive and re-experiencing symptoms. These can feel very debilitating and when you notice that they are starting to reduce because you have greater understanding, have recognised the underlying triggers and learned to manage them differently this is a great step forward in your recovery. The more you allow yourself to get to know them and understand them, the more you will be able to master them and feel in control.

Recognise your achievements and monitor your progress periodically by re-scoring yourself on the scale that appears at the beginning of this chapter. Compare your new score to your old baseline score to see the changes.

Some people experience such overwhelming and strong flashbacks that it is unlikely that this book will be able to resolve these. If you have persevered with the practices in this book and do not notice any significant change in your intrusive, re-experiencing symptoms or their frequency, it is recommended that you seek additional therapeutic help from a trauma specialist. Please be assured that this is not a sign of failure or not having tried hard enough, but simply that your trauma had such an effect that you require more specialist, individualised help to recover.

Summary checkpoints:

- Trying not to think about uncomfortable feelings, memories or sensations related to a trauma doesn't usually work, as it increases rather than reduces these experiences

- The Post-traumatic Stress Disorder Checklist (PCL-5)[2] is a measure used in this book to determine how you cope with your re-experiencing reactions after trauma
- You are taken through the steps that help you take a first measure (baseline) of your reactions, which you can then record in your journal
- If you have scored in the upper mid- to high range, you are encouraged to seek professional help in addition to working through this book
- Intrusive memories and flashbacks are the most prominent index symptoms of PTSD.
- Intrusive memories are vivid recollections in the form of pictures, smells, sounds, and body sensations of what happened just before, during and in the aftermath of a trauma
- During a flashback it feels as if the trauma or aspects of it are happening again and this can be so strong that it disconnects (dissociates) a person from here-and-now reality
- Intrusive memories and flashbacks can both be triggered by a whole array of reminders to aspects of the trauma
- Noticing your triggers can help you make sense of your flashbacks and intrusive memories and the reactions that they provoke in you
- You can then work with specific target triggers using the management strategies and grounding

techniques introduced in this chapter to help you gain mastery over your re-experiencing reactions

- Advice on dealing with flashbacks in sexual relationships is also provided
- Mastering your flashbacks and intrusive reactions is a big step forward on your path to your recovery. Well done!

9

Managing your arousal reactions

As discussed in Chapter 2, a dramatically increased feeling of *arousal* is a major component of the traumatic stress reaction pattern. This was described as the body's alarm system getting stuck on 'red alert', and overreacting to nearly everything. If you have been experiencing high arousal reactions, you will be only too aware of the effects: being constantly aroused interferes with everyday functioning, especially in terms of sleep, temper, jumpiness, nervousness, watchfulness, and a driving need to control everything.

Monitoring your arousal level

It will help if you keep an arousal chart, to gather data on how severely these reactions are being triggered for you. In your journal, make an entry whenever you are startled, snappy, shaky, have an outburst of anger or irritability or experience poor sleep. Describe your reactions quite specifically, using the scales on the next page.

The following questions cover the range of commonly experienced arousal reactions. Please copy these questions into your journal, date the entry and try to answer them as best as you can. The scales 0–4 are explained below:

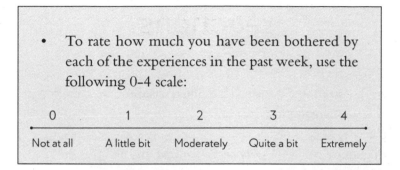

Please answer the following questions by circling the number on each scale which best applies to you:

1. In the past seven days how much have you been bothered by poor quality sleep, either finding it difficult to fall asleep or staying asleep?

    0   1   2   3   4

2. In the past seven days how much were you bothered by having flashes of anger or being easily irritated, quick-tempered or argumentative?

0   1   2   3   4

3. In the past seven days how much were you bothered by poor concentration or problems with your memory, such as forgetting things, losing your bearings, having difficulties reading or listening to conversations?

0   1   2   3   4

4. In the past seven days how much were you bothered by feeling overly watchful, 'superalert' or experienced a heightened concern for the safety of yourself or others?

0   1   2   3   4

5. In the past seven days how much were you bothered by taking too many risks or doing things that could cause you or others harm?

0   1   2   3   4

6. In the past seven days how much were you bothered by feeling more on edge, very jumpy or easily startled?

| 0 | 1 | 2 | 3 | 4 |

Once you have circled the number that best applies to you on each question add the scores from all the questions (1–6). Record these total scores in your notebook.

TOTAL SCORE FOR AROUSAL REACTIONS
ON...................... (date)

Your total score is:..

If your total score is:

6 or below = they are low

7–12 = they fall into the mid-range

13 or more = they are high

Lastly, give an overall rating for how disabling these arousal reactions have been to you in the past week, by circling the number that applies to you on the scale used below (you could also copy this into your notebook):

0	1	2	3	4	5	6	7	8
Not at all disabling		Slightly disabling		Definitely disabling		Markedly disabling		Severely disabling

Now that you have established your own level of arousal reactions you can begin to try to reduce these. Monitor this regularly as you work through the exercises in this chapter and also the rest of the book. If your scores are mid- to high range, specialist trauma therapy could really be useful to you, in addition to working through this book.

Improving your sleep

Since sleep is so vitally important to a person's mood and reactions, our first step is to improve the quality of your sleep. Here are some strategies to help you get a better night's sleep:

EXERCISE 18: IMPROVING YOUR SLEEPING ENVIRONMENT

Protecting your sleeping space

Ensure that the doors and windows of your home have proper locks, and if in doubt invest in new ones. You need to feel that your sleeping space is protected as much as possible from external intruders. If your trauma has resulted from a house break-in or a sexual assault, you may need to consider moving house if you cannot feel at ease where you are living now.

If you need to sleep alone for a while (because of restlessness or crying out during sleep), or need to get up and be alone during the night, discuss this ahead of time with your partner. Explain that this will only be temporary because it is part of your recovery process and that it must not be understood as a rejection.

Coping with internal intrusions

To help with 'internal intrusions' in your sleeping environment, such as difficulty falling asleep, nightmares, waking in the night, try the following:

- changing the position of your bed
- rearranging the bedroom layout, using extra pillows as comforting 'props' to hold or bolster you in bed

- removing wall hangings or posters that may appear scary when you are half-awake in a darkened room
- using a night-light
- removing any upsetting reminders (e.g. photographs of life before your trauma)
- keeping your room at a comfortable, cool temperature

If flashbacks occur while you are in bed, imagine that you are seeing the images on a video screen. You, as the viewer, have the remote control and can freeze the images, turn off the sound and grey out or fuzz the screen.

Taking care of your body

Avoid alcohol, caffeine or other stimulants before bedtime. Caffeine can be found in coffee, black tea, green tea, cocoa or cola drinks, and although you may feel that alcohol relaxes you, it actually has a detrimental effect on sleeping patterns. Do not eat highly spiced or sugary foods late in the evening. Eat something light and not too close to bedtime. Also avoid watching violent television programmes or reading disturbing books before bedtime.

Establishing a night-time routine

Establish a regular night-time routine, for example,

taking a soothing beverage or a herbal tea, such as chamomile or special night-time tea, about two hours before going to sleep. Do not drink anything after this to stop you having to go to the bathroom at night. Try and keep to a fairly regular bedtime. Use your bed for sleeping rather than the couch or other place. Use some easy reading material to help you wind down when you lie in bed. Relaxing music or relaxation exercises or sounds may also help you to calm down. The Relaxed Breathing Method described on page 254 or visualising a scene that has a peaceful and calming meaning for you, may also help you fall asleep. You could connect yourself to your inner sanctuary or safe place (Chapter 4) for this.

To help you get into a positive mindset before sleep, do a 'mental gratitude journal'[1] at the end of each day, as you are getting into bed. Identify five things (big or very small) that you are grateful for from the day. These could be very simple – you might be grateful that on that day you spotted the first snowdrops or you heard a very beautiful piece of music on the radio.

Coping with disturbing dreams

Some people dread falling asleep because of disturbing or repetitive dreams and they don't respond well to relaxation techniques used at bedtime, as they fear 'losing control' by letting their guard down and becoming too relaxed. If this applies to you, instead of the relaxation exercises, you might find it helpful to construct a different, more positive ending for a repetitive dream. First, think of a dream that disturbs you and then try to think of a different ending for it. Concentrate on this by rehearsing it mentally several times before going to sleep.

Alternatively, you could prepare yourself to 'talk back' in your dreams. Imagine ahead of time what you would like to say if that dream occurs and practise it before your bedtime. Say it aloud several times and then imagine saying it to yourself quietly.

You can prepare yourself to cope with bad dreams by reorientating yourself as soon as possible upon awakening. Keep a damp flannel or towel and a bowl of cool water beside the bed for washing your face if you wake up distressed or in a sweat. Mentally rehearse waking up and getting reorientated to the present. Turn the light on; replace your digital clock with a standard analogue clock, as the action of 'telling the time' will help you to shift into wakefulness. You might also like to keep something scented on your night-time table, such as a lavender cushion, the smell of mint, rose, geranium or any other scent that is helpful to you. It has to be unrelated to your trauma.

Remember: you can exert some control over your dreams, especially with practice!

Keep a pad of paper and a pencil by your bed within easy reach. If you want to record your dreams, you can do so without having to sit up and become fully awake, which often causes you to forget details. However, be cautious not to read too much into the meaning of your dreams. They may give you clues to your progress but it might not be helpful to take them too literally. If disturbing themes recur, you might wish to discuss these with a trauma specialist.

Further strategies

1. Introduce pleasant smells, e.g. potpourri, vanilla, amber or other scents (but not those associated with your trauma) into your sleeping environment to create a restful atmosphere. Certain aromatherapy oils, such as lavender oil or other such preparations, may help to relax you. You might want to consult a qualified aromatherapist or you could get yourself a good self-help book on aromatherapy.

2. Physical exercise, during late afternoon or early evening, may also help to enhance sleep. Yoga, qi gong, Pilates or tai chi can be especially helpful. Exercise raises your temperature. As you allow yourself some time after finishing the exercise, your temperature drops and might make you feel sleepy.

3. Alternatively, you might try taking a warm or cool bath, possibly with relaxing bath essences or herbs, before you go to bed. Some people find a hot water bottle very soothing.

4. Remember: If you can't get yourself back to sleep within 30 minutes of going to bed, make sure to get up again and do another activity elsewhere, preferably something very calming, such as reading a magazine or listening to a relaxation script or a light story. After 15 minutes, go to bed again and try to get to sleep. If you still can't fall asleep, get up again and do another activity. Try and do very calming or even boring activities. Repeat this process as long as necessary and only use your bed for sleeping in. Do not take a nap during the day, even if you are tired!

5. Medications for sleep may be helpful on a short-term basis, but should always be prescribed and monitored by a qualified medical practitioner. Alternatives such as herbal remedies, homeopathy, massage, aromatherapy or certain forms of relaxation, mindfulness practice or meditation may be very beneficial, too. You may also benefit if you consult a recognised and well-qualified alternative health practitioner, such as a homeopath or aromatherapist, for advice.

6. Record in your journal any other strategies that you discover to be helpful.

Every person is different and it is quite likely that you will need to try out a variety of strategies and alter and change them until you have found the right one for you. It is important to persevere until you have found the most effective method.

In order to find out if your strategies are helping to improve your sleep, use a sleeping log, like the one in Exercise 19 on page 252.

Relaxed Breathing Method

Exercise 20, on page 254, can be used to lessen tension, promote deeper sleep, counteract the effect of hyperventilation (explained in Chapter 10) or generally help you relax and regain control when you have been overreacting. Try to learn the method, maybe getting someone to read the instructions to you, so you can concentrate on your breathing. Alternatively, you could record these instructions onto an audio-recording device and play them back whenever you wish. When you first practise this method, use it during times when you don't feel too tense. With practice, the deep breathing method will become much more automatic and then you will also be able to use this method during times when you would like to calm down. It can help you correct your breathing pattern to reverse hyperventilation syndrome (Chapter 10).

EXERCISE 19: KEEPING A SLEEPING LOG

Copy this log into your notebook or onto your computer. Use it every day during your sleep-monitoring period and remember to fill it out about 15–20 minutes after waking.

Day	Bedtime routine used:	Before I went to sleep I felt (indicate score by circling one from 1 = very tense to 5 = very relaxed)	I went to sleep at (time):	During the night I woke at (time):	Action taken to get back to sleep:	I stayed awake for (minutes/hours):	This morning I woke at:	When I woke up, I felt (indicate score by circling one from 1 = not rested at all to 5 = well-rested):	The following helped me with my sleep last night:
Monday		1 2 3 4 5						1 2 3 4 5	
Tuesday		1 2 3 4 5						1 2 3 4 5	
Wednesday		1 2 3 4 5						1 2 3 4 5	
Thursday		1 2 3 4 5						1 2 3 4 5	

Day	Bedtime routine used:	Before I went to sleep I felt (indicate score by circling one from 1 = very tense to 5 = very relaxed)	I went to sleep at (time):	During the night I woke at (time):	Action taken to get back to sleep:	I stayed awake for (minutes/ hours):	This morning I woke at:	When I woke up, I felt (indicate score bycircling one from 1 = not rested at all to 5 = well-rested):	The following helped me with my sleep last night:
Friday		1 2 3 4 5						1 2 3 4 5	
Saturday		1 2 3 4 5						1 2 3 4 5	
Sunday		1 2 3 4 5						1 2 3 4 5	

Notice those strategies which seem to be helpful and those that don't have a positive effect on your sleep. Discard the unhelpful ones and keep the helpful strategies. In this way, you can build up your own individualised sleep restoration programme.

EXERCISE 20: RELAXED BREATHING METHOD

When you are anxious or stressed your breathing becomes shallow and you tend to breathe into your upper chest. When this happens, your body is not supplied with sufficient oxygen and the carbon dioxide (CO_2) level in your blood drops. Your automatic response to this will often be to breathe even faster, because it feels to you as if you are not getting enough oxygen. However, the faster you breathe and the more CO_2 you expel, the dizzier and fainter you will feel (see hyperventilation in Chapter 10). This will make you feel less able to function calmly.

In order for you to gain the optimum benefit from your breathing, it should be deep, so that your stomach wall pushes IN as you breathe out, and OUT as you breathe in. This type of deep breathing helps your body to relax and, if used systematically, can make you feel calm and refreshed. The following steps describe how you can achieve such relaxed breathing. You can practise this as often during the day or night as you like. The more you practise, the sooner you will be able to use this exercise wherever you are and whenever you feel a little tense. To start with you might not achieve the desired effect. Don't worry about this and you will soon find that relaxation will be achieved with regular practice.

1. First of all, stop whatever you are doing and concentrate on giving this time to yourself. Tell yourself that nothing else is important at the moment, and that everything can be put to one side for a while, until you feel more refreshed. Ensure that others will not disturb you during this time. If you have a physical disability and can't participate in this exercise as described below, please modify this method accordingly.

2. Find a comfortable chair to sit in or lie down on the floor and loosen any tight clothing. Start by stretching and then try to make yourself as comfortable as you possibly can. Keep your arms by your side and keep them as relaxed as possible. You may wish to close your eyes, since this will help you to concentrate better.

3. Now just sit or lie like this for a while and concentrate on your breathing. Feel your breath going in and out of your body and just stay with it for a while. Don't try to force it, just breathe naturally. See if you can feel the rhythm of your breathing as you breathe in and out. Also notice whether your breath feels warm or cold and keep concentrating on this for a while.

4. When you feel ready, gently put your hands onto your stomach. Now see if you can feel your breath going in and out of your stomach; lifting your hands up as you breathe in and lowering

them as you breathe out. Try and concentrate just on your breathing, making sure that you breathe slowly and evenly. Just feel the gentle massaging action of your breath on the muscles inside your stomach wall.

5. Now take in a deep breath and feel your stomach wall rising. Hold it there to the count of four and then let go, feeling your stomach contracting as you slowly breathe out. Then do the same again and this time, as you breathe out, think of the word 'relax'. Take one or two more deep breaths, hold to the count of four and each time, as you slowly breathe out, think of the word 'relax'. You may also think of your favourite calm colour, a peaceful image or relaxing music as you breathe out. In your own time return to breathing normally, but still think of the word 'relax', colour and/or image and/or sound as you breathe out. Feel a sense of calmness spreading in to all the cells of your body as your stomach muscles slowly go up and down with each breath.

6. You can now take your hands off your stomach if you wish, but still continue to breathe slowly and evenly into your stomach. Just stay with the rhythm of your breathing for as long as you can, relaxing more and more with every breath out.

7. When you are ready, in your own time, count forward mentally, from one to five, becoming gradually more alert, and then slowly open your eyes. Stay seated or lying down for a little while longer and feel how relaxed and refreshed you have become. When you get up, make sure to rise slowly and take some time before getting back to your normal activities.

8. Once you have mastered breathing deeply into your stomach, you can advance this exercise and learn to breathe deeply into both sides of your lung expanding your rib cage which is how your breathing naturally should be. Hold both of your hands on each side of your lower rib cage. Then breathe in gently and deeply into the base of your lungs and expand your rib cage sideways pushing out both hands. You can also try this type of breathing standing in front of a mirror monitoring if your breath manages to push your hands and arms out sideways. This helps to loosen tightness in your diaphragm.

Managing your anger

Another common traumatic stress arousal reaction is an increased feeling of anger. Anger in itself is a very natural response and is part of your body's healthy response system that tells you when to protect yourself. However, the type of anger associated with trauma often feels out of control for people. This may range from general irritability to a deep-seated, explosive rage. You might find yourself arguing with your family or work colleagues over unimportant things or carrying a smouldering hatred toward individuals or larger groups that you hold responsible for your misfortune. This type of anger reaction may remain extremely intense, lasting months or years, and will probably affect your relationships with others. When you are feeling this you are out of your window of tolerance.

While your angry feelings may be quite justified, how you manage and express them is important, both to your own wellbeing and healing as well as to your sense of effectiveness and control. Working on your anger management skills is a positive step towards eliminating the risk of violent behaviour. This ensures the safety of yourself, your family and others and generally helps you to resolve conflict constructively, without alienating others

It's very understandable that you want to blame others for what has happened to you, particularly if the situation could have been prevented or improved by other people's actions. Your feelings of anger may be especially strong if you experienced trauma that involved intentional harm or damage and you may feel a sense of great injustice. You will probably find, too, that your feelings of blame consist of a confusing mixture of guilt, fear, shame, loss of faith in a just society and your own sense of personal vulnerability.

When you have been traumatised, the source of your anger may also be linked with feeling a lack of control over a person, an event or situations, which you may not have experienced before. This is often accompanied by a deep sense of helplessness. The same physical arousal symptoms – a pounding heart, sweating palms, rapid breathing, rising blood pressure – that are present during a situation of tremendous stress, anxiety or fear are experienced when anger is 'on the boil'. Suppressing this chronic anger response has been linked to health problems for both men and women, manifesting in heart attacks, high blood pressure and severe headaches.

Anger can also be useful! For example, when it leads to a struggle against injustice, when it helps a parent to defend a child or when it leads to community action on a problem. Properly handled, it can help you to achieve better, more honest communication through talking rather than shouting. The key is to channel your anger effectively – to feel it, but not to act it out against yourself or others. For example, getting a legal representative to pursue a claim on your behalf allows that person to be angry for you, in an appropriate way, so that you can let go of some of your anger, because you know the issue is being addressed on your behalf.

On the other hand, when anger is bottled up until it explodes, the results can be dangerous and violent and you have certainly moved out of your window of tolerance. Many people who have been wronged have revenge fantasies. They imagine horrible punishments for those that they hold responsible for their tragedy. While it's not uncommon to have such thoughts, it is important to distinguish between fantasy (what you think about) and reality (what you actually do). While a revenge fantasy may act as a useful release at times, to dwell upon it and to consider taking violent action puts you at risk, as well as the other party. Acting out your rage will not erase what has happened, and it could result in serious consequences for you! Resolving your trauma related anger is not easy, may take time and, if very strong, could require specialist trauma therapy.

The people who seem to fare best are those who learn how to understand their own tempers, recognise and express their anger appropriately. Anger is often triggered by some very deep, underlying hurt and by discovering and acknowledging the root of this hurt and taking ownership for it, you can start turning your anger round. You need to get an understanding of what really happened and confront enough of your anger to work out why you are so angry.

Sometimes anger has a deeper root than the trauma itself, even though things during the trauma may indeed not have been fair. Some of the questions and exercises in this chapter may help you find the root to your anger. Be sure to be gentle with yourself and soothe yourself (using the strategies that you identified in Chapters 4 and 6) when examining the deeper causes of your anger. Keep sight of the fact that whatever you discover, whatever happened, however bad it was, has already happened and is in the past. It is important now that the hurt doesn't continue so that healing and recovery can start. By smouldering in your anger, acting it out or hanging on to it, you continue to hurt yourself or possibly even innocent others, such as your loved ones. Even if terrible things happened, even if the justice system failed you and even if enormous losses or suffering occurred, holding on to your anger keeps you bonded to those responsible for causing the injury. Letting go of your anger doesn't absolve others from their responsibility nor does it justify what they have done or belittle the enormity of what happened. It simply releases you from those still holding power over you. It moves you into freedom and back into your own position of control. This chapter introduces strategies that support you with moving on in your life, instead of remaining a victim of your experience.

Rather than feeling 'stuck' in an anger arousal cycle, where every little thing that happens triggers the same overly angry response and you seem to be either suppressing it or lashing out at others, taking responsibility for managing your own anger is a positive step towards gaining control over your life again. When you are able to manage your anger effectively, you will have more choices about how you respond in any given situation.

Techniques for anger management

In this section, you will be asked to work on three steps through the proposed exercises. Each exercise contains at least two parts.

- Step 1 will be to keep your own notes and to ask yourself specific questions, in order to understand your anger and therefore gain more control over it.

- Step 2 will teach you to work with your own body, to notice the signs of tension building up in your muscles, as well as the signs of fatigue or stress that may make you susceptible to a temper outburst. Your goal is to be better able to predict when you are at risk of losing control and of becoming aggressive with others (or even with yourself).

- In Step 3 you will be introduced to some anger management techniques. Try these techniques, at least a few times each: the '*Time-Out*', the '*Thermometer Technique*' and the '*Assertive Exchange*' – and find the ones that work best for you. Regular practise of these will expand your window of tolerance and enable you to feel in better control over your anger and other dysregulated emotions.

EXERCISE 21: STEP 1 – KEEPING YOUR OWN ANGER NOTES

Part 1: Set aside a section in your journal and label it 'Anger Notes'. Draw five vertical columns and in these keep track of:

1. when you get angry
2. what's happened to cause the anger

3. how strong it feels (give it a rating between 0–8, see below)
4. how you think when you are angry
5. how you behave when you are angry.

For example, your thoughts might be: 'I can't stand this!', 'I'll get even for that!', 'They're driving me crazy', 'I can't believe what I'm hearing!' Your behaviour might include making sarcastic remarks, shouting, slamming doors, throwing something, swearing, ignoring others or trying to over-control them.

Use the following scale 0–8 to rate the strength of your anger:

0	1	2	3	4	5	6	7	8
Irritated	Annoyed	Slightly bothered	Agitated	Quite bothered	Angry	Furious	Exploding	Enraged

In your journal you should make entries at least once daily for a period of two weeks or more. Remember that, just like the rest of your journal, these notes are for your own reference and for your eyes alone – so you can be completely honest with yourself!

It is hard to remember things clearly when one is in the heat of anger. Keeping the notes will give you a chance to look back a few days or weeks later and decide if you are managing your anger effectively or if some things still need improvement. Even if you are not a person who usually writes things down, or even if you are uncomfortable doing so, do make an effort to do this. If you really can't keep a handwritten journal use your computer or tablet for this. You will not remember accurately otherwise, and you may even find that the act of writing itself gives your arousal reactions time to CALM DOWN.

Part 2 of Exercise 21 offers some very specific questions to ask yourself in order to help you understand your anger even better.

EXERCISE 21: STEP 1 – KEEPING YOUR OWN ANGER NOTES

Part 2: Ask yourself the following questions and record the answers in your notebook as part of your anger notes as honestly as you can:

1. How often do I feel angry? (Three times a day/ every other day/once a week?)
2. How do I let others know that I'm angry? (By shouting/by being silent/are others even aware/ do I keep it hidden?)

3. What do I look like when I'm angry? (Red in the face/ scowling/face muscles tight/clenched fists?)

4. Is my anger helping me to cope? (For example, does it stop me from feeling sad? Does it give me the drive to deal with legal matters, bank managers, etc.?)

5. Is my anger covering other, deeper feelings that I find difficult to acknowledge? If so, what might these be? What are the feelings lying at the root of my anger that I find hardest to own?

6. Is my anger getting in the way of my recovery? (For example, does it help me to avoid other things that I need to face? Does it alienate me from my family?)

7. What do I hope to gain from my anger? (Confidence/restitution/recognition/revenge?) Are there other ways in which I could gain those things?

8. What is my anger preventing me from doing? (For example, talking to others, forming new relationships, gaining some distance from the trauma?)

9. Is feeling angry different from feeling powerful? (Yes or no) If the answer is 'yes', how is it different? If 'no', does this type of power make me feel better or worse?

10. How did people in my family express anger while I was growing up? Do I use the same ways? If not, how are the ways I use different?

11. How have my ways of handling anger changed since the trauma? (For example, do I throw things now, when I didn't before? Do I shout at the children more?)

12. Have I been hoping to obtain some relief through angry, explosive actions? (Yes or no) If the answer is 'yes', is this a fantasy or a realistic expectation? What other more helpful methods could I use to obtain relief?

13. Do I feel or behave like a victim? (Yes or no) If the answer is 'yes', what is preventing me from claiming my own power back in a positive way and stop feeling less of a victim now?

14. Is it better to 'forgive and move on' or to seek revenge? Are there any alternatives that lie in between those two extremes?

Add any other questions of your own here that you might find useful to ask.

Keep working on your anger notes, make entries daily, so that you can keep track of your feelings and how you are managing your anger in different situations. Try and see if you can recognise a pattern. Write down the date, what it was about the situation that made you angry, and the bodily behaviour signals that told you that you were angry, for example: changes in your breathing, muscles tight in forehead, tightness in your chest or stomach, gritting your teeth, clenched fists, raised voice, pacing, making sarcastic comments. The 'signals' will probably differ with different levels of intensity of your anger. Try to see if you can recognise a pattern in your responses.

Don't expect that this exercise will go perfectly and be patient with yourself, remembering the commitment you made to yourself in Chapter 4. Your anger notes are intended to help you to observe your own ways of dealing with things, and to become familiar with your individual physical and behavioural signals for different levels of anger. Step 2 in Exercise 22 continues this process.

EXERCISE 22: STEP 2 – MANAGING YOUR PHYSICAL SELF

Part 1: To understand your own body, ask yourself the following questions and record the answers in your notebook:

1. How does your body tell you that you are becoming angry?
2. How do you recognise the signals?
3. Does your stomach go into a knot?

4. Do your muscles become tense and stiff?
5. Do you start to sweat or get cold?
6. Does your head begin to pound?
7. Do you feel veins standing out in your neck or forehead?
8. Does your facial expression change?
9. What other signals have you noticed for your anger?

It is helpful for you to get to know your body and your physical responses as best as you can. You could also ask a trusted person what they notice about your bodily changes when you are feeling angry. Many of the physical signs of anger can be very similar to your responses when you are anxious. In fact, unexpressed anger may often be masked as anxiety.

The **Relaxed Breathing Method** that you read about earlier in this chapter will also be useful to help you to reduce your tension and to gain control over your body's responses to anger. When you have mastered your technique, you can begin to employ **Quick Controlled Breathing** described in the next exercise, to help you in situations of high arousal.

EXERCISE 22: STEP 2 – MANAGING YOUR PHYSICAL SELF

Part 2: Control your body's responses to anger with the **Quick Controlled Breathing** *technique*

1. Pay attention to your breathing when you feel yourself becoming angry. Is it sharper? Faster? Can you slow it down by taking five deep breaths?
2. Start by exhaling as fully as you can. Now with each breath, inhale, hold for a second, then exhale slowly, blowing through your mouth. Again, with each breath, inhale, hold for a second, then exhale slowly, blowing through your mouth and counting (silently) backwards from 5 to 1.
3. Remember to exhale fully, as if it was a heavy sigh, then again inhale, hold, exhale slowly, counting 5, 4, 3, 2, 1. Next breath, inhale, hold, exhale slowly, counting 5, 4, 3, 2, 1. As you are exhaling slowly, you might imagine allowing the anger you are holding to flow out of you.
4. Continue three more times and on the last breath say softly to yourself: 'Calm and in control!'
5. As you perform this you should notice a slight drop in your angry feelings. This will help you to think more clearly, so that you can choose how to react. Practise this technique frequently!

In addition to using relaxed breathing, try some healthy physical outlets for your tension if you are able, for example, a competitive sport, a vigorous walk or a run, or even enthusiastic house repair, cleaning or redecorating.

Physical exertion, in the form of exercise or physical activity, is a good outlet for anger and stress. If the traditional types of sport and exercise do not appeal to you, consider some of the less traditional, like the martial arts, tai chi, yoga, qi gong, Pilates. Bowling, swimming or cycling are other possibilities.

One activity it is best to avoid when you are in a temper is *driving*. Instead, a vigorous walk is a good way to calm you down. Make sure you don't engage in activities where you could hurt yourself or others, for example pounding nails with a hammer when angry often results in smashed thumbnails. Throwing hard or breakable objects is also off-limits. Instead, pound a pillow, bounce a soft ball or even blow up balloons (balloons require effort and vigorous breathing, another form of breathing control, so this is not as silly as it sounds!).

If physical injury or disability prevents you from actively engaging in exercise, you can use other means to release anger. You could use singing or sounding to let your anger out, use art or creative activities to externalise your anger, such as painting, making collages of pictures that symbolise your anger, modelling clay sculptures. Alternatively, you can create imagery in your inner mind in which you imagine yourself running fast, swimming a long distance, skiing down a steep hill or engaging in some other form of physical activity that you feel could be a good outlet for your anger. Research has shown that even if our body can't engage in particular exercises, if we imagine vividly in our mind being engaged in them, our brain will respond as if we really are doing them.

Remember to keep track in your journal of what you do and how often, and whether it makes a difference in the way you feel.

EXERCISE 23: STEP 3 – SPECIFIC ANGER MANAGEMENT TECHNIQUES

Part 1: The 'Time-out' technique

Perhaps the most successful and widely used method for gaining control over an explosive temper is known as 'Time-out'. It is particularly useful for traumatised individuals, as it allows them to be 'in charge' of their own anger, paying attention to the body signals of rising frustration and choosing, before they lose control, to take a 'Time-out'. 'Time-out' means leaving the situation so that your anger will not escalate.

If you are at home at the time you feel your anger rising, say out loud to yourself and your partner: 'I'm getting angry and I need to take a Time-out.' Then, you must leave for an hour (no more and no less), during which time you must not drink alcohol and you should not drive. You can use relaxation, soothing and breathing techniques during your time out or anything that is nurturing and helpful to you.

If it is late at night, and unsafe to go out, go to another room and remain alone.

Use the breathing technique or any other techniques, such as physical exercise, to help you calm down. This will help you to deal with things on your return, rather than just reacting to them in an 'out-of-control' way.

Prior preparation

Before you first use this technique, it is important to explain to your partner or others around you that may be affected, that you are trying to learn helpful ways of controlling your anger. Make an agreement with them beforehand that when you are next angry you will take a 'Time-out', but that you will be back after an hour and that they should not worry because you will take good care of yourself during that time. Also explain that your going away does not mean you don't want to be with them, but that there are times when you need to be alone in order to cope better with your anger. Encourage them to respect your efforts at anger control and ask them to give you the freedom to use this technique without stopping you or coming after you when you feel angry, as this would not be helpful.

EXERCISE 23: STEP 3 – SPECIFIC ANGER MANAGEMENT TECHNIQUES

Part 2: The 'Thermometer' technique

This approach draws on your newly developed skills of paying attention to your bodily signals, in particular, signs of temper rising. It has been taught (in various forms) and used successfully for many years by groups such as Narcotics Anonymous, whose participants have often turned to drug or alcohol abuse as an ineffective way of managing explosive tempers. When people are working to overcome addictions, they often feel quite raw and on edge, just as you are likely to be feeling at times, while you work to overcome the effects of traumatic stress.

Here is how it works:

1. Picture, in your mind's eye, a very large thermometer. Try and allow yourself to see very clearly the gradation marks on each side of the glass tube that register the degrees of temperature rising. The mercury inside the glass tube is red. We will use this to represent your temper.

2. When you are calm and cool, there is very little mercury in the tube, just enough to help you pay attention and interact effectively with

others. However, when you start to become agitated, the temperature starts to rise and the mercury level in the tube will go up!

3. Because you are much more in tune with your bodily signals now, you will notice how your breathing begins to quicken when you become just a bit agitated. Your muscles tense, and you become aware that your eyes are squinting a bit, your nostrils are flaring. In short, as your 'temperature rises', you are starting to resemble a charging bull! The mercury in your imaginary thermometer is rising very quickly indeed.

4. Now, all thermometers have some red marks at the top to indicate 'danger' and 'overheating'. As you pay attention to the signals of your rising anger, you can start to picture the thermometer, and you can become aware of how close you are getting to the danger zone. It is time to bring the mercury down before you get into the 'red zone', where you will not be able to think clearly enough to take appropriate action.

5. If you allow your anger to boil over, you will be operating on raw emotion, with very little (if any) rational thought. Those are the situations where you are likely to get into trouble and do or say things that you will probably regret later, when they are hard to undo. Use all your skills to stay out of the red zone of raw emotions.

6. Keep being aware of your temper. Try using the 'Quick Controlled Breathing' technique described on page 269. Take a step back and let the intensity of your voice drop. Wait a few moments, take a 'Time-out' if you need to. Do whatever you need to do to get your anger 'thermometer' to drop the temperature down to a more reasonable and comfortable level.

7. When you have reached 'room temperature' level again, then you can begin to deal with the person or problem on a rational basis.

8. Practise this technique as often as possible. As soon as you find yourself getting worked up, think 'THERMOMETER'! This technique can be very effective, once you have learned it and as long as you use it regularly.

EXERCISE 23: STEP 3 – SPECIFIC ANGER MANAGEMENT TECHNIQUES

Part 3: The 'Assertive Exchange' technique

When you have some mastery over the surges that fuel your temper, the next skill to work on is improving your communication. If the only way you communicate when you are frustrated or angry is to be sarcastic, intimidating, shouting, aggressive, blaming, withdrawing or giving the silent 'freeze treatment', your partner, family members or colleagues are unlikely to want to engage in problem-solving with you! They know you are angry, but they probably stop listening at an early stage and are busy thinking about how to defend themselves. Nothing gets resolved, and the situation tends to repeat itself in a vicious and very frustrating circle.

You can change this by developing your assertiveness skills. The following technique, which we call the 'Assertive Exchange', is based on a method called the D-E-S-Cscript[2]. It has become the basis for most assertiveness communication training.

An easy way to remember our 'Assertive Exchange' formula is to think of the acronym, **'R-E-A-C-T'**, which stands for:

Refer: state directly the issue that is upsetting you and that you want to talk about.
Example: 'James, the television is turned up too loud!'

Exchange: use an 'I' statement here to communicate your feelings.
Example: 'I've spoken to you about this several times already. I'm frustrated that you're not listening.'

Action: be specific about the action you want to take place; what is it that you want the person to do?
Example: 'Turn the television down immediately.'

Conditions: if appropriate, now indicate any stipulations or consequences.
Example: 'This is the last time I'm going to speak to you about it.'

Thanks: express gratitude to the other person for listening.
Example: 'Thank you. I appreciate you turning it down'

This very simple method may feel like a big leap for you, but it is fairly certain to produce positive results, both at home and in the outside world. It works with children, partners, work colleagues and even most bosses and authority figures!

Why is it so effective? Because it emphasises fact, and it keeps emotion in check. It does not focus on the blaming 'you' statement (e.g. 'You make me sick!'), which is more aggressive and puts the other person on the defensive. That is the difference between aggressiveness and assertiveness. When you are being properly assertive, more respect is communicated between the parties and emotions tend to stay in check. The result is that you stay in control and more problem-solving happens. By using this technique, you may begin to feel more understood and more effective in achieving the result that you need.

If you have a difficult exchange coming up during which you need to stay assertive and not explode with frustration, apply this R-E-A-C-T formula in a rehearsal before the encounter takes place. Write out each step of what you are going to say in your journal. Imagine how the other person may respond and visualise yourself staying on track. This imaginary rehearsal will greatly enhance your chances for success even if the actual situation may turn out a little different from the one rehearsed!

Anger reactions and increased risk-taking behaviour

In moments of extreme frustration and high arousal – especially as you are struggling to overcome a trauma, and may feel very helpless to do anything else – it is tempting to take it out on yourself. Banging one's head, putting a fist through the wall or window, destroying things around you, driving recklessly, cutting or self-mutilating are all examples of behaviour that indicates that you have lost control.

This type of behaviour is a sure sign that you are not coping, and that things have become too much for you. You may also engage in behaviour during those times that puts others in danger and at greater risk of harm. This behaviour signals that you are out of your window of tolerance and are struggling with emotion regulation. You resort to self-harm, self-injurious behaviour or risk-taking as a way of trying to cope with your feelings of utter overwhelm.

However, these ways of coping are not helpful as they add further pain and complications to the hurt you are already suffering. They also don't help you to find your way back to your emotional comfort zone. Remember the contract you made with yourself in Chapter 4. As part of helping your mind switch into gear for healing you committed to giving yourself another chance of life now. Remind yourself of this now.

Remove yourself from the situation and from the people who are causing you to want to harm yourself. Remind yourself that such behaviour is a desperate bid for control and, as you have seen in this chapter, there are better ways to achieve control. If this is behaviour that you are recognising in yourself, remind yourself of some of the techniques introduced to you in Chapters 4, 6, 8 and also in this chapter to bring yourself back into your emotional comfort zone. Make an immediate plan of what soothing strategies you commit to using instead of self-harming or risk-taking behaviour. Set aside time in your day to practise these as often as you can, not only when you are in trigger situations. Choose the ones that you find work best for you. Every person is different and what works for one may not work for another. Record these under a separate heading in your journal. Remind yourself of using these each time you are at risk (ideally before this) of wanting to use harmful behaviour.

If you find that you cannot regulate yourself sufficiently to be able to stop self-harming behaviour *you should seek the help of your GP and arrange for treatment from a trauma specialist.*

Other arousal reactions

This chapter focused specifically on managing problems with sleep and anger. You may have noticed from your arousal monitoring questions that there are also other areas in which high arousal can affect your functioning in life. These include difficulties with concentration, feeling 'super-alert' and feeling jumpy and startled more easily. You may also experience panic attacks and these are explored in more detail in Chapter 10 in connection with your avoidance reactions. Many people are very bothered by their poor concentration, difficulties focusing and memory problems.

Sometimes people think that this could be a sign of some form of early dementia. This is unlikely, as concentration and memory problems are linked to the system overload that many people experience after trauma. Your body/mind system has finite resources, like a hard drive on a computer. Currently it is so overwhelmed and preoccupied with trying to keep you safe (as it hasn't properly updated) that most of its available resources go into this. This leaves very little spare capacity for coping with day-to-day demands, such as taking in and storing new information or retrieving information that doesn't seem relevant to your highly aroused survival system.

It is very likely that if you can help your sleep improve and your level of anger to come down that extra resources will become available to you. The more aspects of your trauma you have processed and resolved, the more resources will be become available to you again. You can also build up your concentration by regularly using the resource strategies explored in Chapter 6 and your inner sanctuary as these give your overactive arousal system some respite. You might find that this in itself over time will free resources that can go into attending to day-to-day activities and improving your concentration. Your super-alertness and your jumpiness should also reduce as a result of regular use of these exercises and the processing of your traumatic experience.

Summary checkpoints:

- Reactions of increased arousal are a major component of the traumatic stress reaction and PTSD.
- If you are affected by this it will help to keep an arousal chart to monitor how frequently and how much you arc bothered by these reactions.
- Once you have established your baseline for arousal reactions, monitor this regularly as you work through the exercises in this chapter and the rest of the book.
- Impaired sleep can have a devastating effect on your functioning, mood and reactions. This chapter provides you with a wide range of strategies and a specific breathing method aimed at helping you improve both the length and quality of your sleep.

- In order to benefit from these, you must persevere with these strategies for a while and allow yourself to be patient.
- Increased feelings of anger and irritability are another very common response to trauma.
- This chapter helps you to manage your anger in three steps:
- Step 1 helps you to understand your anger and therefore gain more control over it.
- Step 2 helps you to be better able to predict when you are at risk of losing control.
- Step 3 introduces you to three different anger management techniques which, when practised regularly, can help you widen your window of tolerance and enable you better control over your anger and other dysregulated emotions.
- This chapter gives specific advice on the relationship between anger and increased risk-taking behaviour.
- Other reactions of high arousal, such as 'super-alertness', jumpiness and startle responses and concentration and memory problems are likely to lessen as your sleep improves and your anger resolves.

10

Managing your avoidance reactions

Avoidance arises from your attempt to manage, cope with and reduce the uncomfortable intrusive and arousal symptoms of post-traumatic stress. You may not even be aware of this, as much of this takes place on a subconscious level, driven by the autonomic system and related brain structures. While avoidance in this context is entirely understandable, it can have a severely restrictive effect on your life. It also maintains the PTSD, as your belief and body system continue to act as if you are still in danger. This chapter helps you with getting to know your avoidance reactions and the link to your overactive arousal system. It provides you with strategies and steps which help you tackle avoidance in a gradual manner at your pace, enabling you to stay within your own window of tolerance.

Getting to know your avoidance reactions

In order to be able to manage your avoidance reactions, described in Chapter 2, it will help you to know how upsetting to you they are. Measuring the level of upset of your reactions will enable you to take your *avoidance baseline* (just as you did in Chapters 8 and 9 for your intrusive and arousal reactions).

The following questions cover the two avoidance reactions that people may experience. Please copy these questions into your journal, date the entry and try to answer them as best as you can. The scales 0–4 are explained below:

- To rate how much you have been bothered by each of the experiences in the past week, use the following 0-4 scale:

0	1	2	3	4
Not at all	A little bit	Moderately	Quite a bit	Extremely

Please answer the following questions by circling the number on each scale which best applies to you:

1. In the past seven days how much were you bothered by efforts to avoid memories, thoughts or feelings that reminded you of or that are closely associated with your traumatic experience(s)?

0   1   2   3   4

2. In the past seven days how much were you bothered by efforts to avoid reminders of the stressful situation (for example, people, places, conversations, activities, objects or situations) that arouse distressing memories, thoughts, or feelings about or closely associated with the traumatic event(s).

0   1   2   3   4

Once you have circled the number that best applies to you on each question, add the scores from both of the questions (1 and 2) for each of the two categories. Record these total scores in your notebook.

Lastly, give an overall rating for how disabling these avoidance reactions have been to you in the past week, by circling the number that applies to you on the scale used below (you could copy this also into your notebook):

TOTAL SCORE FOR AVOIDANCE REACTIONS ON................... (date)

Your total score is:...

If your total score is:

2 or below = they are low

3–5 = they fall into the mid-range

6 or more = they are high

0	1	2	3	4	5	6	7	8
Not at all disabling		Slightly disabling		Definitely disabling		Markedly disabling		Severely disabling

Now that you have established the baseline for your avoidance reactions you can begin to try to reduce the level of these. You may also find that professional help would be useful if your scores fall into the mid- to high range.

The avoidance–panic connection

Although panic reactions are really rooted in responses of heightened arousal, such as anxiety and fear, in this book they are discussed in this chapter because they are so directly linked to avoidance behaviour.

If you have ever experienced a panic attack, the sudden shortness of breath, severe chest pain or feeling that your head was expanding may have led you to wonder if you had a serious illness or were going mad. The feelings are so dreadful that immediately you begin to worry about this happening to you again and as a result you are 'on the look-out' for the slightest signs of increasing nervousness within yourself. In order to reduce the chances of a recurrence, you might begin *to avoid* situations, places and activities that you think are likely to make you feel uncomfortable or uneasy, and bring on a panic attack. This is also referred to as safety behaviour. The cycle of anxiety leading to avoidance leading to the anticipation of more anxiety leading to more avoidance has begun. The diagram on page 288, shows you what happens:

When you have experienced a trauma, anything related to that experience, its aftermath, the further consequences of it, and even your internal sensations about it, might act as a trigger. Once you have been triggered, a message of 'danger or threat' is relayed via neural pathways. This is then registered and stored by arousal structures in your brain. These are wired to be in charge of protecting you and this is a process that happens automatically and that is not under your conscious control.

Specific neurochemicals are then pumped into your body to prepare you for the perceived threat. These momentarily change your body chemistry and you might notice this

Diagram 4: Panic and Avoidance Cycle

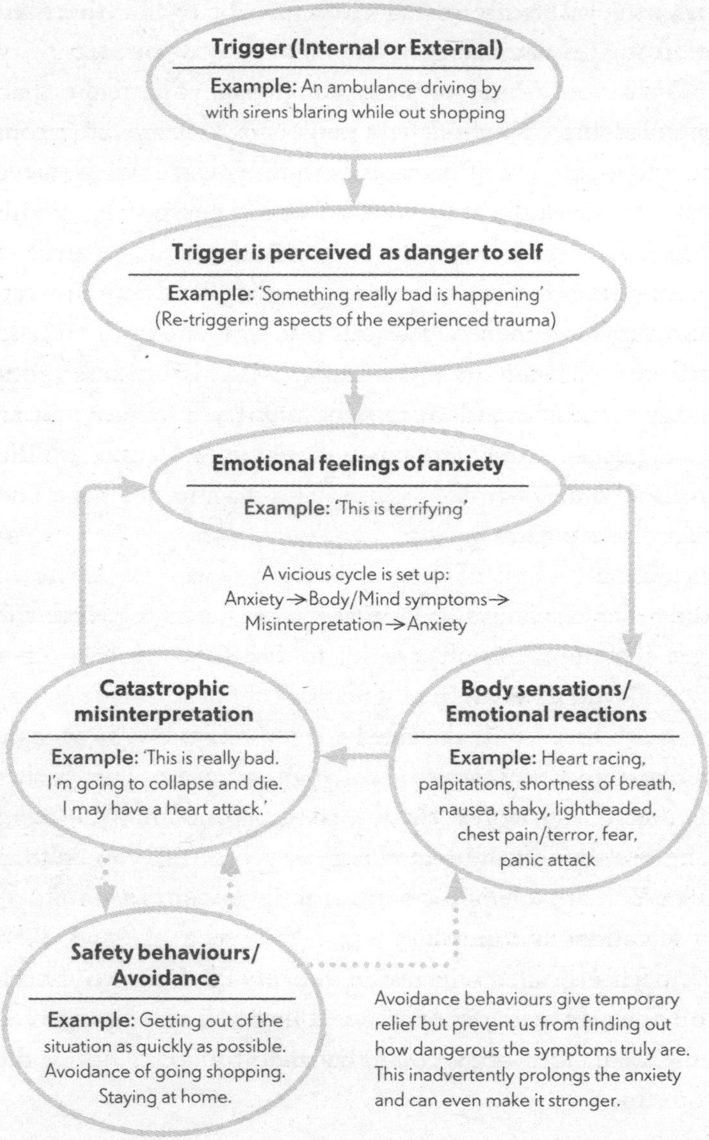

Trigger (Internal or External)

Example: An ambulance driving by
with sirens blaring while out shopping

Trigger is perceived as danger to self

Example: 'Something really bad is happening'
(Re-triggering aspects of the experienced trauma)

Emotional feelings of anxiety

Example: 'This is terrifying'

A vicious cycle is set up:
Anxiety→Body/Mind symptoms→
Misinterpretation→Anxiety

**Catastrophic
misinterpretation**

Example: 'This is really bad.
I'm going to collapse and die.
I may have a heart attack.'

**Body sensations/
Emotional reactions**

Example: Heart racing,
palpitations, shortness of breath,
nausea, shaky, lightheaded,
chest pain/terror, fear,
panic attack

**Safety behaviours/
Avoidance**

Example: Getting out of the
situation as quickly as possible.
Avoidance of going shopping.
Staying at home.

Avoidance behaviours give temporary
relief but prevent us from finding out
how dangerous the symptoms truly are.
This inadvertently prolongs the anxiety
and can even make it stronger.

because you pick up uncomfortable body sensations, such as for example, a sense of 'tightness in your chest', 'shortness of breath', 'heart racing' or 'tightness in your throat'.

Once you perceive these sensations, you might then interpret them as a threat and think that these are dangerous and might cause you harm, for example, you might believe that 'you are suffocating' or 'will have a heart attack'. This then causes you feelings of anxiety and the arousal structures in your brain register this as even further danger and threat, pumping more neurochemicals into your body to try and activate your 'fight' or 'flight' responses. This intensifies your bodily sensations and you might also start to have internal images of something really bad happening to you like it did during the trauma (flashbacks or intrusive memories). You might notice feeling 'your head going fuzzy or blurred or expanding', 'sense of intense heat or sweatiness','sense of coldness and shivering', 'dizziness', 'chest pain as it feels the chest is getting tighter', 'gasping for breath' or various other uncomfortable sensations.

At this stage it is likely that these sensations or images are the only thing that you are noticing. You probably don't notice that in reality you are safe now and nothing dangerous is actually happening to you at this moment in time. You are totally focused on these uncomfortable bodily sensations and mental images. They seem to have taken over. This is called selective attention. The selective attention focusses you on only one thing, on your perceived sense of danger and your belief that you could even die from this.

It is understandable that all you want to do at that stage is to get out of this particular situation in order to make the sensations stop and feel safe again. You probably use safety behaviour that either makes you do something that gets you out of this particular trigger situation or something that shuts these feelings down, because it feels so unbearable to you in that moment. This is where the avoidance comes in. Not only might you be avoiding the particular trigger situation, but you might also be learning to use strategies that help you avoid these sensations, for example not talking to people about certain things that could trigger such feelings. This is because you are likely to have misinterpreted these uncomfortable sensations as dangerous.

You might even ruminate about what other people might think of you when they see you like this in a particular situation. These catastrophic misinterpretations make you feel even more out of control and increase your sense of anxiety. While all these reactions are totally understandable, you are inadvertently teaching those arousal structures in your brain which register danger that all this is really dangerous. These then become even more sensitised to potential triggers and to your own sensations which leads to a vicious cycle. Your selective attention to those things that you think are dangerous, not only increases your chances of further catastrophic misinterpretation in the future, but leads to an ever greater range of avoidance strategies and safety behaviours to help you manage the situation. You are stuck in a vicious cycle of panic and avoidance. There are many things you can do to change this pattern and move out of this vicious cycle of panic and avoidance once you become aware of it and this chapter helps you with this.

Hyperventilation

You will be aware that your breathing changes in response to a trigger and these often very subtle shifts in your breathing pattern can lead to hyperventilation or overbreathing. Hyperventilation can also be caused by body postures that may be related to feeling threatened or vulnerable and are assumed to protect oneself, such as hunched shoulders, head and neck thrust forward, clenched teeth, puffed up chest. It is caused by the tensing of muscles of the neck, throat, chest and abdomen in response to stress, anxiety and worry.

During the rapid and frequently shallow breathing pattern that ensues, carbon dioxide (CO_2) is expelled faster than the body is producing it. This blood CO_2 drop leads to constriction in certain blood vessels resulting in less oxygen reaching the brain, heart and extremities, and a change in blood acidity levels, causing less oxygen to reach the body tissues and the release of certain irons, which flood them. This leads to a number of very distressing symptoms, which are highlighted in the table on page 292. One of the problems is that once hyperventilation has been present for about ten days, the body makes adjustments to the low CO_2 level and restores the blood's acid–base balance. This enables the breathing initially to calm down, but now the system has become sensitised, which means that even a single deep breath or sigh can trigger symptoms, which will feel even more pronounced. This leads to respiratory alkalosis and some people may suffer from the symptoms of this most of the time, others only in times of stress.

Table 1: Symptoms of Hyperventilation
• Breathlessness and chest pain • Headaches and migraine • Dizziness, unsteadiness and instability, feeling faint, visual disturbance (blackouts and blurred or tunnel vision), paresthesia (numbness, pins and needles, burning limbs) • Muscle pains, cramps, tremors, twitching, weakness and stiffness, lower back ache • Digestive Problems, such as irritable bowel syndrome (IBS), flatulence, belching, bloating, abdominal discomfort • 'Hiatus Hernia' • Impaired concentration, memory and sleep, emotional sweating, woolly head • Allergies • Fatigue and exhaustion

The symptoms of hyperventilation are quite varied and distressing. Frequently they lead to repeated medical consultations, examinations and misdiagnoses, while the actual cause remains unrecognised. If you breathe more than fourteen breaths per minute you may be suffering from hyperventilation. Another symptom is breathing mostly through your chest with very little abdominal movement.

You can recover from the unpleasant symptoms of hyperventilation. You can re-train your breathing patterns so that your CO_2 level becomes more balanced or you can engage in exercise and increase the amount of CO_2 produced by your body. Yoga or mediations are helpful practices to rebalance the CO_2 level. The Relaxed Breathing Method (Exercise 20, Chapter 9) is helpful for re-training your breathing pattern.

Overcoming the cycle of panic and avoidance

Though panic feelings are very unpleasant, they are quite natural and do not cause you actual harm. They are caused by a temporary surplus of neurochemicals in your bloodstream, which are released because arousal structures in your brain registered (incorrectly) that you are in danger and they want to protect you. It is just that you don't really need this protection because you are in an 'ordinary' situation rather than in a dangerous or threatening one. Therefore you don't need any of these surplus neurochemicals to deal with this situation and as you don't use them up they stay in your body. This, together with the consequences of your hyperventilated breathing pattern, gives you these uncomfortable feelings.

These 'ordinary situations' might be public activities, like shopping, meeting other people, using public transportation, going to the theatre or cinema or they might be private activities, such as opening an official letter, such as from a solicitor, watching something on TV or hearing something on the radio, or even just thinking what it felt like when you had your last panic attack. Driving could become a problem as well, if you start to fear that you will have a panic attack while in traffic or on the motorway. You may no longer trust yourself to stay in control and feel that you are no longer safe to drive. This is called a driving phobia. Avoidance of driving is often even more intensified if your trauma directly involved a road traffic or transportation accident.

As a result of your trauma your body and mind have been conditioned to perceive danger even in situations seemingly unrelated to the traumatic event. Thus, you may find yourself avoiding more and more things and life can become very limited. Frequently, people come to regard this far more limited life as their new norm and they often forget all the things that they may have been able to do before the trauma.

Recognising the scale of your avoidance

It is always useful to take stock. Part of this involves you finding out how much your life has really changed since your trauma. Although it may be hard to discover at first, knowing what you are actually dealing with is very helpful, as it puts you back in control. You can't change anything if you don't recognise, acknowledge or know it. It takes courage to look at your life honestly. If you can pluck up the courage and do it, it may be well worth your while as part of your commitment to give yourself another chance of life (Chapter 4 – Moving towards your path of recovery). Exercise 24 will help you with this.

EXERCISE 24: TAKING STOCK OF THE SCALE OF YOUR AVOIDANCE

Allow at least 45 minutes for this exercise and find an undisturbed place, such as your special safe place, in which to practice it. Have your journal ready for recording your answers. Some of what you discover may bring up emotions. Have something with you that can soothe or comfort you, such as a cosy blanket to wrap round you and a box of tissues.

1. Settle yourself comfortably into your seating and think back to a time before your trauma when you felt most connected with life. Try and think about this as if you were observing your former self through the eyes of a neutral observer. Write your answers down in a section of your journal, which you label: 'Me before the trauma'.

2. Notice what your life looked like when you were at your most energised. Think about the person you were then and observe from this

neutral position what a typical week or month would have looked like for you. What would you have done during this time? Which things interested you? What hobbies did you have? What things would you get involved or engaged in? How often would you go out in the evenings? What were your favourite activities?

3. Notice now what most motivated you in your social interactions. How did you relate to other people in your life? How would others have described you in terms of your social interactions? Did you feel more energised by interactions with just a few good trusted friends or were you the kind of person who would thrive in larger groups and be the life and soul of any party? What worked best for you in your interactions with others? Consider your interactions with your close loved ones. What were these like? How did you relate to them and what made you feel the best? Look at this former self closely and note all that may be significant for you to recognise about your preferences.

4. Now look at your working life. What were the things you enjoyed most, what did you do that energised you? What fulfilled you most? How did you relate to your boss and your colleagues? What did your boss and colleagues value about you? What were the skills or characteristics that

made you unique? What activities did you most enjoy at work? Notice anything else that may be relevant.

5. When you have got a really good picture of the person you were then and have recorded all the things that made you feel good, stop. Thank the person you were then for showing you all this and bring yourself back to the here-and-now.

6. Now reflect, as objectively as you can, on how your life is now after the trauma. Go back to the same questions and consider your answers for the present moment in time (e.g. what most motivates you now in your social interactions?). Allow yourself to stay with any emotions that this may bring up for you, but try and keep on task. Be as non-judgmental as you can. Just notice your observations and write them down in your journal, creating a section that is labelled: 'Me after the trauma'.

7. When you have done this, make two lists in your journal: a. All the things that you used to enjoy, but no longer do because you truly can't do them any more because of an actual physical injury or physical disability relating to your trauma. b. All the things you used to enjoy and could still do, but have stopped doing because you avoid them (regardless of what the reason for your avoidance is).

8. Then create a new section in your journal, entitled 'Overcoming my vicious cycle of avoidance'.

9. In relation to your listings in 7a, consider what alternative activities, hobbies or interactions to the ones you used to enjoy could be done within the range of your current physical limitations. Be aware of not closing yourself down to new possibilities. Write all of these down in a new list, even if you feel that you are not quite ready to do them yet.

10. Use your listings in 7b. and 9. as the baseline for moving yourself into a meaningful life beyond the trauma. To start with, choose only one of those items on your lists to focus on. Choose those that might come easiest or most natural to you. Exercise 26 will guide you further on this.

Well done for completing Exercise 24. This has enabled you to recognise the scale of your avoidance. Out of this recognition you have been able to create a baseline of activities which you could now, one by one, use to practise overcoming your vicious cycle of panic and avoidance. Exercise 26 on page 303 will show you how to do this. You owe this to yourself as part of your commitment to give yourself another chance of life.

Strategies to help you overcome your panic feelings

It has been explained why panic feelings arise and their connection with hyperventilation, and you have been helped to recognise the scale of your avoidance. You can overcome the vicious cycle of panic and avoidance in several ways. One is to use strategies that reduce your feelings of panic. The panic feelings are a sign that specific arousal structures in your brain are overactive. In order to cope with these panic feelings, and to reduce your fears in anticipation of them, it can be helpful to remind yourself that the situation is not dangerous now and these uncomfortable feelings are there because your arousal system has misinterpreted the situation. This is called cognitive re-framing through 'psycho-education'. Speaking to yourself in a reassuring manner, orienting yourself to the safety of the here-and-now and explaining why you are feeling like this can help soothe those overactive arousal structures. Slow down and balance your breathing while you do this. You can also write reassuring messages to yourself in your journal or memos that you stick around the house that remind you that you are safe in the here-and-now. This usually helps best when you are just a little anxious and would like to calm that anxiety. Some of the exercises introduced in Chapter 6 on methods to soothe your disturbed nervous system could also be helpful to you for this. All this is less useful if you are already in the middle of a panic attack. However, the more often you practise the above the less likely you are to experience a panic attack.

For those times during which you might still experience a panic attack, you can learn strategies that help you gain confidence in managing those panic reactions. You can focus on controlling your breathing, count down slowly from 10 to 1 and congratulate yourself on small successes ('I was able to stay out shopping for half an hour before I began to mind the crowds'). Once you are no longer frightened by them, and give them less attention, the panic attacks will usually disappear on their own. Exercise 25 helps you with this.

EXERCISE 25: QUICK TIPS FOR HANDLING YOUR PANIC

1. Remind yourself that you understand what is happening to you now, and that there is no real need to be frightened. Remember these symptoms are uncomfortable but not life-threatening!

2. Begin to concentrate on your breathing. Blow out first, as slowly as you can. The next breath in will be deeper. Try to breathe out to the count of 10, then in again to the count of 10, breathing from your diaphragm (belly) and not from the top of your chest. If you can't manage to the count of 10, breathe in and out to the longest count of breath you can manage.

3. Repeat a coping statement to yourself – 'I can get through this' or 'This feeling will pass in a few seconds if only I stay with it!'.

4. Slow down a bit and continue doing whatever you were doing, as calmly as possible. Try not to rush home.

5. Then find a place where you can stop, possibly sitting down with your feet flat on the floor. Block your ears with your thumbs (resting the fingers on the top of your head) or your index fingers. Breathe in strongly and quite quickly through your nose and then slowly breathe out, making a low humming sound that is soft and deep. Try and keep your awareness inside the head while you do this (you can close your eyes also if you like and it is safe to do so). Continue this way for about 10 to 15 rounds. When you have finished, keep your ears closed for some time and listen to any after sounds within your head. Observe them until they fade and then lower your hands. This breath is very calming and can help to instill a state of calmness and peace in your mind and nervous system. It is called the **humming bee breath** (*bhramari*) and comes from yoga practices for trauma[1].

6. If the feelings still continue, try singing! If you are alone in the car while driving, sing out aloud and if you are with others, hum a tune or sing softly under your breath. Try to pick a song that makes you feel good or strong or cheerful!

7. Congratulate yourself on continuing your trauma recovery journey. It can be hard work, but you are not giving up! It will be worth the practice.

8. When you are in a comfortable place again, practise the Relaxed Breathing Method (Chapter 9, Exercise 20), and allow yourself to let go of the built-up tension.

It will also help if you keep a record in your journal for a two-week period, noting when you feel panicky or anxious and what was happening at that time. For example, were you in a particular place, or with certain people, or especially tired or upset?

Then from your list of things that you have been avoiding (Exercise 24, 7b. and 9.) select *one* to work on. Decide what *gradual steps* you could take to try that activity. Order them from *easiest* to *hardest*, and start to work on an easy step first. This should just make you feel a little bit uncomfortable, but not overwhelmingly so. Record your progress and successes in your journal. Use Exercise 26 and the examples which follow to help you.

EXERCISE 26: GRADUAL STEPS TO COPE WITH PANIC AND AVOIDANCE

1. Keep a record of your panic attacks in your notebook. Rate them in terms of their strength (using a scale between 0 = none and 8 = absolutely overwhelming) and monitor them on a daily basis. Here's an example of what your panic diary might look like for a one-week period:

Panic Diary							
Time	Sun	Mon	Tues	Wed	Thur	Fri	Sat
a.m.		Panic = 7					
noon					Panic = 4		
p.m.				Panic = 3			

Notes:

Monday: Went shopping, felt anxious and nauseous, quite strong, therefore I came home.

Wednesday: Had doctor's appointment, tried to go by bus, panicked and took taxi instead.

Thursday: Upset because of an argument at home, panicked while doing the shopping.

2. Next, look at your notes in your panic diary and notice what caused the panic. Once you can identify the triggers, decide on an activity that you have been avoiding but would now like to try to master again. Choose an activity that won't be too easy but also not completely overwhelming.

3. State precisely what it is that you would be able to achieve if you were to master this target activity. For example, based on the panic diary:

Target activity: To go on the bus, by myself, when it is crowded, with a reasonable level of comfort.

4. As you are working through your target activities always ask yourself three core questions. The first is 'What do I think will happen?' Ask this always before you engage in a chosen practice. Write down what your answer is. Then you can engage in your chosen practice (using the guidelines below). During this, observe the second question, which is: 'What actually happens?' Write this down in your journal when you have completed your practice. Now is the time to ask yourself the third question, which is: 'What have I learned about what may be

helpful to do the next time when I practise and have an anxious thought?'

5. List the steps (from easiest to hardest) that you have to take to be able to achieve your target activity.

Example list of steps towards that goal:

a. *Decide which bus route is least threatening and most pleasant.*

b. *Walk to the bus stop at a time when it is not crowded, and just wait there for a while. If a bus comes by, don't get on. Leave to go back whenever ready.*

c. On a day when feeling particularly well, ask a friend to come along for a short bus ride (one or two stops only). Pick a non-crowded time and route.

d. Practise taking short rides alone. If the bus looks too crowded when it arrives, wait for the next one. If I become too uncomfortable, I'll get off at the next stop and wait a little while until I come back on another bus.

e. Gradually I will begin to practise getting onto more and more crowded buses. If sometimes this is too hard for me, I have to just get off that time but try again another time, with a slightly less crowded bus.

f. The most important aspect of all this is that I persevere and don't give up trying, even when at times I have to take a step backwards rather than forwards.

g. The more often I practise the more likely I am to master the target activity!

The same technique of setting one target at a time, and identifying a series of small, very gradual steps towards a goal will work for any number of feared activities or situations. It is very successful, for example, with driving phobias, which are very common after a road traffic trauma.

In the case of a driving phobia, you would also prepare a hierarchy of steps, ranging from easiest to hardest, that you would need to master in order to achieve your target activity. For example, your list might look something like this:

- Open car door and just sit in it (easiest). (Wait until you feel ready to move to the next step.)
- Turn the key while sitting in the car. (Wait until you feel ready to move to the next step.)
- Put the car into gear and drive a few yards down your road and back (or if your road is really busy, ask your partner or a friend to drive you

to a quiet area where you can practise driving a few yards). (Continue practising until you feel comfortable to move to the next step.)

- Drive down the whole of your street and back. (Continue until you feel ready for the next step.)
- Drive round your neighbourhood and back. (Continue until you feel ready for the next step.)
- Go for a ten-minute drive in the car, while it is light. (Continue until you feel ready for next step.)
- Go on a drive along a major road to visit a friend (hardest) – and so on.

For your driving practice you can ask yourself the same core questions as outlined for Exercise 26.

- Before your practice, ask yourself: *'What do I think will happen?'*
- Monitor during your practice: 'What actually happens?' and write this down when you have finished.
- After your practice reflect on: *'What have I learned about what may be helpful to do the next time when I practise and have an anxious thought?'* Write this down in your journal to help you remember for your next driving practice.
- It would be helpful for you to monitor and record your level of anxiety or panic each time you practise these steps, so that you can notice any changes.

After each practice engage in a nurturing or soothing activity, such as the body postures, to calm your disturbed nervous system introduced in Chapter 6. Make sure that you congratulate yourself on the progress you have achieved each time and expect progress to be gradual. Confidence comes through a series of small but increasing successes.

When you are engaging in driving practice, ensure that you plan your exercises in a way that keeps you and others safe. Do not take any unnecessary risks. Inform your partner or a friend about what you are going to do. Make arrangements that you can call them and they would come out to you if you need help. If you have a panic attack or flashback during your practice, pull in and stop and park up as soon as you can safely do so. Use those grounding techniques that work for you (see Chapter 8, Exercise 17) and engage in the 'humming bee breath' (Exercise 25, 5. in this Chapter) or the relaxed breathing method. Ensure beforehand that you know which strategies work for you and prepare yourself by writing down what you will do in those situations that might help. Resume your practice only when you are calm enough to do so. If you are finding it really difficult to regulate and calm down, call the person you arranged this with for help and ask them to help get you home.

This is probably a sign that you are not quite ready for the step you were practising. For your next practice start lower down on your hierarchy, with something that you can definitely master. Build your confidence back up this way and only go back to the step during which you experienced a panic attack or flashback, when you have comfortably mastered the steps before. Easy does it! Allow yourself to be patient and consistent and you will attain mastery.

Coping with safety behaviour during driving and other activities

When you have been in a trauma that occurred while you were engaged in an activity, like driving, it is more than likely that you will now associate a certain amount of fear with that activity. This might lead you to be extra cautious when you are driving, or doing whatever you were doing at the time of the trauma. Many people start to adopt these so-called 'safety behaviours', which we already referred to earlier in this chapter (page 288), when they subsequently try those feared activities. For example, if your fear concerns driving, you might now look more frequently in the rear-view mirror, get really panicky before a sharp bend, avoid overtaking, use only the 'slow' inside lane on the motorway, find yourself braking too frequently and sometimes unnecessarily, only drive during daytime hours, never use busy roads and so on. You might even find yourself behaving in strange ways when you are a passenger in the car. Your partner might find your constant comments about his/her driving irritating. You might scan the road ahead of you very alertly or clasp your seat very tightly, you might even be pressing an imaginary brake pedal while someone else is driving.

This behaviour is linked to your panicky feelings and may be so distressing that at times you are tempted to avoid driving or travelling as a passenger altogether. It is important to recognise that such behaviour is the body's attempt at protecting itself from something that has in the past been a danger! The arousal structures in your body remember that danger and want to warn you because they think that the danger is still around now. In order to overcome this pattern of behaviour you will need to teach yourself that the feared situations are no longer dangerous.

Make a list in your notebook of all the kinds of protective behaviour that you find yourself using. Tackle them one by one, telling yourself that you do not need them, even if you feel uncomfortable at times when you do the activity concerned. Try using relaxation and breathing techniques instead and resist these over-anxious responses, which are actually making you less safe. Stay within your individual window of tolerance (Chapter 6) when you tackle them gradually. This helps you to achieve mastery rather than putting you under too much stress.

Once you have mastered some of your avoidance of trauma-related external reminders, you can also practise noticing the times when you avoid your thoughts or feelings. You might notice that whenever something reminds you of your trauma, you stop what you were doing and engage in another activity. Or you may notice that you switch topics or evade people when they ask you about your trauma. Start to monitor yourself and notice what strategies you use. You can then use the same steps described above and try out what happens if you don't avoid your thoughts or feelings. What happens when you stay with your feelings just for a moment longer? You can use reassuring self-talk and controlled breathing while you experience some of your feelings. The methods you learned in Chapter 6 to soothe your disturbed nervous system can further support you with this. The more you can allow these feelings or thoughts the easier it will be for you in the long run. It takes a lot of effort to avoid your thoughts and feelings and when you don't have to do this any longer it will be a huge relief to you.

Whatever avoidance or safety behaviour you are tackling at the moment, the same technique of gradual exposure – taking things bit by bit, one step at a time – is applied. In all situations, your goal is to achieve containment of your reactions within your own window of tolerance. You have already had your coping abilities overwhelmed by the traumatic experience(s) you have been through. This book aims to help you develop strategies to enable you to deal with your reactions without feeling 'wiped out' and experiencing setbacks to your recovery. Tackle things within your own pace. If you begin to feel overwhelmed by the work you are doing with this book, it may be a sign that you are trying to do too much too fast or that it is time to talk to a professional. The key is to be patient with yourself and recognise the progress that you have already achieved! Even just engaging in this book and trying to reclaim your life is amazing progress! Healing rarely occurs in a straight line.

Summary checkpoints:

- Avoidance reactions are part of the symptoms of traumatic stress reactions and PTSD.
- They fall into two groups:
  - Avoidance of trauma-related thoughts or feelings
  - Avoidance of trauma-related external reminders (people, places, conversations, activities, objects, situations)
- Once you have established the baseline for your avoidance reactions, monitor this regularly as you work through the exercises in this chapter and the rest of the book and note down any changes.
- The feelings of panic and avoidance are often closely linked and can lead to a vicious cycle, which is explained further in this chapter.
- This chapter offers several strategies on how to overcome this vicious cycle:
  - Strategies to soothe the overactive arousal structures of the brain
  - Reassuring 'self-talk'
  - Orienting yourself to the safety of the here-and-now
  - Cognitive re-framing through 'psycho-education'
  - Controlled breathing

- Using a Panic Diary for self-monitoring
- Gradual exposure to the avoided situations or activities

- This chapter also provides help on managing your safety behaviour and driving phobia.

- It is important that you progress at a pace that is manageable for you and that keeps you in your window of tolerance at all times. Gently, but steadily, does it!

11

Managing negative changes in mood and thought patterns

The range of trauma-related changes in mood and thought patterns can be quite diverse, as outlined in Chapter 2, and you may not easily be aware just how much you have been affected. This chapter helps you to get a sense of how prevalent these difficulties are for you. This knowledge enables you to focus and work on those aspects most relevant to you. This chapter and Chapters 12 and 13 provide guidance on helping you manage specific areas of changed mood and thought patterns.

Getting to know the changes in your mood and thought patterns

In order to be able to manage the negative changes in your mood and thought patterns it will help if you know how these are bothersome to you. This enables you to take your *baseline* (just as you did in Chapter 8, 9 and 10 for the other symptoms of PTSD) to prioritise those that are most relevant to you. Keep a mood and thought diary to gather data on how severely these reactions are being triggered for you. In your journal, make an entry whenever you observe yourself experiencing any of the specific reactions described in the scales, below.

The following questions cover the range of commonly experienced changes in mood and thought patterns. Please copy these questions into your journal, date the entry and try to answer them as best as you can. The scales 0–4 are explained below:

- To rate how much you have been bothered by each of the experiences in the past week, use the following 0-4 scale:

0	1	2	3	4
Not at all	A little bit	Moderately	Quite a bit	Extremely

Please answer the following questions by circling the number on each scale which best applies to you:

1. In the past seven days were you bothered by having trouble remembering important parts of the stressful experience?

| 0 | 1 | 2 | 3 | 4 |

2. In the past seven days how much were you bothered by having strong negative beliefs or expectations about yourself, others or the world (for example, having thoughts such as 'I am bad', 'there is something seriously wrong with me', 'no one can be trusted', 'the world is completely dangerous')?

0   1   2   3   4

3. In the past seven days how much were you bothered by blaming yourself or someone else for the stressful experience or what happened after it?

0   1   2   3   4

4. In the past seven days how much were you bothered by strong negative feelings (for example, a sense of fear, horror, anger, guilt or shame?)

0   1   2   3   4

5. In the past seven days how much were you bothered by loss of interest or participation in activities that you used to enjoy before the trauma?

0   1   2   3   4

6. In the past seven days how much were you bothered by feeling detached or estranged from others?

0   1   2   3   4

7. In the past seven days how much were you bothered by trouble experiencing positive feelings (for example, happiness, satisfaction, pleasure or loving feelings?

0   1   2   3   4

Once you have circled the number that best applies to you on each question, add the scores from all the questions (1–7). Record the total score in your notebook.

TOTAL SCORE FOR CHANGES IN MOOD AND THOUGHT PATTERNS ON ...... (date)

Your total score is:...

If your total score is:

7 or below = they are low

8–14 = they fall into the mid-range

15 or more = they are high

Lastly, give an overall rating for how disabling these negative changes in mood and thought have been to you in the past week, by circling the number that applies to you on the scale used below (you could also copy this into your notebook):

0	1	2	3	4	5	6	7	8
Not at all disabling		Slightly disabling		Definitely disabling		Markedly disabling		Severely disabling

Now that you have established the baseline for your negative changes in mood and thought patterns you can begin to try to reduce the level of these. Monitor this regularly as you work through the exercises in this chapter, Chapters 12 and 13, and also the rest of the book. Additional specialist trauma therapy could be useful if your scores fall into the mid- to high range.

This chapter explores the effects of emotional numbness on your life and provides you with guidance on how to reclaim your sense of emotional awareness and reintroduce closeness into your personal relationships. It introduces you to the concept of mindfulness and explores the factors that may maintain your emotional numbing as well as providing exercises that help you to feel again.

Chapter 12 focuses on helping you transform feelings of guilt, shame and self-blame and to make a realistic assessment of the responsibility that you feel you may be carrying in response to particular aspects of the traumatic event/s. It explores how you can reclaim self-respect through finding acceptance and forgiveness of yourself.

Chapter 13 helps you recognise and better understand your feelings of loss and explores what you can do to gain healthy adjustment.

Managing emotional numbness

Feeling emotionally distant or estranged from others and being unable to feel positive emotions such as happiness or love indicate that you may be experiencing emotional numbness and shutdown. This is common after trauma and is an attempt (driven by neurophysiological processes and relevant brain structures) to avoid emotional overwhelm. It can also happen in response to utter emotional exhaustion and burn-out. It is part of the hypoarousal responses of the 'window of tolerance' explained in Chapter 6, which include 'shutdown' and dissociation from feelings and body sensations. While this may seem adaptive and even provide you with some temporary relief, essentially it is a way of opting out of life and the world.

You might not notice or might not even care how much this keeps you away from others. Frequently it is people's loved ones or close others who notice how much the person has changed. Relationships frequently suffer, especially if the capacity for physical closeness and intimacy has been affected. You could be perceived as 'cold' or 'unapproachable'. You may try 'not to let on', but it is likely that those close to you notice your sense of estrangement. The numbness is often self-perpetuating. The more numbness you feel, the more you avoid and opt out of connections to life and closeness to others and this further reinforces your numbness. You may also notice that you fluctuate between periods of significant emotional numbness and shutdown and periods of considerable emotional overwhelm. This is common after trauma and the latter is part of a hyperarousal reaction. Both indicate that you are outside your emotional comfort zone or 'window of tolerance'. These feelings may feel quite out of your control and may be very unsettling. Sometimes they are misdiagnosed by professionals as a 'bi-polar disorder'.

It may not until now have been apparent to you that the numbing could be linked to your trauma. If you feel emotionally closed off and empty inside, as described in Chapter 2, you could begin to ask yourself (gently): 'What am I trying not to face?' Often this type of reaction indicates that your mind is trying to protect you from an emotion that you are afraid of, for example: 'I am afraid to love again', 'I am afraid to trust again', or 'I never want to feel that bad again'. In effect, you are hiding from your emotions, for fear they will overtake and destroy you. It may be that you carry emotions in relation to the traumatic experience which you haven't at this stage been able to connect to and assimilate. You may therefore want to avoid any experience that could elicit those unprocessed feelings. Your avoidance is therefore more likely to be linked to aspects of your past experience rather than the situation you may be numbing yourself to now.

While your numbing is very understandable and makes sense, it stops you from reclaiming your life and keeps you not only away from others but essentially also from yourself. If you can't feel yourself because you have shut down, you are less responsive and safe, because you can't access your feeling system which provides you with important information about day-to-day life.

Once you are safe in the here-and-now, you may very gently explore how to re-engage your feelings and sensations to help you reconnect to yourself. There are several things that can help you with this. The practice of mindfulness introduced next can help you gradually melt your sense of numbness and reconnect you to yourself. You will then be guided to explore aspects of your traumatic experience that you may not have been able to connect to because they have felt too overwhelming or difficult for you to face.

Moving into Mindfulness

Mindfulness practice has gained a lot of attention in recent times and it is now being taught to people in many areas of life, including to children at school. It has been recognised that mindfulness can reduce many types of mental and physical suffering, including PTSD[1,2]. Mindfulness is a concept that has grown out of ancient, well-established Eastern meditation practices. It can usefully be integrated into every person's day-to-day life[3].

Mindfulness is a special kind of awareness that everyone can acquire, which enables total acceptance of the present moment. It proposes that the only time we can ever have any control of is each present moment. The practice of mindfulness therefore encourages you to focus on what you are aware of in the present moment, or in the here-and-now.

You are invited to become aware of all your inner and outer experiences, including your painful memories, associated thoughts, feelings and body sensations. Mindfulness proposes that we have two different mind systems. Our ordinary mind (also called the 'monkey mind' because of its constant chatter) is preoccupied with painful feelings, thoughts and sensations, keeps us stuck in auto-pilot and rushes us through life often with little awareness of what is actually happening in the here-and-now. In PTSD it catastrophises, focusing on painful thoughts and emotions, for example: 'I will never get better!', 'I won't be able to cope!', 'My life is ruined!' It also judges harshly, such as, for example: 'It is all my fault!', 'I am broken!', 'Why can't I just get over it?', 'I should pull myself together!' This part of your mind keeps you connected to your pain and keeps you stuck in a cloud of negative gloom, which may feel so bad that you numb yourself. While the ordinary mind is running our life we are not aware that we also have another, much deeper mind or part of self that we can access. We can call this our wise mind (or Core Self or True Self) and this part of us takes a much wiser, more compassionate and enlightened overview of our life. This part does not judge, but feels compassion, kindness and unconditional love towards us whatever our life might have been like. When you are connected to your wise mind, everything feels peaceful inside and you feel a sense of deep acceptance rather than the resistance that is part of your ordinary mind.

For most people it takes time to find the connection to their wise mind and it is a matter of gentle practice and perseverance. Two mindfulness exercises that you can try are described in Exercises 27 and 28. One asks you to focus on one object or activity a day to give your full mindful attention to and the other brings awareness to your body and breath. You can try these exercises many times over and each time you will notice something different; you can record your observations in your journal afterwards. These exercises can connect you deeper and deeper with your wise mind, but do give this time and practice. This doesn't usually happen immediately. It is like a beautiful flower that takes time and requires the right care for each of its petals to open.

For more guidance or practice, it may be beneficial to join a mindfulness meditation group or find a specialist trauma therapist who incorporates this approach into their work. People frequently experience that once they have started practising mindfulness they can apply it to many aspects of their daily life, until it becomes part of their natural way of being, which is usually much lighter, more joyful and calm.

EXERCISE 27: DEVELOPING MINDFUL AWARENESS

Choose one object or activity each day that you would like to give your full mindful attention to. This could be anything: washing the dishes, eating a strawberry, a dried plum or an ice cream, picking a beautiful flower and attending to it, going for a walk, watching a sunset, feeling the wind or rain on your body, talking to a friend, or even the way you engage in your bedtime routine. You can choose.

Follow the instructions below for guidance. Once familiar with their intention, you can change them to suit your particular chosen object or activity. If you have a physical disability please adjust this exercise to what is possible for you, paying attention to your particular needs:

1. Decide on the amount of time that you will give yourself to mindfully attend to your chosen activity. Start with a short amount of time like 5 minutes. As it gets easier to do, you can lengthen your practice time.

2. Initially, start by selecting an *edible object*, such as a fruit, fresh or dried, or a vegetable, to give your full attention to. As you become more familiar with mindful attention, you can

advance to other objects and more significant activities or relationships.

3. *Holding:* Explore your chosen object as if you have never seen it before in your life. Imagine that you have just landed on this earth and found this object. Hold it in your hand and notice what it feels like? Can you feel its weight? Does it leave a contour in your hand?

4. *Seeing:* Notice its colour. Does it just have one colour or several? Look at it with great care and let your eyes notice every detail. Notice the shades of colour, its texture, the hollows, the folds and the ridges.

5. *Touching*: How does it feel between your thumb and your forefinger? Does it feel different when you touch it with different fingers of your hand or when you change hands? Feel every bit of the connection. Even as you approach it with a finger notice when your finger very first becomes aware of the connection.

6. *Smelling:* Now approaching it with your nose, notice with each in-breath. Does it have a scent? Let it fill your awareness. If there is no scent or very little notice this as well.

7. *Positioning:* If your chosen object is edible, pick it up and position it in your hand. Focus your whole attention on how you do this. Notice that your hand and arm know exactly how to hold

it. Move it towards your mouth and notice how your mouth opens and how your hand positions the object into your mouth. Notice what your tongue does to receive it. Without chewing it, simply explore the sensations of having it on your tongue. Gradually explore the object with your tongue, really feeling it.

8. *Chewing:* When you are ready, consciously bite into the edible object and notice the effect on the object and yourself. Notice any taste that it releases. Notice how your tongue responds to this. Feel the texture as your teeth bite into it. Notice if it releases any fluid as you continue to chew it without swallowing it yet. Notice what is happening in your mouth.

9. *Swallowing:* Notice the first intention to swallow some of this edible object as it arises in your mind, experiencing it with your full awareness without swallowing yet. Notice what happens in your mouth to prepare you for swallowing. Bring into your full awareness how your tongue moves before you swallow. Consciously follow the sensations of swallowing and notice if you can sense the edible object as it moves down into your stomach. If you don't swallow it in one go, deliberately focus on the next swallows that follow until your mouth is empty.

10. *After-reflections:* Notice consciously what your mouth feels like without the edible object in it. How does its absence feel? Is there still an after-taste? Do you notice a tendency to look for another bite?

11. *Journaling your experience:* Write down what you noticed. Persevere even if at first you think this is weird or silly or you can't really feel anything. Notice if this changes with repeated practice.

EXERCISE 28: DEVELOPING MINDFUL BODY AWARENESS

Find a comfortable position for your body, sitting or lying down, in a place where you can be undisturbed for the next 20 minutes. Your external safe place might be very suitable for this. Follow the instructions below for guidance. If you have a physical disability please adjust this exercise to what you can comfortably do. Once familiar with the instructions, you can expand them to intensify and deepen your mindfulness practice.

1. Make yourself comfortable in your chosen position. If sitting, allow your back to be in a

comfortably aligned but straight position. If lying down, let your legs be uncrossed, with your feet falling away from each other and your arms lying alongside and slightly away from your body, so that the palms can be open to the ceiling if that feels comfortable. Let your eyes be closed if that is comfortable for you. If any of this does not feel possible, adjust your posture accordingly so that you are comfortable doing this exercise.

2. *Bring your awareness into your body:* From the point between your eyes focus inwards into your body. From this point of your inner mind notice where your physical body ends and where it makes contact with another object, such as with the floor or whatever you are sitting or lying on or with a blanket if that is wrapped around you. Allow yourself to spend a few moments time to explore these points of contact and the sensations that go with that for you. Notice how your body responds to that contact.

3. *Now bring your attention to your feet:* Notice your toes, how they touch and relate to each other. Spend a few moments really feeling into your toes. Then focus your attention to the soles of your feet. Notice what this feels like. Can you feel a tingling underneath the soles of your feet? If so, just notice. Notice any other sensations or

lack of sensations on the soles of your feet. Then bring your awareness to the heel of each of your feet, then the tops of your feet. Allow yourself to become aware of the physical sensations in your feet, moment by moment. Notice if they feel the same in each part in each of your feet or if they feel different? Observe how the sensations might change as you attend to them. If you notice that you feel very little or numb in all or particular parts of your feet then attend to this. Observe that there is numbness. Free yourself from any expectations. There is no right or wrong, you are simply attending to how it feels in the parts of your feet at any given moment in time.

4. *Bringing awareness to the rest of the body:* Expand your awareness to any physical sensations in other parts of your body. Attend to your legs, the various muscles in your legs, feel into the different parts of your legs, such as your ankles and your knees. Spend a few moments just noticing what sensations you find in those parts. Then attend in turn to the different parts of your torso – from your pelvis area and hips right to your shoulders. Spend a moment focusing on each part of your lower and upper torso, even on how your internal organs feel. Then move your attention to your arms and hands,

first on your left and then on your right and then noticing if they feel the same or different. After this, shift your focus to your neck, your face and the rest of your head. Notice all the sensation in those parts of your body.

5. *Observing just what is:* As you focus on the different parts of your body notice how it is to allow your body to be just how you find it. If you observe a tendency to want to change the feelings you experience or you find yourself judging, then notice this without passing any further judgement. Most people find that after a while their attention drifts into thoughts. If this happens to you just notice and focus your attention back to your body. Notice how liberating it feels just to accept your body as it is in this moment in time without wanting to change anything. The more you accept your body's sensations at any moment in time the more you come into contact with your body. Over time this can be an effective exercise to transform numbness into feeling.

Facing what you have kept 'hidden' from yourself

When you have become more familiar with the practice of mindfulness you will notice that it starts to get easier to stay connected even with uncomfortable emotions, painful sensations and memories when they come up. Mindfulness involves staying with your feelings and emotions. It is important that when you first practise mindfulness you take things slowly and always work within your emotional comfort zone. Your numbing can melt away gently as and when you are ready and it feels safe to do so. It is important for you not to be overwhelmed, as that is likely to cause a setback. Be wary of highly charged emotional situations for this reason. Working slowly and privately – by yourself or with the help of a trauma specialist – you can then begin to acknowledge the parts of your experience that you have found difficult to face. Exercise 29 is aimed at helping you recover your emotional awareness. Answer the questions by recording them in your journal and allow yourself sufficient time for this exercise. If you don't manage it in one go, come back to it again another time.

EXERCISE 29: RECLAIMING EMOTIONAL AWARENESS

- What has been the meaning of the trauma for you?
- Are you still closing yourself off from painful emotions linked to the trauma?

- Ask yourself which emotions you are avoiding? Write down as many as you can.
- Explore why you are avoiding those emotions:
    - Are you too preoccupied with survival that you never stop to take the time to feel?
    - Are you frightened to feel any of those feelings because you fear that it would be too overwhelming and you might lose control?
    - Do you fear that there are so many conflicting emotions that you don't know where to start?
    - Are there spoken or unspoken messages in your family, social or work environment that convey that emotions are a sign of weakness and you are coping by 'staying strong' or 'being tough'.
    - Have you never been very good at recognising your feelings even before the trauma? Maybe you were never encouraged or never learned how to express emotions healthily in the family you grew up with?
    - Do you consider it dangerous to experience emotions because you have witnessed close others expressing their emotions in damaging or uncontrolled ways?
- As you are working through these questions, memories and feelings might come up. This is fine and allow yourself gently to stay with these and record your memories in your journal.

Once you are aware of why you may be closing yourself off from your emotions, you can work on increasing the range of your emotional awareness. If you discovered in Exercise 29 that even before the trauma you have never been able to feel or express emotions very well, then this may be a longer process for you and you may benefit from the additional help of a specialist trauma therapist.

Reclaiming emotional awareness is very important for your healing process because feelings signal to you if something is good or not so good for you. They have a protective function. Start to become aware of your feelings and name them. Even if all you can initially perceive is a sense of numbness, then name this perception. Recognise your level of numbness and as you monitor it, it is likely to change in gradation from being very strong at times to being milder at others. Ask yourself if there could be other feelings underpinning your numbness. Maybe there is frozen rage or anger, sadness or irritability hiding underneath.

Start to develop an emotional language for your feelings. Write your emotions down and name them. This will enable you to feel greater control over them. If you want to share your emotions with others, the most constructive way is to name them, but not to act them out. 'I' statements are the most effective, such as for example: 'I feel rather sad today.' You can then give yourself a rating for your level of sadness between 0 (no sadness) to 10 (the saddest). Use your journal to enter into an emotional dialogue with yourself and if you notice tears, just allow them and comfort yourself. Let them come without judging yourself. If you find that you automatically judge yourself, just observe this and write it down. Notice that this is your judgement and it is unlikely to be an accurate assessment of the situation. It can be very healing to allow your emotions to be.

Allow yourself to develop a real curiosity about how a particular feeling might have arisen in you. Feelings are there for a reason. They are your response to particular thoughts or triggers in your environment or internally. They help you to gauge a particular situation in terms of its effect on you. The more aware you can become of your feelings the more in control you will feel and the better able you will be to create conditions in your environment that are life-affirming and healthy for you.

Your trauma healing process could be leading you to greater levels of emotional awareness than you may have had before. You may now be experiencing feelings that you could never understand in others before the trauma. This could lead you to becoming more tolerant and accepting towards yourself, but also towards others. The key is to be patient with yourself! Healing rarely occurs in a straight line and greater emotional awareness develops gradually.

Emotional numbness does not usually go away on its own. It requires your attention and willingness to work with. It can be related to many factors. You may still be in shock about what happened and haven't adjusted to how you now perceive this to have affected your life. It can be linked to a significant loss that you have experienced, perhaps even a sense that you have *lost your previous identity* through the trauma. You may have responded during the trauma in ways that you didn't think you ever would or could. This may have shown you an aspect of yourself you didn't realise you had. You may have lost your job or your ability to work or your place in a professional group (such as a military unit, or fire fighters' team), or important others that formed part of your identity. This may have changed your plans for the future. You may still feel so consumed by the changes, including those to your physical body, that you cannot see a different future for yourself, yet. Loss of hopes and dreams or no longer seeing yourself as the person you had thought you were or were hoping to become is very difficult and you may have shut yourself off from the emotions linked to these losses.

EXERCISE 30: REDISCOVERING YOUR PERSONAL IDENTITY

Ask yourself the following questions and reflect on your answers to them in your journal:

1. Who am I now, after the trauma?
2. Do I see myself differently now than before the trauma?
3. What personal expectations did I have before that I no longer think I can achieve?
4. How do I compare myself with others now after the trauma?

5. Have I been treating myself like a 'broken person'?
6. What is it that I am afraid others will see?
7. Is there anything that I am afraid to admit to myself?

You might like to review some of the work that you did as part of Chapter 5 – 'Your life before the trauma', to remind yourself of the life events which helped to shape your sense of personal identity before the trauma.

Numbness is often experienced as part of a *grieving response* for a lost loved one, even if that loss has occurred some time ago. To turn feelings back on after they have been turned off completely, feels frightening and sometimes disloyal to the person or people you have lost traumatically. Chapter 13 on grief reactions may also help you to recognise these patterns in your own responses and the exercises there will assist you in dealing with your loss more directly, rather than suppressing your feelings by staying numb.

Dependence on alcohol, drugs, comfort eating or other addictive behaviour

Emotional numbness is one way our nervous system and the subconscious parts of our mind respond to overwhelming emotional pain. But that reaction is designed to be short-term, to provide immediate protection to the traumatised person. What often happens is that we artificially extend the numbness reaction by the overuse of alcohol, drugs, comfort foods (the severe restriction of food intake, *anorexia nervosa*, may also begin as a reaction to a traumatic experience) or a wide range of other addictive behaviours.

After a trauma, it takes a remarkably brief time for what seemed like a short-term coping strategy to become a dependency, and thus further problems are created. It is therefore essential to confront any substance dependency or addictive behaviour problems that might have developed if you are to make any headway in reducing your emotional numbness reactions.

Try to gauge whether you have a problem with dependency by asking yourself the following questions (answering as honestly as you can):

1. Am I using any substance or other addictive behaviour – alcohol, drugs, sleep medications, comfort foods, gambling, excess shopping, excessive or unusual sexual or bonding behaviour, etc. – in a different way than I did before the trauma?
2. What is the difference?
3. How much more am I using substances or engaging in addictive behaviour?

4. Do I try to block out pain, fear, anger, sadness or other stressful emotions with the use of substances or addictive behaviour?

5. Does that work?

6. What price am I paying? What are the side effects of this?

7. Do I now use alcohol, drugs, food or another dependency to numb emotions in order to sleep?

8. Would I be embarrassed to admit to someone else (like my medical practitioner) how much more I am drinking, or eating, or taking drugs (or any other addictive behaviour) now? (If the answer is 'yes', that is a clear indicator of an overuse problem.)

9. Am I anxious at the prospect of having these substances or this addictive behaviour less available in my life? (Again, a 'yes' indicates dependency problems.)

Substance dependency is often closely linked with difficulties regulating your emotions. If you recognise your own behaviour in the preceding questions, it is very important for your own wellbeing and healing that you set aside any feelings of embarrassment and talk to someone who can help you with this. Nearly every community, no matter how small, has access to resources for people who are struggling with substance abuse or addiction problems. If you are seeing a specialist trauma therapist, they may be able to help you with your addictive problems alongside trauma therapy. Sometimes, depending on the degree and nature of a specific addiction, you may be advised to tackle your addiction first before engaging in trauma therapy. Your medical practitioner should be able to advise you about suitable services or you may find resources to help with addiction advertised in your local library or by searching the internet.

Managing feelings of alienation and problems with intimacy

If you feel you have lost the capacity to connect to the world and to your loved ones as a result of the trauma, you might feel very lonely and isolated. As a result of your experience the world may feel numb, cold and alien – it becomes a place where you survive, but no longer thrive. Whatever the root of your trauma, whatever its deepest meaning, it is truly personal and it may seem impossible for anyone else to even begin to understand how much you've gone through and are still going through. While you are feeling like this it might seem logical to think that to remain alienated from others is the best way to avoid further risk. Such post-traumatic reactive thinking is based on beliefs such as: 'I can never trust again', 'No one can understand me', 'I will never let anyone get that close to me again' and

'To feel again leaves me open to further hurt'. Without a doubt, every time we enter into a trusting or intimate relationship with another human being there is an element of risk. It is normal for most people to feel a sense of greater vulnerability as they allow themselves to experience more closeness with another person. The challenge is not to let that sense of vulnerability and even fear of loss of control deter you from seeking closeness to others. If you let your fear control you it will perpetuate a sense of alienation by maintaining a restricted, narrow emotional world which can be a very lonely place to live in.

This chapter invites you to venture out from this lonely place and re-engage in life again, at your own pace in your own time, as long as there is forward movement. As before, to reduce avoidance behaviour, decide on a specific target or goal and identify a series of very small, gradually increasing steps towards that goal. The **Mindfulness Exercises** in this chapter, as well as the **Relaxed Breathing Method** and **Assertive Exchange Technique** (see Chapter 9) can support you with this work. For example, if you are living alone, with few friends and no family members to give you emotional support, your target could be 'to increase the number of social interactions that I have with people during the day'. To achieve this, your steps might include:

- Go outside the house, for a walk or an errand, every day.
- Smile at a minimum of three people and greet them if they look likely to respond. Notice your eye gaze and posture and allow yourself to look up and hold yourself upright.
- When queuing to purchase food or other items, make small talk or exchange pleasantries with other customers.
- Go to the library or park and join groups if there are opportunities to do so.
- Find out information about volunteering opportunities from your favourite charities. Talk to a charity and find out how you could get involved. Many of them offer a great range of potential opportunities suited to your current level of ability.
- Give yourself small rewards and lots of encouragement for the efforts you are making.

The sense of alienation will not go away on its own. It takes interaction with people and your own efforts in challenging your current patterns. When you start to approach people again, be they strangers or your own friends or loved ones, be mindful that you don't place too much weight on each single encounter so that it becomes an 'all or nothing' event! The term 'all or nothing'[4] means that (knowingly or unknowingly) you are putting the other person to the test. They must perform perfectly, according to your specifications, or you are likely to say to yourself: 'There! I knew it! People always let me down. It's just not worth trying. I'm never doing this again.' The result is that you give up, after the first (or a very early) try. Remember that very few things in life are immediately successful! Remind yourself of your commitment to give yourself another chance of life, which you made in Chapter 4. Therefore it is very important that you persevere with your efforts, take your time and approach encounters with others as open-mindedly as you can without prior expectations. The concept of mindfulness can again be very helpful to you here. Observe every new encounter with an open-minded curiosity and stay present in yourself whilst you do this as best as you can.

Dealing with the avoidance of intimacy is doubly challenging, because your partner is also unsure what to expect from you, just as you are unsure of what to expect from yourself. The tips for a partnership on 'surviving the trauma together' in Chapter 3 may be helpful reading for you both. Again, be wary of 'testing' your partner or your friends, by expecting them to 'prove' their caring for you. Such behaviour is manipulative and assumes that you know what the other person is thinking, and what has influenced his or her behaviour. Your assumptions might not be accurate, so be mindful of such behaviour in you. Use your journal to monitor and record your interactions with others and notice how you behave and what feelings or thoughts may be underlying your particular patterns of interaction. Once you notice you can experiment with using a more positive interactive style.

Most of us, even at good times, experience fears of rejection, especially when we are establishing or re-establishing new relationships. The fears may be connected to feelings of unworthiness or fears of abandonment if our partner found out what we were really like. It is harder work to stay with a relationship and try to negotiate the bumpy parts than to walk out in order avoid facing the bumps.

Allow yourself to face your fears, realistically appraise what your responsibility is for something that has gone wrong, and free yourself from carrying responsibility for those parts that fall into other people's control. Think of yourself as a worthy partner for someone. It is time to discard any thoughts of yourself as 'damaged beyond repair'. The better you start to get to know yourself and the more you learn to accept and like yourself, the better a partner you will be to others. Recognising, understanding and taking ownership of your own emotions will make you a better partner and friend.

Discover any nourishing and enriching qualities that you can find in your relationships (with a spouse, partner, friend, co-worker, etc.), focus on the positives that are there or are still working, and build from there. While you will need to acknowledge aspects of your trauma and talk about it some of the time, it is also important to have some periods of time together, however brief, that feel 'normal'. Your partner should not be a replacement for a therapist. Although they may be very supportive it is not your partner's job to heal you. This falls into your domain and it is important that it does. Try talking about mundane things – the weather, football, home decorating, an article in a magazine, etc. This gradually will help bring your life into balance again and enable you to relax and enjoy other people's company. Your life will start to feel fuller and richer again.

Summary checkpoints:

- The range of trauma-related changes in mood and thought patterns can be quite diverse and you may not be aware how much you have been affected.
- Recognising those reactions that are most prevalent to you enables you to transform them.
- This chapter focuses on helping you manage feelings of emotional numbness, which is a common response to avoid emotional overwhelm.
- The concept of Mindfulness is explained as a way of helping you overcome your emotional numbness and safely connect you to feelings.
    - Practical exercises are provided to support you with this
- You can then work on increasing the range of your emotional awareness and developing a language for your feelings.

- Substance dependence and addictive behaviour are often used to cope with emotional over-whelm, but it maintains the emotional numb-ness and causes additional problems.
  - This chapter offers you an opportunity to assess whether you have a problem with dependency
- A loss of capacity to connect to others, feelings of alienation and loss of intimacy are all common responses after trauma and can lead to isolation and loneliness.
- This chapter invites you to re-engage in life again by overcoming the above problems. Practical exercises and management strategies are explored to help you with this.

12

Guilt, shame, self-blame and self-respect

Whatever the circumstances of your trauma, as you have worked through the preceding chapters in this book, you have probably found your feelings gradually shifting. For a while, you may have noticed only your fears or your rage, but as you found different ways to cope with those strong emotions, other feelings (like guilt or shame, for instance) may have begun to emerge from the shadows and demand your attention. These feelings are part of the negative changes in mood and thought patterns outlined in Chapter 11. The purpose of this chapter is to help you recognise and better understand these emotional reactions and explore what you can do to find relief from them.

Difference between guilt, shame and self-blame

Guilt, shame and self-blame are all emotions that can feel extremely unpleasant, quite stuck and not easy to shift. People also easily confuse them. Guilt relates to feeling uneasy about something you believe you did or didn't do. It therefore relates to a behaviour (or lack of it) that you think was 'bad' or led to an 'unfortunate' outcome and which you now feel uncomfortable about. Shame, in contrast, goes much deeper. It connects you to an internal belief that your character is 'flawed' and that you are 'bad' or 'unworthy' as a person. Shame is frequently linked to a boundary violation, for example, victimisation or abuse trauma. Self-blame can arise from both guilt and shame, because you hold yourself overly responsible for a past behaviour (or lack of it) or because you belief that things happened because you are such a 'bad' or 'flawed' person. Rather than leaving what happened in the past and coming to peace with it, self-blame keeps it alive and active in the present. It will be helpful for you to explore whether you are affected by any or all of these emotions. Use your journal to note this down. This chapter focuses on these emotions and on the unhelpful thought patterns that keep these active and provides you with guidance on reclaiming self-respect, inner peace and acceptance of yourself.

Guilt

Trauma by its very nature is not planned and you can't prepare yourself for it. It confronts you with chaos and dilemmas where your choices feel very limited. Even in situations where you are trained to deal with traumatic events as part of your profession, such as being an emergency service professional, an A&E doctor, nurse or psychotherapist (Chapter

18 in the Addendum on useful guidance is written especially for professionals and carers), you never know beforehand how things will turn out, and even with the best training, preparation and years of experience behind you there may still be situations that can catch you out. Trauma can affect anyone. It takes you over the threshold in which planned, intentional action submits to the realm of instinctive, autonomic responses controlled by your innate survival system. When you look back at the situation afterwards you may not recognise yourself or understand why you have acted in that way. You may feel regret over how you have acted and horror at the consequences that arose and this now makes you feel guilty. You need to understand that under these specific circumstances you could not act from the perspective of your usual 'in control' self, as you were taken over by a part of your nervous system that noticed you had come out of your emotional comfort zone. Its aim at that stage was simply to ensure your survival regardless of the consequences.

Survivor guilt

For some people guilt can be especially strong if the trauma involved the deaths of others. Initially, these feelings of guilt may be related to surviving when others have not. You may feel unworthy of living, when someone else, whose life you thought was important, has died. This is especially difficult if the person might have died because you couldn't or didn't help at the time or they ended up in a particular position, which you had been in before or should have been in instead, or they died while they were trying to help and rescue you. If the death involved a young or helpless person survivor guilt is even stronger. If you were the victim of a violent attack, an abduction or a hostage taking you may be surprised that you might even feel guilty if you witnessed your aggressor subsequently being killed, for example by Special Force Police during the rescue operation. Although you may be relieved that you were rescued, you may at the same time feel guilty that death couldn't be avoided. You may feel very confused about your mixed emotions.

Later on, you may feel guilty for beginning to enjoy yourself again. Engaging in normal social interaction, relaxing and temporarily forgetting about the past may feel like a betrayal of others who were lost or left behind or whom you consider to have suffered even more than you did. These are feelings of *survivor guilt* and you may try to take complete personal responsibility for the way in which you made your decisions before or during the trauma.

When family members or friends encourage you to come out with them or to try something new, you may react with anger at their expectation that you should be getting on with your life when, to you, that seems impossible. You may find that you avoid activities that you would have participated in without hesitation, like a neighbourhood barbecue or your child's school sports day. Somehow now it doesn't feel 'right' for you to be there. Although you might put on a brave face, inside you feel as if you've been marked, or singled out in some way to permanently carry the burden of responsibility for the tragedy that has occurred. Most people find it very difficult to confide their guilt to others. It can be so pervasive and makes them feel so bad that they fear that others judge them in the same way or maybe even worse, as they are judging themselves internally. This of course is an internally held assumption, which may not be at all true. However, when guilt is kept hidden it cannot get disconfirmed.

You may blame yourself for the way you acted and consider yourself weak. Sometimes it is easier to take the blame than to acknowledge that some things just happen and are beyond our immediate control. The idea that no matter what you do, how hard you try and how watchful you are, certain terrible events are bound to occur, can be a terrifying thought.

Nicole's description of her feelings of survivor guilt sums this up.

> I lost my husband Tim in a sailing accident. I still can't forgive myself that he is no longer here. We were both very experienced sailors and I had originally agreed to go with Tim on the trip that afternoon. However, some friends called by unexpectedly and Tim decided to go with my friend's husband, Pete, instead, so that the two of us could stay behind and chat. Pete was not an experienced sailor and when the boat unexpectedly got caught up in very strong crosswinds, he panicked and completely froze and couldn't do the things that Tim asked him to do to regain control over the boat. In the end Tim fell overboard after having been hit by the boom

of the sail. Although Pete tried to save Tim, he could do little to pull him out from underneath the boat where he had got caught somehow. Tim had been knocked unconscious and then drowned. I just could not forgive myself that I hadn't insisted on all of us going together. The pleasant memory that I had of the afternoon with my friend was completely over-shadowed by my feelings of utter self-blame and survivor guilt. I feel that I am responsible for Tim's death, because I am sure this would never have happened had I been there. I feel that Tim died because of my selfishness and that I will never be able to forgive myself. Life is not the same without Tim and I shall never experience any joy again. Tim can't and therefore I don't deserve to either!

Nicole

You may have felt similar to Nicole after your own experience. These are very understandable and natural feelings and are linked to the human wish to be in control of one's life and destiny. Your thoughts that the trauma might not have occurred if only you had acted differently before or during it give you the illusion that you could have controlled the event. These thoughts make your healing and recovery process very difficult because they stop you from accepting and coming to terms with the trauma. You cannot rewrite history, no matter how much you may long to do so: disasters and accidents *don't* make sense and you cannot control or plan for them. If guilt is linked to having survived when another loved person didn't or feeling responsible for the death of another, these feelings are hard to shift.

It involves learning to accept that under the circumstances you made certain decisions and, even if you had some doubts in your mind at the time, decided to follow a specific course of action. At the time you could not anticipate the outcome of the event, even if some part of you may have felt some sense of unease about your decision. Until you allow yourself to accept that you cannot control your own or other people's destiny, much as you would like to be able to do so, you won't ever be able to heal properly. This is a very difficult concept to accept because it puts us in touch with our vulnerability, fragility and the impermanence of our life as human beings. It takes time to find acceptance and inner peace with this recognition, but when you can it connects you to a deeper, and more spiritual understanding of life.

Blaming yourself

In your attempts to create meaning from what has happened there is a danger that you will develop a heightened degree of self-blame, holding yourself responsible for a tragedy which got out of control at the time.

It is a natural human tendency to want to find a reason for things. Guilt relates to your sense of conscience. Guilt is not a useless emotion. It helps to navigate you towards what is moral, life preserving and aligned with your integrity. Without any capacity for guilt you would be ruthless and hold no respect for other people's boundaries. Guilt enables you to evaluate your degree of responsibility in any given situation, learn from the outcome and adjust your actions accordingly. This resolves the guilt and enables you to move on with your life.

After a trauma, the memories of the event often are not fully accessible and your perception of what happened can become distorted. If you experience unrelenting feelings of guilt or self-blame this is usually an indication that you have not fully processed, come to terms with and accepted what has happened. You may still internally feel stuck in particular scenes of the trauma, think in some way that it is your fault, that you *should* have been able to anticipate or prevent it or, in some *superhuman* way, have been able to minimise the harm that arose. Although you may carry some responsibility for what happened, frequently the standard of behaviour we expect from ourselves in such situations far exceeds what we would expect from any other human being. Your assessment of your level of responsibility may not take into account the reality of the circumstances at the time. You may be overly harsh and self-blaming. Your current trauma may also have brought up older feelings or patterns of guilt or shame that were already there before in your life, as will be explored in the next section.

Reading the next section could be quite emotional for you as it might bring up memories of experiences and feelings that you have sought to bury for a long time or may have even dissociated from. Make sure that you are in your external safe place and remind yourself beforehand of the resources that you have learned to use to ground yourself. If the next chapter triggers things in you or you get too overwhelmed, stop and soothe yourself. Write your responses down in your journal if you can. Only go back to reading more of the next chapter when you feel internally grounded enough.

The origins of guilt and shame

Some people are more susceptible to a guilt or shame response than others and the answer often lies in their earlier childhood experiences. For instance, a common practice in child-rearing is inducing a sense of guilt in children as a means of teaching them the difference between right and wrong. While this may be necessary and important in order to pass on a moral code of conduct (for example, if they have injured another child deliberately, it is appropriate for them to feel guilty, in order to learn responsibility for their actions), unfortunately it often tends to be over-applied, even to simple mistakes or accidents. As a result, guilt is perhaps one of the most over-learned emotional responses[1]. Often the child ends up feeling responsible and guilty for anything bad or negative that happens to others around him or her[2]. Depending on the child's developmental age when this starts, the frequency and the degree of blame applied, these feelings can turn into shame. This happens when the child in response to blame begins to view him- or herself as intrinsically bad or negative. The child may feel the cause of misfortune for others, just by being there or by not trying hard enough to control what happens. This elicits deep-seated beliefs of shame in a child.

1. Was guilt a feeling commonly encountered when you were a child? How were things handled when you got things wrong or made mistakes? Were you shamed? Did this influence your early sense of self? What messages did you receive from your parents about your self-worth? About taking responsibility?

Sometimes parents who administer harsh punishments, or who abuse their children physically or sexually, will tell the child, 'You made me do this', 'If you weren't so bad, I wouldn't do this' or 'Now you're getting what you deserve'. Even though the child has been hurt and violated, at some level he or she starts to think that the parent must be right, and begins to take responsibility for the parent's abusive behaviour, as if somehow he/she 'brought it on'. Frequently, parents are repeating their own abusive child-hood experiences of being blamed and shamed, without being aware how they have learned their behaviour. This is due to the tendency to dissociate from overwhelming and distressing experiences, which have nevertheless been stored in subconscious memory systems. These are now projected onto the child, who inadvertently acts as a trigger to the parent, because it has justified, unrelenting needs. Sometimes parents attack and shame their children as selfish for even the most basic levels of healthy self-interest[3].

> 2. Have you ever thought that abuse was your fault? Are you still even now taking all, or most of, the responsibility for others' bad behaviour? Is it safer for you 1) to listen than to talk, 2) to agree than to dissent, 3) to offer care than ask for help and 4) to elicit the other to talk than to express yourself, and 5) to leave choices to the other than to choose for yourself?[3]

As children grow older, this pattern of reacting in a guilty or self-deprecating manner begins to be more widely applied, sometimes to any new situations that the child or adolescent experiences. Fears of making mistakes, and thus 'causing' everything to go wrong, may make the growing teenager overly watchful and perfectionistic in their outlook. Pete Walker[3] has introduced the concept of trauma-induced codependency. This is when a person finds it difficult to exist in their own right and they neglect or deny their needs in service of others (often abusive partners). He describes this as a fear-based inability to express rights, needs and boundaries in relationships. This often sets up trauma-based coping patterns in which people hide behind their helpful personas, seek safety and acceptance in relationships through listening and eliciting. They invite the other to talk rather than risking exposing their own thoughts, views and feelings. They ask questions to keep attention away from themselves, because their parents taught them that talking was dangerous as their words would inevitably prove them guilty and unworthy.[3] This safety response is designed to minimise the risk of further humiliation or abuse from others through almost total negation of the self. Sadly, in reality this pattern often leads children who carry this pattern into their adulthood regardless of gender to be at higher risk of falling prey to further abuse. Pete Walker describes this survival-based coping response (after fight, flight and freeze) as the 'fawn' response (in Chapter 5 also referred to as the (be)-friend response).

In adult life, women and men sometimes channel their guilt or shame feelings in different ways. Women can find themselves more often in caring roles, where they take on a great deal of the responsibility for others at the risk of no longer feeling and losing themselves. For men, the feelings may be as strong, but may be masked by a super-conscientious work performance or a tendency to blame others to conceal their secret blaming of themselves.

3. Have you recognised any of your own patterns of behaving described in this discussion? As an adult, have you continued patterns that were established in your early years? Allow yourself to write these down in your journal when you can. If emotions come up for you in relation to any of the above give yourself time and space for these. Be gentle with yourself and stop and use grounding and soothing strategies if you feel too overwhelmed.

Obviously, guilt and shame are complex emotions. They keep us stuck in the same patterns of reacting and generalising over and over again. They are often connected to secrets – things that we have been too afraid to admit, even to ourselves.

4. What have you been keeping a secret? Is there something, some bit of your traumatic experience, even a thought or a feeling, that you have considered so terrible you could never tell anybody about? Something that you are ashamed of or feel humiliated about?

5. Try to write it down, say it aloud (when alone), or even audio-record it so you can hear it played back to yourself. Do this without making any judgements. Try to read or listen to it with the same level of understanding that you might offer to a friend or someone you would care for, by standards that are less harsh than those you have used in the past for yourself. Nurture and soothe yourself gently if emotions come up.

The act of putting guilt or shame *outside of yourself* may help you to look at it more objectively. You may try and use Exercise 31 in this chapter to determine how much responsibility really belongs to you and how much was actually beyond your control or part of the responsibility of others or your ability to predict what would happen.

If, after reading this section, you feel that many of your feelings of guilt or shame seem to be linked to early negative childhood experiences, it might take you longer to shift your sense of over-responsibility to the current trauma. Your responses now are likely to be based on deeply embedded feelings of guilt, shame or self-blame and although it may be helpful to recognise and understand this, this book may not sufficiently meet your needs. You may really benefit from working with a therapist who is familiar with the effects of complex developmental trauma and who can help you address and change these early core beliefs and help you discover your non-traumatised, authentic sense of self.

Layer after layer

During the aftermath of a trauma, many people find themselves *ruminating* over what happened. Again and again, they blame themselves for what was done or not done, regret actions taken or generally feel responsible for it all. The disorientation and uncertainty that accompanies a trauma can act as a trigger for the guilt or the feeling of over-responsibility. If the phrase 'dwelling in guilt' seems to describe how your thoughts are stuck at this moment, you may be looking at past situations or actions in the same way, over and over again. Just telling you not to think about it would *not* be helpful. You have the right to interpret your part in the traumatic experience as you see fit and there is no intention to minimise how profoundly you may be affected by what happened to you or to others. It is also important that you recognise those aspects that may indeed have been part of your responsibility. At the same time, it is helpful for you to recognise that guilt is such a familiar emotional response that it can be over-applied to situations where things go very wrong. In this way, guilt becomes the surface emotion or the primary way you interpret your role in events.

If you think of your emotional reactions as having layers, like an onion, it might make sense to look underneath the 'guilt layer' and work out what other emotions you are experiencing. Is there a layer of anger? A layer of hurt? Are there layers of sadness, regret, confusion, despair? Try to identify as many other emotions as possible and record them in your journal.

Looking at guilt and shame in a new way

If guilt or shame *are* a very familiar emotional response to you, then assuming that *you* are responsible for bad outcomes is likely to be the first conclusion you jump to. While you can't prevent your thoughts from going in that direction in the first place, you *can* keep yourself from stopping there and looking no further.

While your learned response may be to shoulder all the guilt and feel shame, there are four other possible ways of looking at what happened:

1. It may be that you share only part of the responsibility as there are others involved who do, too
2. There was no way you could have predicted what was going to happen
3. You did what you could under the circumstances
4. What happened was utterly beyond your control.

You can use the 'four other possible ways of looking at it' strategy any time you are having a strong emotional response to an aspect of the traumatic event you feel guilt or shame for.

Exercise 31 (loosely based on a model developed for shifting guilt with war veterans[4,5]) further helps you to assess more objectively your level of actual responsibility. Set aside at least an hour of your time in an undisturbed place for this. Do the exercise in several stages, coming back to it and working through each of the different aspects you identify separately. When you have covered them all you can pull it all together in terms of your actual responsibility. Although we are using percentage ratings for the responsibility, don't worry if you are not great at maths. It's not important to add it up perfectly; what counts is that you develop a different perspective on the actual responsibility you carry for the traumatic event or aspects of it. Have your journal and pens ready with you. If emotions come up as you go through this, allow them, comfort and soothe yourself. Emotions are a great release when you can allow them without judgement or resistance. If this exercise gets too overwhelming or you have flashbacks, stop. Use grounding techniques and try again another day when you feel ready.

EXERCISE 31: THE RESPONSIBILITY RATING

Connect to your trauma experience and (as you did in the reliving work in Chapter 7) either write it down again or read through what you have already written down.

Try, as objectively as possible, to determine the level of responsibility that you are feeling now for the situation by assigning it a number, from 0 to 100 per cent. For example, if you have no feelings of responsibility related to your trauma, or you are bothered very little by any sense of guilt, the number you choose would probably be between 0 per cent or up to 20 per cent out of 100 per cent. If you are troubled by a sense of responsibility and guilt some of the time, but feel that other emotions are much stronger for you, your rating might be between 21 and 40 per cent. If you feel responsibility and guilt regularly your ratings maybe anything between 41 and 60 per cent. If you feel responsibility and guilt a lot of the time your ratings maybe anything between 61 and 80 per cent. If your level of responsibility and guilt is so overwhelming that you dwell on it nearly all of the time, can't think of anything else, feel you are marked by it for life, then your rating probably would be between 81 and 100 per cent.

If you find that you experience responsibility related to shame rather than guilt, or indeed both use the same ratings described above. Shame is explored later in this chapter.

Record your rating in your journal with today's date. For example:

My level of felt responsibility on 9th August 2016 at 12.15pm is 85 per cent.

(Remember that you are measuring your level of felt or perceived responsibility throughout this exercise. This is your subjective rating and has nothing to do with how others perceive things.)

Write down the answers to these questions in your notebook:

1. Connect yourself to the traumatic event. State as clearly as you can what exactly it is that you feel responsible or guilty for in relation to the event? Write down everything that comes to your mind. For example:

   a. *'I feel responsible that I didn't run into my neighbour's house when it caught fire and rescue their baby from the upstairs bedroom!'*

   b. *'I feel responsible for underestimating the gravity of the situation and for not calling the Fire Service earlier but instead listening to my neighbour and helping him try tackle the fire on our own first.'*

> c. *'I feel guilty for panicking and not thinking clearly as the fire got out of hand.'*
> d. *'I feel guilty about avoiding my neighbours since the fire and for not knowing how to talk to them about the death of their baby and my role in it.'*

2. Then assign your felt responsibility ratings (0–100 per cent) to each of the aspects that you have listed. (For the example, for the aspects above, you might rate your responsibility at: a. 90 per cent, b. 60 per cent, c. 80 per cent, d. 90 per cent)

3. Now examine each of the aspects separately (possibly at a different time, only dealing with one today) by asking yourself the following questions, answering them as honestly as you can:

    • If you could have done things differently, what would you have done instead?

    • Do you think that, by doing something differently, you could have prevented what happened?

    • What prevented you from taking that/ those action/s at the time? Consider all the things that went on at the time that prevented you, and assess them fairly.

    • Did you do anything intentionally designed to cause harm to yourself or others? If so, truthfully assess what made you do so at the time and how that affected the situation? Reassess your level of felt responsibility for that (0–100 per cent) (E.g. in the example above, the answer to this is '0 per cent'.)

- Were others involved in the event that also shared some responsibility for the situation? Was there somebody who deliberately caused harm, such as a perpetrator? (E.g. in the example above: the neighbour, his wife, her father, the other neighbours in the street, the delivery man (unintended perpetrator) who had carelessly thrown away his cigarette and driven off, etc.)

- Now assess your perception of what their responsibility was for each of the aspects that you listed and what they could have done differently, but didn't? Assign them each a responsibility rating (out of the 100 per cent). (E.g. in the example above for a: the neighbour = 40 per cent, his wife = 80 per cent, her father = 20 per cent, other neighbours in the street = 5 per cent, the delivery man = 50 per cent; then do the same for aspect b, c, and d, etc.)

- Now consider any other circumstances or factors independent of you and those others holding responsibility that also contributed to the event turning out the way in which it did. Assign your perceived felt responsibility ratings (out of the 100 per cent) to those factors. (E.g. in example above: the age, structure and build of the neighbour's house, the weather conditions, the fact that it was already dark and visibility was poor, etc...)

4. Having considered all those other factors above in depth, now go back and assess again your role and what you did and didn't do. Imagine watching the whole scenario on a screen with all the people and circumstances that were involved and assess fairly who carries what level of felt responsibility out of a total responsibility level of 100 per cent for each of the aspects you listed. Then assess fairly out of the 100 per cent what realistically, having considered all the other factors in this, is your actual felt level of responsibility for each aspect and your total is now. (E.g. in the above example, maybe a. 10 per cent, b. 15 per cent, c. 20 per cent, d. 50 per cent and the overall felt responsibility rating now is: 25 per cent). Please note that the total score is not the average of a., b., c., and d. The total score represents your subjective feeling of responsibility after having taken into consideration a large number of factors

(e.g. like in the above example, age of the house, weather conditions, etc.). It does not have to be mathematically totally accurate but rather represent your shift in feelings.

5. Now explore how much you have already suffered and punished yourself for the level of overall responsibility you had believed you carried for this event (e.g. in the above example, the initial total felt responsibility rating was = 85 per cent, but now the actual reassessed overall felt level of responsibility is only 25 per cent). How does your level of suffering, guilt and self-blame over all this time compare given your actual level of rated overall responsibility now? Does it feel: 'not adequate', 'adequate' or 'more than adequate' (e.g. in the above example, it would seem that the suffering, guilt and self-blame since the trauma far outweighs the actual rate of responsibility. It is probably: 'more than adequate').

6. Now explore if there is any positive action you would like to take to make amends. It is important that this is non-punitive and life-affirming to counterbalance the destructive energy of the trauma. (E.g. in the above example, it may be to plant a tree in memory of the baby, or if appropriate, talking to the neighbours and apologising for not having

been able to stay in touch after the trauma, or volunteering for some relevant cause, etc.). Whatever you may choose to do, it is important that there is a positive outcome and you gain and learn something from the action you take. It is also good if others can benefit from the positive action you engage in.

7. Allow yourself to let go of your guilt now. It has had its purpose and now something more positive can grow out of it for you and the community you live in.

Reclaiming your self-respect

How did you get on with Exercise 31? Did you take time and go through all the aspects that you held yourself previously responsible for? When you considered the 'bigger' picture did you notice a shift in the amount of actual responsibility you hold? If so, that is great and you may have noticed that it has already made you think differently about yourself and something feels as if it has lifted.

If there is no shift in your perceived level of responsibility, even though you have fairly and realistically assessed all the other aspects contributing to the traumatic event/s then there are two possibilities. One is that you haven't scoped far or deep enough, for example, examining where your behaviour or action in this situation may originally have developed from. None of us exists in total isolation, or even if you do now, there would have been a time and people in your life that would have had an influence on and shaped you. Go back and consider all the factors that have made you into who you are today and attribute them their due ratings of responsibility. Then re-examine the situation and notice if something does shift. This is not a way to talk you out of your responsibility; it is only a way of looking at the 'bigger' picture and considering the factors that led you to where you are today. The other possibility is that you are indeed truly responsible for the amount of responsibility that you have taken on.

There may be some situations when you carry most of the responsibility for some terrible event. Should this be the case for you then guilt, shame or self-punishment are not helping. They are now keeping you trapped and stuck and this doesn't help you or others. It is a matter of changing yourself and the way in which you interact with yourself and the world now. You may want to engage in positive, life-affirming amends, even if this takes you out of your usual realms of doing things. You may want to start finding out who, beyond all that has been damaging and destructive, you really truly are. You may need to seek professional help from someone who deals with complex trauma and who can work with you to enable you to find this out. Your commitment to give yourself another chance of life, which you made in Chapter 4, might involve planning out what you will do differently so that if you look back in five years' time at your life you can meet a person who you truly can respect. You can't change the past, it is also not helpful to walk away from your responsibility, but there is scope to reinvent yourself, by finding out who, under all the layers of pain and coping strategies, you truly are. This may require your genuine commitment to deeper-level therapeutic work and an expert therapist who understands the complexity of your presentation and who can help you to make these steps if you truly desire to do so. You might also find the Ho'oponopono practice[6] described in the next section helpful to apply.

Guilt, shame and self-blame are such important emotions to shift. Rather than meeting the world from 'underneath a blanket' or 'several centimetres smaller' than you truly are, shifting these emotions brings you into healthy alignment with yourself and on par with other people. In order to reclaim your self-respect, it is not only important to release your guilt, shame or self-blame, but to develop a way of deeply accepting what happened and your own particular role in it.

Acceptance, forgiving and reclaiming self-respect

It may be very difficult to accept what has happened to you and it may be even more difficult for you to accept the role you played in it and the person you have now become. There have been changes and your mind may be refusing to accept these changes. You might have found out things about yourself, through your actions or your lack of action, or your reactions, that have appalled you. You may have believed about yourself that however severe the circumstances, somehow you would rise to the occasion and act wisely and well, however, this 'bubble of safety-thinking'[7] may well now have burst. Perhaps you expected that, if a bus came screeching around the corner with no brakes and out of control and a small baby was directly in its path, you would throw yourself in front of the baby? To some degree, we all expect the best from ourselves in extreme circumstances. *But what if that doesn't happen?* Often, how we react in a life-threatening situation is not the way we planned to or imagined we would, if we had even ever thought about it. Trauma mobilises your body's autonomic survival responses and these take over. Perhaps you couldn't move, but instead stayed frozen to the spot, or maybe you ran away or broke down in fear and cried. Whatever happened, however different it was from how you would like it to have been, it is now time to accept what happened, forgive yourself and reclaim your self-respect in order to start living your life as it is now.

Acceptance is very closely interlinked with the concept of forgiving. Forgiving is often very misunderstood and can be used in an unhelpful way. Both acceptance and forgiving do not entail that we condone an action that was damaging, hurtful or harmful by thinking that once we have forgiven, the things that happened were acceptable. Children are often made to forgive another child or an adult who has hurt them. Often there is the assumption that once forgiveness happens everything is fine and nothing more is to be done by the perpetrator and things can go along as they have been until another boundary violation happens and renewed forgiveness is requested. This is an unhelpful way of practising forgiveness. The person made to forgive in this way often doesn't internally feel ready to forgive, because it requires of them to suppress their own legitimate feelings of anger or hurt. People often feel resistant to forgiving in this way because it makes them feel that somehow the person who harmed them has won and got away with it while they are still hurting or having to live with the consequences of the damage that was done.

It is never alright to hurt, harm or damage, although no human (regardless of position, rank, power, status, wealth, etc.), by nature of our shared fallibility, is immune from ever having hurt or potentially hurting somebody. Forgiving means that you have deeply accepted what has happened, even though it was harmful and damaging, and you are now ready to no longer be hurt by it. Ready for letting the hurt leave your system.

Forgiving is not about the other, such as the perpetrator of a crime or the one committing the hurt. How they deal with their part of the responsibility for what they have done needs to stay with them and you can't actually make it better for them, even if you truly feel ready to forgive them. Also, by not forgiving them you are not actually making them more accountable if they are not themselves ready to take responsibility. All you are doing is allowing the hurt to continue to fester inside yourself, which ultimately can make you feel bitter and unwell. Forgiving is for yourself. Only ever for yourself! It involves giving yourself permission to move on and to be no longer stuck in the pain that may have been inflicted upon you or that you may have inflicted upon yourself. It is letting go now of what might have immobilised you for a very long time. This clears negative emotions that you might still have been carrying inside and helps restore your self-respect.

Readiness to forgive, to let go and to move on can take time and you can't force yourself into it. It needs to come from an inner place of acceptance of all that has been and that is. Mindfulness practice, which connects you to being in the 'here-and-now of what is', can help you to develop this level of acceptance within yourself. However, this may take time and requires your willingness and regular practice to be effective.

Another method which you might like to explore is Ho'oponopono[6]. This is part of an ancient Hawaiian healing practice for forgiving yourself. It involves using four phrases in relation to an experience that still causes you pain and which you would now like to let go of.

Ho'oponopono was first recognised in the West, through the work of Dr Len, a clinical psychologist, who accepted a post as head of a ward for the criminally insane at the Hawaii State Hospital. This was a position nobody was eager to work in, as the atmosphere was heavy and dangerous with high absenteeism and poor staff retention. Dr Len asked to see each patient's files and shut himself away in his office every day insisting that nobody disturb him. Although people thought it strange that he didn't see the patients directly, they respected his request. After about three months it was noticed that the atmosphere in the ward and the relationships between patients gradually improved. When staff noticed and asked Dr Len what he had done, he explained that he had studied each client's file and cleansed the memories in himself that he had in common with each of the patients. For this he used the four phrases which are part of an ancient Hawaiian forgiveness practice and which are outlined to you in Exercise 32. Staff were incredulous and puzzled by the effect that something so seemingly simple seemed to have. Dr Len stayed in his post for almost four years after which time the psychiatric ward closed down, because the patients had either been cured or it was no longer necessary for them to remain in that ward. When Dr Len was questioned he explained that the practice is based on the understanding that everything in our lives, everything that happens to us, is connected to us and hence it is possible for us to let it go.

Although the above concept may seem a bit strange and somewhat alien to you, you may like to try it out and keep an open mind. It may seem strange to us in the West, but this practice has been effectively used and passed on for centuries. It would probably not have survived if it had no substance. Exercise 32 describes how you can apply the ancient practice of Ho'oponopono for the purpose of forgiving yourself in order to let go.

EXERCISE 32: HO'OPONOPONO[6] FORGIVENESS PRACTICE

Create a moment's space for yourself, where you can be undisturbed. Think of an aspect of your trauma experience that you would now like to let go of. Picture this aspect in your mind's eye. Now say either aloud or silently the following four phrases:

1. **'I am sorry'**
   (This is a 'sorry' to yourself and not to another, about any pain you may have created, any errors you may have made, or for anything that has felt harmful or hurtful to you.)

2. **'Forgive me'**
   (This is a 'forgiveness' to yourself, because you were not aware of that aspect inside yourself and you are now ready to let it go.)

3. **'Thank you'**
   (This is a 'thank you' to yourself for allowing yourself to release and cleanse this memory now.)

4. **'I love you'**
   (This is a message to your inner self, meaning that 'you love your inner self' – essentially you can understand this as an acceptance of how you are in the here-and-now. You can also remind yourself that this is linked to the contract you made with yourself in Chapter 4 to 'give yourself another chance of life' and 'to develop a language of loving kindness and compassion towards yourself'. This is one way of practising this. You need not link this to your usual concepts about love, which may feel difficult for you because of conflicting feelings you may associate with this.)

If you notice emotions coming up as you say these four phrases, just notice and allow them. Do not judge yourself.

Allow yourself to try this practice with an open mind. Do not have any expectations, just observe.

You can say these phrases as often as you like whenever you are confronted by a conflict or anything else that causes strong negative emotions to surge up within you which you would like to let go.

Regardless of whether you practise mindfulness to find a place of forgiveness towards yourself or try out 'Ho'oponopono', it is important that you keep an open mind and do not place expectations on yourself. This creates unnecessary pressure and may make it more difficult for you to allow yourself to let things go. Just keep an open mind and observe, you cannot do anything wrong with this. Follow your commitment to developing a language of kindness and compassion towards yourself and when you notice that you are not, rephrase the way you talk to yourself. Allow yourself to be patient, as forgiveness for yourself unfolds over time. You may gradually notice that you feel internally stronger, more positive towards yourself and self-respect is restored.

Take a moment to review whether you feel any change in yourself now compared to when you first started reading Chapter 12. Note in your journal, what most touched you in this chapter and what, if anything, enabled you to progress and shift in how you feel about your level of responsibility and aspects of the trauma now.

Summary checkpoints:

- Guilt, shame and self-blame are part of the trauma-related changes in mood and thought patterns. People easily confuse them.
  - Guilt relates to feeling uneasy about something you did or didn't do.
  - Shame connects to an internal belief that your character is 'flawed' and that you are 'bad' or 'unworthy' as a person.
  - Self-blame can arise from guilt or shame when you hold yourself responsible. Self-blame keeps the guilt and shame alive and active rather than allowing it to shift.
- Survivor guilt arises when you may feel unworthy of living, or later on enjoying yourself, when someone else whose life you thought important died.
- Healthy guilt serves an important function of navigating you towards what is moral, life preserving and aligned with your integrity.
- The overuse of guilt or the use of shaming during childhood creates fears of making mistakes and lays the foundations for becoming overly

responsible and easily triggered into guilt, shame and self-blame.

- In children who are attacked and shamed as selfish for even their most basic levels of healthy self-interest, this creates a 'fawn' response in a person leading to trauma-induced codependency[3]. This is characterised by negating one's own needs and self-neglect in favour of other people's demands or expectations.
- People can hold an unrealistic sense of their level of responsibility in relation to the trauma as they cannot access the full picture due to the fragmented nature of the memories.
  - This maintains guilt and potential feelings of shame.
  - It is therefore important to establish a realistic sense of actual level of responsibility, which specific exercises help with.
- To reclaim your self-respect it is not only important to release guilt, shame or self-blame, but to develop a way of accepting what happened, your role in it and forgiving.
- Forgiving is only ever for yourself. It involves giving yourself permission to move on and be no longer stuck in the pain that may have been inflicted on you or that you may have inflicted upon yourself.
- This chapter suggests mindfulness practice and the practice of Ho'oponopono[6] to support you with enabling forgiveness and letting go.

Grief, loss, sadness and emotional pain

Whatever the nature of a trauma it usually results in change. Things will be different and not the way they were before and as such, loss is a very common part of the changes initiated by trauma. Realistic concerns for immediate survival or recovery from injury after trauma can make it difficult for grief, sadness and emotional pain to be given appropriate space following loss. Yet healthy adjustment to trauma requires that these feelings are dealt with and given due space. If this has not happened or not been possible they can linger on unprocessed and become part of the negative changes in mood and thought patterns, outlined in Chapter 11. The purpose of this chapter is to help you recognise and better understand your responses to loss and explore what you can do to enable yourself to adjust in a healthy manner.

Coping with loss

Your traumatic situation might have involved the death of a loved one or an injury to yourself that resulted in a temporary or permanent change to your body, or perhaps the loss of your personal sense of safety and security. Whatever your experience, it is important to acknowledge the loss that you have experienced and to allow yourself to grieve for it.

When you completed Exercise 2, the 'Climbing Chart', in Chapter 5, you might have been surprised to notice that many of the significant events from childhood to adulthood on your chart involved the loss of something. It is common to feel shattered by a loss and to have difficulties coming to terms with the fact that someone or something that you were very attached to is gone from your life. While the death of a friend or loved one is a bereavement that is obvious to everyone, there are many other kinds of loss that can also affect a person deeply but might not be acknowledged as real experiences for grieving. These could be, for example, a miscarriage, stillbirth, loss of position, role or status important to you, being made redundant, loss of trust as a result of infidelity, cheating or other betrayal, the break-up of a relationship, divorce and having to move away from your home, culture or home country because of traumatic or adverse circumstances. If you have experienced any of these or a similar personal loss, you may find it harder to cope because of the lack of recognition of your pain by others. Exercise 33 asks you some questions about the losses that you may have had and how you have coped with these in the past.

EXERCISE 33: YOUR OWN EXPERIENCE OF LOSS

Acknowledging the losses

Identify in your journal how many and what type of personal losses you have experienced in your life so far. You could do this by going over your notes from Exercise 2 in Chapter 5. Remember that these should be events that involved a feeling of loss for you. Do not be influenced by what others thought about these events. Follow your personal experiences and feelings.

Coping with your losses

Now address the following questions in your journal:

1. How have you coped with your losses in the past? Did you just 'get on with things' and 'pulled yourself together' or did you acknowledge your sadness and give yourself space to grieve?

2. Did you make some type of memorial gesture to mark the loss? What was it?

3. If these losses involved death, did you attend funerals or other ceremonies marking the passing away of this person?

4. Which loss has been the hardest for you? What made it feel this way for you?

5. Are there other things you still need to do to honour the loss, now that some time has passed?

6. You may have done some things to comfort yourself, like eating too much or spending money on things that weren't really necessary but that helped you to feel better for a short time. People commonly use such coping strategies to help them get through a time of grief. What was particularly helpful to you when you were trying to cope with a loss?

7. What was not helpful about your coping behaviour? Did you turn away from others or towards them for help? Did you try to share with others what the loss meant to you?

8. Are there any things that you would have liked to have done differently, with hindsight?

If a loss has been significant, most people will experience feelings of shock and disorientation immediately after the event. Sometimes this is accompanied by a brief or a prolonged period of denial ('It didn't really happen . . .', 'He can't really be dead!', 'I keep waiting for him to come through the door . . .'). The loss feels too painful and overwhelming to acknowledge and we can't quite take it in. Therefore we tend to shut it away from us as long as possible. Another way of coping is to minimise the loss ('It wasn't really that important!', 'I'll be fine!', 'He (or she) is much better off . . .' or to deny our own feelings ('I'm not upset . . . nothing's changed!', 'I'll have to just get on, be strong and cope'). This can also manifest itself as a shutting off of *all* emotion. When there is so much to do and take care of, such as the practical arrangements for funerals or taking care of the family or other tasks, you may have found yourself carrying on functioning quite automatically, like a robot. On the inside, you may be feeling numb and others may experience you as seemingly untouched by what is happening, your face may look blank and you may feel unable to cry. Others may even feel that you are strong, but actually you just feel numb and shut down.

- Did you experience any of these feelings? Are they still with you?
- What do you have a hard time acknowledging, even now, about your loss?
- Has the reality of your loss sunk in? Does it still feel too overwhelming? Is that very hard to cope with?

When the reality of the loss *does* sink in, it is common for people to feel very angry towards others – including those who have been directly involved – as well as at well-wishers who make unhelpful or insensitive comments. If someone close to you has died, you may even have felt angry towards that person for leaving you and then ashamed or guilty for having felt that way. Actually it is very normal to be angry for a while with the person who has died and left you in so much pain. If you have lost trust as a result of being the victim of infidelity, betrayal, having been cheated on or conned, it can be equally painful and distressing. You may feel angry but also blame yourself for not having noticed, and, more encompassing, you may have lost trust in the good of human nature altogether.

- Have you experienced angry feelings that you are now ashamed of or feel guilty about?
- Are those feelings preventing you from moving on and dealing with your loss?
- Have others made you feel angry because of insensitive or unhelpful comments? Have you felt that they are trying to help but don't really seem to understand what you are going through?

Set aside some time to be just with yourself and use your journal to reflect on the feelings of anger, resentment or bitterness that may have been coming up for you. Allow yourself to be entirely honest even if you feel embarrassed or guilty about some of what has come up for you. Get yourself into a state of mindfulness (Chapter 11) and just observe your feelings and allow them without any judgment. If they feel very intense you may want to take some drawing pens and make a drawing out of them. Again don't hold yourself back. This is not a drawing that needs to meet artistic standards, but you could, for example, just draw doodles or paint brush strokes as a way of sharing your angry feelings with your journal, if you find it difficult to express them into words.

Feelings of anger may gradually give way to *despair and depression*. Feeling deeply sad, you may have withdrawn from social contact, either physically by cutting yourself off from other people, or emotionally by putting on a brave face and pretending that all is well and you are coping. Inside, though, you may be feeling miserable and isolated. When you are in such a frame of mind, it often seems that things keep going wrong. Everyday problems, such as having the car in front of you take *your* parking spot, become very stressful when added to the major loss you are trying to cope with. Your 'personal shield' feels very thin, everything feels a struggle and you may even start to wonder if life is worth living.

- Do you recognise these feelings?
- Can you identify everyday stresses that have felt like too much to cope with as you struggled with despair?
- Have you had other experiences where things have gone wrong since the loss?

- Even if things feel hard and a struggle at the moment, remind yourself of your commitment to give yourself another chance of life (Chapter 4) and make a deal with yourself to choose to see this life through. Actively protect yourself from any drastic actions until you feel able to cope again.
- Notice also the language you are using with yourself. When things go wrong and you struggle it is especially important that you treat yourself with compassion and kindness. Speak to yourself as you would with an injured child. Be patient and calm. You need time to heal and you are hurting just now.

All of these emotional reactions are normal stages of the grieving process that most people pass through (though not necessarily in the same order) after experiencing a significant loss. The length of time will vary from person to person. There is no right or wrong. Grief has its own timetable – one that is often quite different from society's idea of how long it *should* take to recover from a tragic loss.

Complex grief

Sometimes it may be more difficult to move through your loss, especially if it is associated with layers of conflicting feelings. This can be the case if you had a very complicated relationship with the person you lost through trauma, for example if the person was both your carer and abuser. In this case the loss may elicit feelings of both sadness and relief, which you may feel guilty about. Also, now that your abuser is dead or no longer present in your life it may be the first time that you can connect with the extent of your own suffering. This can elicit complex and confusing feelings, depending on the type of your relationship and the length of your suffering. Your ability to move through this kind of loss will be influenced by the extent to which you can work through the abuse trauma that you have experienced.

Grief can also be complicated if the person you lost died under very violent circumstances and the body was disfigured. You may feel stuck with this last image in your mind and the suffering that your loved one had to endure rather than being able to hold the image of the way the person looked before the trauma. It can also be very difficult to grieve if the body is missing altogether and the remains may never be found, for example, if the person died at sea or in an aircrash. This can be even harder and elicit very confusing emotions if you don't know if the person that is missing has actually died or if there is a chance that they may have survived and could still be found somewhere. You may be very unsure if and when to move on.

Another circumstance when grief can be very complicated is when the person you lost died at their own hands, for example, if they committed suicide. You may be overcome with huge waves of anger as well as sadness and guilt, because a part of you may feel you should have been able to predict this and save them. You might find it very hard to forgive yourself and move on. If this is the case, or if you have experienced trauma that is similar to any of the above examples, you are advised to seek out the help of a trauma specialist as you need a more individualised therapeutic approach that is tailored to your specific circumstances. This can help you to work this through so that you can find peace within yourself, move on and reclaim your own life.

Problems may also arise if you get stuck at one stage in your grieving process and can't allow healing and resolution of the loss to occur. An example of this would be refusing to acknowledge that a loved one is really gone. For example, by keeping a living 'memorial' – continuing to set a place at table, refusing to change the arrangement of their possessions and maintaining everything 'exactly as it was'.

When you are grieving, you may feel reluctant to let go of your painful loss and begin to enjoy your life again, for fear that you would be betraying the memory of the person or the thing that was lost. You may feel unable to say goodbye or may torment yourself about things that were left unsaid or undone. You may also worry about appearing to others as if you had not really cared about that person or that situation. You may fear others judging you and this may make you feel insecure and cautious about how to move on.

You may find it helpful to address some of the questions that follow in your journal. It is important that you start to trust yourself and not listen to others. Only you truly know your feelings and your relationship to the person or thing that you have lost. However hard it is to accept, you cannot undo what has already happened by holding back your grief and hanging on.

- Did you recognise any of this in your own feelings or behaviour as you were reading through this section? If so, describe them in your journal.
- Allow yourself to explore what may be preventing *you* from healing and resolving your loss.
- Write down anything that you may be holding yourself back from because you feel you may betray the person you have lost.
- Notice any of your behaviour that may be stopping you from working through your grief and letting go of your painful loss.
- Ask yourself if it is helpful now to either yourself or the person you have lost if you are continuing to hold yourself back from life?
- Consider what you would have wished for the person you have lost if it had been you that had left them behind. Would you have wanted them to move on with their lives after a period of grieving? If so, what is holding you back now from also enabling yourself to do this? Are you treating yourself differently to how you would expect or even wish for others to act in such a situation?

While you are working on these questions give some thought to the type of commemorative or 'goodbye' ritual that would be personally meaningful to you. Think of something that is just for you to help you to honour and acknowledge the depth of your loss, so that you can gradually move on. Remind yourself of ways you have said goodbye in the past that you might have forgotten to use. Explore if any of these may be suitable for this loss or design something totally different to reflect the situation now.

Memorial rituals

Here are a few ideas for memorial rituals that other people have found helpful:

A night to remember

Spend an evening looking at photographs or clippings. Allow yourself to cry, have some pleasant memories, think about the things you miss and the things you don't miss. Put your photos in order in an album or folder and label them with the date and time and whatever else you remember about the occasion. Make this night very memorable: have a special candle burning and use aromatic scents, such as sage, sandalwood or rosemary, fragrances that are often used for commemoration. Or you could have the person's favourite perfume or aftershave around you. Buy some flowers, play some music that you and the lost person may have liked. Celebrate the time you were able to share together with this person. Allow yourself to feel gratitude for what this person added and brought to your life. Make space for the feelings that come up and use safety, grounding and soothing strategies (Chapter 4 and Chapter 6) to comfort yourself. Be kind, compassionate and patient with yourself and acknowledge that your feelings are human and give yourself all the time you need to work through them during this special memorial ceremony.

Writing a special letter

Write a letter to the person who has died (or left you behind), saying on paper all the things you would have liked to have said to him or her were they still alive. Tell that person what you have been through, what he or she meant to you and what you are going to do now to get on with your life. Allow yourself to experience all feelings that need to come out while you are writing this letter. They are part of the grieving and natural healing process. Be compassionate and kind with yourself and give yourself as much time as you need for this process. 'Send' the letter by burying it in a significant place, burning it and scattering the ashes or by depositing it near the person's remains. In the case of a very recent death, the letter could also be enclosed in the coffin.

Group memorial

If you are part of a group that has experienced a traumatic loss, the group can have a ritual of 'letting go' together. For instance, each member could write a personal goodbye message which is inserted into a helium balloon and then all the members of the group release their balloons at the same time and watch them rise and disappear into the air.

River of life

Another ritual, called the 'river of life', can be carried out individually or as part of a group. It involves making small paper boats that each contain a candle and an individual message. The candles are lit, and the little boats are set afloat in a large stream or river. This can also be done with flowers or some other significant or symbolic object. Messages are attached and the objects are then set afloat.

Keep notes in your journal as you work through your own grief and loss. When you are ready, proceed with your own 'goodbye' healing ritual. There are also some useful books that might help you listed in the resource section at the end of this book. If you feel really stuck and your feelings of loss don't seem to be shifting, seek professional help to support you with this process.

Expect your grieving to be a gradual process that requires time. As you move on it may feel easier most days, but then when there are special occasions or memorials you may suddenly feel overtaken by grief again. This is entirely normal and not a sign that you are going back. You are just experiencing another layer of emotional pain which has not been processed yet. Go through this in exactly the same way as you moved through your pain before. Comfort and soothe yourself, keep yourself safe and allow your feelings. Commit to proceeding at your own pace and do not put yourself under pressure to move through this quickly. It will take however long it needs, as long as you are allowing your feelings and remain kind and compassionate with yourself. Although painful, grieving is a natural process and as you move through it gradually you will feel stronger again and new possibilities, experiences and a new sense of openness can emerge for you in your life. Well done for staying with yourself in this process and through this enabling yourself to grow into new strength.

Summary checkpoints:

- Whatever the nature of trauma it usually results in change, and loss is a very common part of this.
- Healthy adjustment requires working through and grieving for the loss.

- It is common to experience feelings of shock and disorientation immediately after.
- Later feelings of denial that it happened may occur and when the reality does sink in anger, resentment, bitterness, sadness and despair can follow.
- Grief has its own timetable and the length of time will vary between each person and is often quite different from society's idea of how long it should take to recover from loss.
- Some experiences of loss may not be acknowledged by others and you may find it harder to cope because of the lack of recognition of your pain.
- Sometimes the nature of loss is such that it causes complicated grief, which is not easy to shift and work through without professional therapeutic help.
- Memorial rituals can be a very helpful way of honouring and acknowledging the depth of your loss to enable you to start to gradually move on.
- Grieving is a natural process. Allow yourself to proceed at your own pace and do not put yourself under pressure to move through your grief quickly.
- Comfort and soothe yourself, be compassionate and kind towards yourself, keep yourself safe, allow your feelings and take as long as you need.

14

Changes in the body and physical pain

Learning to live with the physical scars of trauma

When your body has been injured and the trauma has left permanent physical changes, you will need time to heal from the emotional scars as well as the physical scars. Chapter 13 could also be very relevant to you as your losses may encompass your previous physical self, your level of fitness and your health. Complete healing from the physical injuries may indeed not be possible, but *in order to move on with your life and make it livable again, your challenge will be to find ways of accepting and getting to like your new self.* That this is not an easy task goes without saying, as Antonia describes:

For me the hardest was to learn to live with (yes and even love!) my changed physical self. I had been a model and my whole livelihood was dependent on my perfect body image. The trauma was a road traffic accident, in which my boyfriend Allen drove our Mercedes Coupe into a large tree, after coming off the road round a very sharp bend under icy driving conditions. Allen broke both his legs and had various other fractures, on his arms and ribcage, but otherwise his body image remained intact. Things were worse for me. A branch had come through the window on my side of the car and caused a serious large cut right across my face. It also tore off one of my arms, so that it had to be amputated later. Friends and family were relieved that I had survived and told me so in the hospital. I couldn't share their feelings. I felt I would rather have died than look like this. I hated my swollen face with the huge scar running across it. I looked completely grotesque, disfigured like a monster out of Frankenstein, and certainly not like me any more! Even worse was the complete loss of my left arm. It is not possible to put into words the heart-wrenching pain I felt at the loss of this. I have to honestly admit that there were several times when I really felt like ending it all. I hated everything – Allen for not having prevented it, the world for being such an unjust place and most of all myself! I could see no purpose in living any more, I had lost everything, there seemed no reason to carry on, there really seemed no point!

What stopped me? I think somewhere inside me was a tiny voice that urged me not to give up, to stay strong. Although this voice was very small and quiet, it was strong enough to put me in touch with that part of myself that felt I would be wrong to kill myself. I had to completely readjust. I had to change most of my social circle. I no longer belonged to the glamorous and glitzy 'showbiz' world. I went back to college to retrain as a business administrator. Gradually, as I stopped avoiding people all the time, I learned that people responded positively to my personality. People seemed to like my open yet sensitive manner. I learned that aside from my previously beautiful body I had other qualities that had not been destroyed by the trauma. I had never really noticed these other sides of myself and I now think nobody else really valued them before the trauma. After all, I had lived in a world that was more about image rather than personal qualities. I also found a new partner, Luke, who helped me a lot towards learning to accept myself. Luke was somebody with whom I could share all my feelings. He understood my anger and rage and my feelings of loss, sadness and despair. He also taught me to appreciate a different kind of beauty, other than the one that concentrates purely on physical image. I learned to appreciate the beauty of human friendships, I rediscovered my talent for painting. By taking up walking I learned to appreciate the beauty of all the elements around me. My sense of self changed completely.

All this happened very gradually and was by no means always easy. For example, I often automatically did things that would require the use of my left arm. Although I do carry a prosthesis now, I can no longer use that arm. It took me a long time to accept that I would never get my normal arm back and I sometimes still really miss it. It has got much easier though and I can say that I even love myself again, much more consciously than ever before!

Antonia

Antonia's account demonstrates how damaging the effect of trauma can be, but also that it *is* possible to enjoy life again, even if this means a complete change of lifestyle. Indeed, adjustment to the physical injuries caused by a trauma often demands those changes in your life; it may no longer be possible for you to go back to your previous work or to pursue the old hobbies or sports that you enjoyed before the trauma. As in Antonia's case, your circle of friends will often change, too. People frequently say that during a crisis your true friends emerge. People often find that those whom they thought of as friends before the trauma turn out not to be true friends, and yet new, more understanding friends emerge instead.

Like Antonia, you may discover that although you have to make significant life changes as a result of your trauma, it could be that these will be more aligned with the person you actually are. Although difficult and painful, because of the trauma and the resulting physical changes you may no longer be able to keep up the appearances or 'image' that you had been so used to displaying to the outside world before the trauma. This may now help you evaluate who you really are, including getting to know your personal qualities, beyond your external self-image.

Sometimes, because of the physical injuries, there can also be a real sense of isolation, because you may not be able to get about as much or as easily as you did before your trauma. So, the first step towards learning to live with the physical scars is often to *accept* that you will have to make certain changes in your life. The next exercise is designed to help you look at those areas of your life you may need to change.

EXERCISE 34: IDENTIFYING YOUR AREAS OF CHANGE

1. Take your notebook and write down all the things you used to be able to do before the trauma. Then give yourself a score anywhere between 0–10 for your past quality of life (where 0 = poor and 10 = very high quality of life).

2. Now write down all the things that you are doing now. Again give yourself a rating anywhere between 0–10 for your present quality of life.

3. Calculate the difference between your score of past quality of life and your score for present quality of life and make a note of this. What do you notice? Did you expect there to be such a difference in scores? Is this discrepancy really justified? Or would you like to try to redress this unequal balance? (Or maybe you are one of the few people who have already mastered this and the scores are not all that different after all!)

4. Now write down all the changes that you would like to make to help increase your present quality of life and support your process of healing. Of course, these need to be realistic and to take into account any changes in physical condition. Nevertheless, there are probably many things that you could be doing despite the

physical changes, which so far you have not tried. Give yourself an estimated rating between 0–10 for your quality of life if you really managed to make these changes. Also, rate using the same scale 0–10 the extent to which these changes would support you with your healing process? Would you be satisfied with this score? If not, maybe you could think of some further changes to make or areas of life you would like to explore.

5. Order the changes that you have listed in terms of how easy you think they would be to achieve. Select the easiest change first and write down in your journal what you have to do to achieve this first change and how and when you will have done this.

6. Try to work towards the easiest changes first and once you have mastered them, advance to the more difficult ones in your own time. It might be helpful if you could get a partner or friend to help you achieve those changes.

Also don't forget to re-rate your quality of life at intervals and remember the challenge is to improve your quality of life, regardless of the physical changes you have experienced!

Learning to accept your body as it is now

Now that you have begun to work on reinstating quality into your life despite the physical changes, it would also be helpful if you learned to reconnect with your body and reintegrate the hurt or changed parts with the rest of your body. Your goal is to learn to accept your body and yourself as it is now.

After severe physical injury it can be very difficult to accept the changes to your body image and to start to see yourself as a whole person again. It is quite understandable that you find it hard to accept your new self and your altered physical image. However, your old body image *has* changed and now you need to give yourself a chance to get to know and familiarise yourself with your new body image.

The following exercise is designed to help you with this. Take as much time as you need and only work on this when you feel ready. It is very normal and even necessary to allow yourself to experience any feelings that may come up for you during this exercise. In order to manage these use the safety and grounding resources (Chapters 4 and 6) that work for you. Remind yourself to be compassionate and kind to yourself. You have already been through so much. Whatever happened, however you currently feel about yourself you deserve patience and compassion with yourself. This exercise gives you the opportunity to explore your present body as it is, in order to welcome and learn to accept each part of yourself.

EXERCISE 35: RECLAIMING YOUR BODY

1. The task is for you to reclaim each part of your body separately. Start with those parts of your body that you feel either positive or neutral about (do not choose any parts that carry any negative feelings for you), for example you could choose to start with your elbow or your wrist (if those parts of your body haven't been changed by the trauma and you don't feel negative about them).

2. Set aside 5 or 10 minutes every day and work on your chosen part of the body. When you were a baby you spent hours just looking, touching and exploring each part of your body in order to get to know and to familiarise yourself with them. Just as when you were a baby, allow yourself to discover that chosen part of your body all over again. Examine how the skin looks, is it smooth or rough? Allow yourself to feel it, touch it, stroke it. Feel and experience it like you have never noticed or experienced it before. The principles of mindfulness (described in Chapter 11) can assist you with this. Think about its function and how it has served you over the years that you have been together. Do this every day for the next three days and allow any feelings that come up for you. Just be with them and notice.

3. By day three start writing a letter of appreciation about this part of your body. Acknowledge what a wonderful functional part of your body this is. Write down all that you appreciate about this part of your body, make friends with it.

4. On day four allow yourself to buy a small, inexpensive present for this part of your body, for example, some cream or oil, a feather or a ribbon. It should be something that you can put on it, use to stroke it with or even give it a little massage, to show your appreciation and care. Let it know in that way that you accept it as a part of yourself.

5. When you are ready to like and accept this part of your body, move on to other parts of your body. If you are not ready for writing your letter of appreciation on day three, give yourself more time. However, do move through all the stages above until you feel ready to learn to accept those parts that have been damaged by the trauma.

6. When you are ready, go through the steps of this exercise with your injured or changed parts as you did with all other parts of your body. Allow yourself to really get to know those injured parts, to look at them closely, to feel them, to touch them and in your own time to welcome them back as part of your own body. It is very

likely that when you first start to connect to your injured or changed body parts that feelings come up in you. These are necessary and important. They are part of a grieving process that is important for you to allow and move through as it will enable you to readjust to the changes. Take as much time as you need. You can also revisit Chapter 13 to explore if any other of the information or exercises there could be helping you to move through these feelings of loss.

7. Move to your letter of appreciation only when you feel internally ready to do so and when what you write feels genuine. You may then recognise how brave that part of your body has been and how hard it must have been to be rejected and unloved for so long. Explore, if you can, ways to love or like this part of your body.

Remember: *those damaged parts are with you now in this way because your body has accepted them after the trauma. So, it is not your body but your mind that has rejected them! Your task now is to help your mind to find ways of befriending and accepting them as part of your new whole being.*

Learning to live with the pain

When physical pain following injuries becomes chronic and persistent it can seem like an inescapable and constant reminder of the trauma.

The sensation of pain is a natural signalling system indicating that something is not right for our body. Initially, the pain is likely to have been a direct response to your physical injuries. These can take a long time to heal and modern medicine with its emphasis on efficiency frequently doesn't allow for a longer natural healing process. Therefore, it could be that your pain is simply an indication of your body still recovering and needing more time to heal from the injuries. This can take months or sometimes years.

If that may be the case for you, it is important that you create an appropriate healing environment for it. You may want to be aware of any factors in your environment that may hinder or stand in the way of your healing. For example, do you consume any substances that aren't very healthy or caring for your body? For example, cigarettes, coffee, black tea, alcohol, recreational drugs, conflicting or many different medications? Notice carefully if there are any other factors that may stand in the way of your physical healing. Observe your diet and notice if you consume any foods that may not in fact be so healthy or healing for your body. Also become aware of the way in which you treat yourself. Although we tend to differentiate between physical and emotional pain, in bodily terms the same neural pathways may be involved in both.

Rather than avoiding or fighting your pain, it is usually more helpful to start to get to know it and then learn to manage it differently. Familiarise yourself with the quality of your pain sensations and their level of intensity at different times during your day. Observe if there is a pattern to them. Notice what else may have been happening for you during the day that could have had an effect on your pain perception. You might find the following questions helpful to consider:

- Have there been any factors that may have been aggravating your pain?
- How have you been responding to your pain?
- Do you withdraw, shut down or stop engaging in activities?
- Do you overdo things, find it hard to recognise your limits or push yourself too hard at times?
- How have you been treating yourself?
- Does your pain respond differently when you are harsh and impatient with yourself compared to when you are compassionate and gentle with yourself?

Start noticing what is going on with your pain and how it may fluctuate in response to different internal or external factors. You may find it helpful to keep a pain diary in which you report the pain together with other factors, both internal and external that may be present at the time. The Pain Diary on page 408 gives an example of how this might look. You may find that your pain fluctuates and this way you may get a clearer sense of what may be intensifying and what may be reducing or soothing your pain.

Diagram 5: Example of a Pain Diary

Date	Time	Type of pain How severe is the pain? (0 – 10 worst)	External factors	Internal factors	Action taken & effect	Severity of pain now (0–10)	How helpful was this?
02 June	8.00am	Gnawing pain. 7/10	Betty just left for work	I feel useless and blame myself for not being able to work.	I do a mindfulness practice and feel calmer in myself.	4/10	Helpful – would like to be able to do more often
	11.00am	Stabbing pain 8/10	Letter from my solicitor re the Court Proceedings	I have flashbacks to the assault during the trauma. Feel really agitated and hyperalert.	I feel I can't cope and drink 3 glasses of wine. Feel lousy.	6/10	Unhelpful. Numbed me out, don't feel good. Feel less in touch with myself.

4.30pm	Piercing pain 7/10	Children came back from school	I can't cope with their noise and the thought of cooking tea for all of us felt overwhelming.	I decide not to push myself and sit down with the children. Together we come up with a plan and work out how to do a 'pop-up' café for this evening's meal. They feel excited and want to all join in.	3/10	Really helpful. I feel great. Rather than isolating myself, I got involved in the action with my children. It helped take the focus away from the pain and I even laughed. It helped with our bonding.

Keeping a regular pain diary enables you to notice over time which factors might be aggravating or soothing your pain. You can then monitor which actions are helpful and healthy for your recovery, reducing your pain and enhancing your well-being.

At this stage there may not be any medical solutions to remove your pain completely, but you can still learn ways of managing the pain, rather than allowing it to control you and your life.

Although I recovered reasonably quickly from the two operations, following the fractures to my hip and upper thigh, it was this constantly gnawing pain that was crippling me. It seemed to be worse every time I moved and subsequently I withdrew more and more from doing anything. Claire, my wife, was a keen walker but even when she asked me to come out with her to take a gentle stroll through town I refused. Eventually, I ended up staying mostly at home, doing very little but sitting and eating, which started to have its effect on my weight. I felt very miserable about myself and was internally angry for having let myself go. In the end Claire had had enough. She sought advice from a friend, who was a physiotherapist. Together they got me onto a programme where very slowly I learned to increase my activity levels again. I now feel so much better. The pain hasn't stopped, but I am more mobile and active again and this gives me a sense of achievement. I am actually doing things for myself again. Also when I focus on something I enjoy doing I am less aware of my pain and it gives me relief for a short time. Even if I am

slow and pace myself carefully, it is better doing something
than nothing at all!

Joe

If you are suffering from chronic pain, you might like Joe
be avoiding life and have found yourself withdrawing more
and more from normal activities. If you feel that the pain has
taken over your life, the following exercise might be helpful:

EXERCISE 36: TAKING CONTROL OF YOUR PAIN

1. If you are suffering from chronic pain, ask yourself how many activities you have stopped doing
   because of the pain.
2. Ask your partner or another person who knew
   you well before the trauma what they have
   observed you giving up as a result of the pain.
   Make a note of all those activities you have lost
   in your notebook.
3. Now look at your list of lost activities and
   decide whether there may not be one or two of
   these that you could modify so that with time
   you might be able to manage them once more,
   despite your pain.
4. Write yourself a programme to help you towards
   achieving this.

For example:

Aim: To walk into town again.

a. Work out how many steps you can manage presently (e.g. 300 steps).

b. Next, decide what number of steps you would like to have increased your mobility by for the next week. Decide on a small increase (e.g. 350 steps).

c. Now practise walking a little more every day until by the rest of the week you have mastered 350 steps. Congratulate yourself if you manage this. If not, be kind and gentle with yourself and give yourself more time. It is not a race and what matters most is that you are trying. Continue to try for another week or longer, until you have achieved this goal.

d. Then work out what your aim for the following week is and continue in small steps until you have mastered your aim of walking into town. You might need to arrange for resting stations along the route.

e. Once you have achieved your first aim, set yourself another aim to work towards.

f. When you suffer from chronic pain it is important that you set yourself small and achievable goals and not push yourself unreasonably hard. It is important to pace yourself carefully.

5. If you can't identify anything from your list of lost activities that you would like to work towards, think of an activity that you haven't done in the past but that you would like to be able to master. Proceed in the same way with small incremental steps.

Keeping your pain diary (see page 408) in combination with setting yourself gentle activity goals will be helpful. It can also be a guide as to how you have been treating yourself internally while you engaged in your activity goals and how that affected your level of pain. It is really important that you engage with yourself in a compassionate manner and gently pace yourself rather than pushing yourself unduly into action.

Now that you have taken steps to work with your pain rather than allowing it to take over your life, you could explore some additional techniques to help you manage your pain.

EXERCISE 37: IMAGINATIVE TRANSFORMATION OF THE PAIN

1. When you next experience a pain, try the following:

   a. Notice your pain and identify where exactly you can feel it in your body.

   b. Give a rating of how strong it is now 0–10 (0 = no pain, 10 = the worst you have experienced) and write this down in your journal.

   c. Notice what type of pain it is. How would you describe it in words? E.g. gnawing, biting, crushing, etc. Write this down in your journal.

   d. Where in your body is it? Located right inside or more on the periphery?

   e. Notice the edges and parameter of your pain sensation. Where does it start and where in your body does it stop?

   f. Notice what shape it is.

   g. Notice the size of this shape.

   h. Become aware of the surface of this shape. Is it smooth or rough?

   i. Feel into the edges of this shape. Are they round or jagged?

   j. Notice if this shape feels solid, liquid or like a gas?

   k. Notice its temperature.

l. Notice its colour.

m. If it could make a noise, what noise would it make?

n. How loud would that noise be?

o. Now give yourself another rating of how strong your pain is now (0–10) – write this down in your journal. Notice if you can feel a difference to your initial rating.

2. Now explore possible changes to this image. Feel into how your pain's image might like to change in order for the pain to be less intense or powerful.

- Sense into which colour might be a more healing or soothing colour for your pain?
- Notice which shape and what size would feel more manageable to you?
- Notice what the smallest size is that you could imagine your pain changing into?
- What temperature would it need to be to feel more comfortable for you?
- Imagine it turning into a liquid and sense it flowing out of your body deep, deep down into the earth where it will get recycled and turned into nourishment.
- Imagine whatever might be left in your body changing into lots of tiny little parts, which feel far less intense.

- Explore sending each of them off in their own tiny balloon and notice these lifting up into the air until you lose sight of them.
- Or imagine yourself breathing these out of your body and as they scatter into the air notice them dissolving into sparkles that turn into air.
- Explore any other changes that might help your body transform this pain into a less intense and more manageable sensation. For example, imagine cooling it down if it feels hot or stingy or soothingly warming it if it feels icy.

3. Allow yourself to be as open and explorative with the changes to your image as you can. You may find that the less you concentrate on the actual physical sensation of the pain, the less you notice it and the more likely it is that some of the pain intensity can be reduced. In order to achieve this it is important that you make your image as strong and powerful as you can.

4. Practise this exercise as often as you can (several times a day if possible). Give yourself a rating between 0–10 for pain intensity again after you have completed this exercise.

It could also be very helpful for you to engage in regular mindfulness practice (as described in Chapter 11), which has been found to be very effective in the management of chronic pain as it helps you focus your attention away from the pain. The breathing exercises that are described in Chapter 6 of this book could also be supportive to you. You may additionally want to consult a physiotherapist, cranial osteopath, acupuncturist or a chiropractor for support with your pain management. Gentle exercise, such as Pilates, tai chi, qi gong or yoga carefully tailored to your level of ability might also be supportive.

Finally, recognise that your decision to take more active control over your pain is a very positive one and constitutes the first big step toward mastery of that pain.

Summary checkpoints:

- Your losses may encompass changes to your previous physical self, your level of fitness or your health.
- The physical changes brought about by trauma require you to accept that you will have to make changes to your life.
    - Rather than your life being taken over and dictated by those changes, allow yourself to consciously evaluate what changes you

would like to make so that they can support your healing process and enhance your quality of life.

- Finding ways of accepting and getting to like your changed physical self will help you to make life liveable again. Reclaiming the different parts of your body can help you with this.

• It requires time to heal from the emotional as well as the physical scars and sometimes pain can become chronic and persistent.

- This could be a signal indicating that you are still recovering and healing from injuries, which can take month or even years.

• Support this process by creating an appropriate healing environment for yourself.

• Keeping a pain diary can help you recognise which factors are healing for and those that might be aggravating your pain.

• Setting yourself gentle and paced activity goals will help you work with your pain rather than allowing it to take over your life.

• Other strategies, such as imagery transformation of the pain, mindfulness and breathing exercises can also help as they enable you to master your pain by focussing your attention away from it.

15

Reclaiming your life – opting for positive life choices

The final stage of healing from the effects of your trauma is to reclaim control of your life. You may not have been aware of just how much your trauma has impacted on your life until you picked up this book. You may have noticed that you have not been feeling well, but the changes resulting from the trauma may have just crept into your life and you took them as given, assuming that this was how it was going to be from now on. You may have felt that you had no choice as things felt out of your control. You may not even have noticed how narrow and confined your life may have become and how much you have lost agency of yourself. This is common for many people who have been affected by trauma.

This chapter invites you to reclaim control of your life. You are invited to evaluate the changes that have occurred for you in your day-to-day life and consciously choose how you would like to live your life now. You could transform the trauma-driven changes into positive, healthy life choices for you. Life choices that support your healing and may be more aligned to your true values and authentic needs. For example, Antonia, who was mentioned in Chapter 14 on page 396, discovered that although she had to make significant lifestyle changes as a result of her trauma, eventually these aligned more with the person she actually is. She found out who her real friends were and she discovered that the world she had operated in before the trauma had been much more about image rather than her personal qualities. In that sense although she would not have ever wished for the trauma to have occurred, it brought her closer to who she really was.

You have now reached a stage in this book where you are invited to embed what you have learned about yourself during your recovery process into your day-to-day life. You may choose to aim towards creating a life that despite, or possibly because of, the trauma could be a much fuller, healthier and rewarding experience for you than it may have ever been. The benefits arising from a life well lived not only enhance your emotional and physical wellbeing but also optimise your physical health and with this the functioning of your brain. This maximises brain plasticity thus aiding and accelerating your healing process.

This chapter invites you to revisit the principles that you committed to in Chapter 4 and that have underpinned the whole of this book. These are:

- To develop an open curiosity towards yourself

- To give yourself another chance of life now
- To develop a language of loving kindness and compassion towards yourself

This chapter helps you shine a spotlight on various areas of your life to enable you to examine your current lifestyle or habits, bearing in mind the above principles. You are invited to evaluate to what extent you are content with and how much in control you feel in each of these areas of your life. You are encouraged to identify areas or habits that do not benefit your healing process, are not healthy for you and do not serve you well now. You can then explore what you might try to do differently to bring about more positive choices in this particular area of your life.

Spotlight 1: Diet, nutrition and eating habits

You may be wondering why diet, nutrition and eating habits feature in a book on overcoming traumatic stress. Body and mind are intricately connected, and the food you eat as well as how you eat it can greatly affect and influence your physical health but also your capacity to heal. A poor diet causes stress to your body, further compromising your resilience and making you more vulnerable. A diet rich in antioxidants, minerals and vitamins protects your brain, improves immune function and optimises the health of your brain, heart and body-cell functioning. This section does not propose any particular diet, but it provides you with general established nutritional guidelines and invites you to examine your current eating habits and explore what healthy lifestyle changes you may wish to make.

Nutritional guidelines for optimising your health:

- Minimise animal fats and eat meat sparingly. If you choose to eat meat, select lean meat, poultry without skin or fish. Avoid red or processed meats, high fat dairy products and fast food. If you choose to stop eating meat altogether change gradually to a vegetarian diet. Seek further nutritional advice on how to replace the necessary proteins and nutrients with plant-based foods or meat alternatives (such as tofu, beans, pulses, nuts or seeds).
- Eat a diet rich in plant foods, such as vegetables, fruits, beans, pulses, grains, nuts, and seeds.
- Ideally buy fresh, seasonal food, which is grown locally and organic.
- Fresh, lightly cooked, warm food is easier to digest than raw, uncooked food. In order to retain the full nutritional value, it is important not to overcook vegetables or fruit. Freshly prepared smoothies, green smoothies, fruit or vegetable juices are a great way to supply your body and brain systems with concentrated amounts of fibre, antioxidants, minerals and vitamins. They also help detoxify and clear your gut and we now know that the health of your gut determines your overall health.
- Use unsaturated fats and avoid hydrogenated,

polyunsaturated or trans fats commonly found in commercially produced bakery, snacks, crisps, margarine or fast foods. The best fats for this are coconut oil, butter or ghee and extra virgin olive oil. Reduce your overall intake of fried food.

There are some guidelines below. You might also like to start to read a little more about healthy food, life style and nutrition. There is a lot of information on the internet that you could explore.

- It is helpful to get your body used to three really healthy nutritional meals a day with your main meal at lunchtime. Start with a healthy breakfast, eat your main meal at lunchtime. Ideally this should be a cooked meal, accompanied by a salad and completed with a healthy pudding. Eat your last meal of the day early in the evening and keep it light.
- Your body responds best to modest amounts of food taken at regular intervals to keep your blood sugar levels steady throughout the day. Try not to skip meals. Should you find yourself feeling tired or irritable, this could be an indication of your blood-sugar levels dropping. In this case introduce healthy mid–morning and mid–afternoon snacks.
- If you have digestive problems, it is possible that you may have a food intolerance and it could be helpful to consult your GP or a nutritionist for advice.
- As a general rule eat modest amounts of food and

stop eating when it tastes best. Chew your food well before you swallow.

- Cook food that tastes good, is fresh and full of nutritional value. Love the food you eat and enjoy the process of eating it. Make time to sit down with your meal and create an eating environment that appeals.

- Then focus on your food and the process of eating it. Allow yourself consciously to taste every bite of your food as you chew it. You might like to use the mindful awareness technique described in exercise 27 in Chapter 11 of this book. If part of your PTSD symptoms includes a numbing of your taste buds, eating mindfully is a really good opportunity to recover your taste for food.

- If cooking is not one of your strengths, you might like to join a cooking course or an internet guided cooking school, which could be a positive life choice arising out of the entertainment, leisure and hobbies spotlight that follows.

- Drink adequate amounts of water regularly throughout the day to keep you well hydrated and maximise your body functioning. Depending on your body constitution, it is recommended that men drink about 13 cups (3 litres) and women 9 cups (2.2 litres) of water per day.

- Avoid concentrated, processed or sugary drinks, tea, coffee, alcohol, and energy drinks containing caffeine. Also avoid nicotine. Tobacco increases the risk of depression and anxiety and brain imaging studies have shown that any of these drugs can adversely affect brain functioning. Try drinking herbal teas, freshly pressed fruit or vegetable juices, smoothies, coconut water or warm water (ideally spring water) as a healthy choice for your body.

Now assess your current eating habits, food and drink intake. Notice if there is anything that you might like to do differently as part of a more positive life choice to support your trauma healing process. Start with one aspect that feels manageable to you. Make a note of this in your journal. Be specific about what you will try do differently. Set yourself a realistic time frame for this and define what exactly you need to do to achieve this.

For example:

> 'Over the next month I would like to start the day with a glass of warm water with a slice of lemon, followed by a healthy cooked breakfast. To achieve this I will prepare and soak some grains the night before. I will need to allow 15 minutes more every morning for the preparation and cooking process of my breakfast. I commit to make space for this extra time and effort as it forms part of my life-affirming choices.'

Monitor the changes that you are planning to make using a simple diary chart in your journal. For example:

Day and date	Description of desired goal/s:	'Yes' if goal met & any observations you want to add, if not, state what happened
Monday, 28.11.	1. Start day with warm water and a slice of lemon 2. Healthy cooked breakfast	Yes – strange taste Forgot to soak the grains night before
Tuesday, 29.11.	1. As above 2. As above	Yes – still tasting strange Yes – delicious.
Wednesday, 30.11.	1. As above 2. As above	Yes – starting to get used to it Yes – felt far less hungry during the day.
Thursday, 01.12.	1. As above 2. As above	Yes – quite soothing today Yes – yummy. Less moody.

Spotlight 2: Physical health, exercise and fitness

It is important to take good care of your physical health whatever condition your body is in, regardless of whether it has been injured during the trauma or not. Chapter 14 already touched on helping you recover from the physical scars. This section provides you with some general guidelines and invites you to evaluate which aspects you might like to try out as part of your commitment to your trauma healing programme.

Guidelines in taking care of your physical health, exercise and fitness:

- Your health is very important! Seek treatment for any medical conditions that can cause or exacerbate your PTSD or psychological health. This includes obstructive sleep apnoea (OSA), which is caused by partial or total blockage of the airway during sleep and leads to regularly interrupted sleep. The symptoms of this are loud snoring, noisy and laboured breathing and repeated short periods where breathing is interrupted by gasping or snorting. This can increase the risk of developing other conditions, such as high blood pressure, stroke or heart attack. It can make you feel exhausted, sleepy, depressed and significantly affect the quality of your life. Other conditions to watch out for are thyroid problems, such as an over- or underactive thyroid, which can lead to depression, constipation, weight gain and tiredness. High levels of cholesterol can lead to symptoms of depression in some people, high blood pressure can result in micro bleeding in the brain, diabetes can be associated with memory problems and gum disease can increase the inflammation in the brain. If you suspect that any of these conditions might be a problem for you ask for a consultation with your GP or your dentist in the case of gum disease. If your trauma-related problems make it difficult for you to consult a doctor or seek medical help, you might need a trauma therapist first to enable you to work through these difficulties.

- Consider the side effects of prescribed medication that you may be taking. For example those from a group of medications that have anticholinergic properties, such as sleeping pills, antihistamines, ulcer medication, benzodiazepines, cardiovascular medication, gastrointestinal medication, antipsychotic medication, antivertigo medication, muscle relaxants and tricyclic antidepressants. These medications block the action of acetylcholine which is an important neurotransmitter in the brain and can have considerable adverse side effects. These can be especially disabling if several medications with these properties are taken for different conditions and in elderly people. You may consider consulting a mental health professional about replacing or substituting such medication or replacing this with non-pharmacological treatments.

- The focus on preventative healthcare in the UK is minimal and patients are encouraged to visit their GP only if their body is already suffering or they are ill. However, there is the possibility to check and optimise your health through the use of private medical care or complementary healthcare practitioners. If you seek advice from the latter, ensure you check their qualifications, registration with a recognised professional body and that they carry professional liability insurance. Personal recommendations are often helpful.

- While you will be responsible for paying for such consultations, consider this as an investment in your health and wellbeing. Even if you have to manage on a tight budget you may be able to allocate small amounts of money to this as part of your commitment to your healing process.

- You may also want to consider having regular massages or other types of complementary body treatments. The health benefits of these can be relieving aches and pain, improving muscle tone, stimulating circulation and bringing more oxygen and nutrients into the muscle, keeping your body tissue subtle, detoxifying and cleansing your cells, soothing depression and anxiety, improving sleep, boosting your immune system. Body treatments can help you ground and reclaim your connection to your feelings and sensations and counteract the sense of trauma-related shutdown, numbness and dissociation. For the latter it is important to work with a body therapist experienced in recognising the symptoms of trauma and dissociation.

- Regular, moderate, physical exercise has many health benefits including releasing stress, reducing blood pressure and the risk of cardio vascular problems, improved respiration, energy and vitality, maintaining a balanced metabolism, strengthening bones and muscles, relieving tension, stress and returning to a more restful state, increasing stamina, protection from injury, controlling weight and improving mental health.

- As part of your trauma recovery programme you are encouraged to set aside time to engage in regular, moderate physical exercise, if you are physically able to do so. For example, regular, low-impact aerobic activities can be helpful to distract or control the mind. These could include jogging, brisk walking, biking, circuit training, dancing, aerobics, skating, swimming, some racket games, workout with a hula hoop. You may also consider trying yoga, qi gong, Pilates, tai chi or other practices aimed at helping to increase your flexibility. These have the added benefits of increasing your core strength and protecting you from injury if practised gently and within your particular ability and pace. If you suffer from pain problems or severe physical limitations seek professional advice as to what exercises you may safely engage in.
- Choose an exercise programme suited to your needs and start small. Setting aside even 10 minutes a day and building up gradually is helpful. Build several short, regular periods of exercise into your day. If you are disabled consult a physiotherapist for guidance on physical exercises that could be helpful and enjoyable for you.
- Work within your pace and ability, try out different activities and select those you most enjoy and that

give you pleasure. Be patient and gentle with yourself and do not push yourself in harshly. Choose exercises that help reduce your stress levels rather than those that exert more stress on your body. Design your exercise and fitness building programme so that it becomes an enjoyable treat for you.

- Establish a healthy balance between periods of activity and engagement and periods of rest and sleep. Ensure that your sleep hygicnc is good so that your body can rest sufficiently. Regular exercise can help with this. You may also go back to Exercise 19 in Chapter 9, which helps you to monitor your sleep patterns and gives you advice on how to establish a healthy sleep pattern.

Once you have read the general guidelines above, assess your current level of physical health and your level of current fitness. Notice if there is anything that you might like to do differently as part of a more positive life choice to support your trauma healing process. Start with one aspect that feels manageable to you. Make a note of this in your journal. Be specific about what you will try do differently. Set yourself a realistic time frame for this and define what exactly you need to do to achieve this.

For example:

'I used to love dancing. I don't quite have the confidence to join a dance class at the moment, but I would like to try

dancing to some music for at least 10 minutes every day.
To achieve this I will select music I like, ensure that I will not
be disturbed by others in my family and spend at least 10
minutes dancing every day. The best time for me to do this is
mid-morning, as I am usually on my own.'

Monitor the changes that you are planning to make using a simple diary chart in your journal. For example:

Day and date	Description of desired goal/s:	'Yes' if goal met & any observations you want to add, if not, state what happened
Monday, 28.11.	1. Dance every day for 10 minutes to music I like	Yes – strange at first. Felt quite self-conscious even though nobody was in the house
Tuesday, 29.11.	1. As above	Yes – felt a bit more relaxed
Wednesday, 30.11.	1. As above	A friend called round and asked me to spend time with her instead. Couldn't do the dancing. Felt a bit annoyed as I was already missing my dancing
Thursday, 01.12.	1. As above	Yes – had fun today. Chuckled to myself as I thought the dancing is my little secret to feeling well and keeping fit

Spotlight 3: Leisure, hobbies and personal interests

When did you last go to the cinema, theatre, a concert, an interesting talk, a show, an exhibition, a sports performance or any similar leisure activity? Are such activities still a regular feature in your life or do they seem to have dwindled away or are even non-existent now? Do you have a hobby or interest that you regularly pursue? What keeps your creativity and mind active? Leisure activities, entertainment and hobbies that you enjoy form an important part of a balanced and fulfilled life. They keep you engaged in life and stimulate the release of endorphins allowing you to feel happy. They might also introduce new meaning to your life and encourage your personal development. If your current life is lacking of such activities this section encourages you to claim back leisure activities, hobbies and personal interests into your life.

EXERCISE 38: RECLAIMING LEISURE, HOBBIES AND PERSONAL INTERESTS

Find a place in your home where you can be undisturbed for at least 30 minutes and sit down with your journal.

Now think back to at least five years before the experience of your trauma or to a time when you still enjoyed some leisure activities. Transport yourself back to that time in your inner mind.

1. Remind yourself what activities gave you most pleasure then. Remember what made you laugh or happy. What caught your interest and kept you engaged? Were these solitary activities or did they involve other people? What type of hobbies did you have? Did they evolve around a common theme or were they all different?

2. What type of entertainment engaged you most? Did you go out and attend certain places for this or did you engage in this at home or with friends? What were you good at? Did you have any skills that others appreciated about you and that you enjoyed applying? If someone else who knew you well at that time would describe you what would they have noticed about you?

3. Were you an initiator or did you need others to inspire you? Did you make things for others or more for yourself? What were your real strengths? Write down as many characteristics about yourself and your leisure activities and entertainment interests as you can in your journal, noticing especially those that made you feel great and really caught your interest.

4. Now reflect on your current life for comparison. How many of those leisure activities and hobbies are still active in your current life? Make a note of those which are. Is there a discrepancy between those you were engaged in previously and those now active in your life.

5. If so, analyse why there is a difference and how big the gap is between things you are engaged in in your current life and your life then. Is it because those activities would no longer interest you now? If so, have you replaced them with other leisure activities and hobbies in your current life?

6. If not, what other reasons are there for this gap in this area in your current life? Notice if those reasons are genuinely valid or if they might be part of a trauma-driven avoidance or opting out of life? Record your observations in your journal and allow yourself to be as honest as possible with yourself. Give yourself a rating for your level of overall satisfaction with regards to the leisure or entertainment aspects in your life. (10 would be totally fulfilled and happy and 0 would be not at all happy). Record your current rating with the date of today in your journal.

7. Now devise a list of those leisure activities that might still capture your interest even if you can't feel this right now. Write down potential leisure activities, hobbies or personal interests that you might like to pursue. This could include activities that you have never tried but might like to try out. Allow yourself to be as curious and explorative towards new hobbies or areas of personal interests as you can. Step out of your box. Give yourself permission for creating new, life-affirming choices that carry meaning for you.

8. Then choose one leisure activity, hobby or personal interest choice from your list that you would like to try out or reintroduce into your life first. Devise a realistic plan of how you could start to introduce this into your life. Start small and then build up. The aim is to enjoy without pressure rather than being overly ambitious.

9. Monitor how this new activity or hobby feels to you. Even if at first you feel little benefit, persevere with it for some time and assess what you might like to improve to gain more pleasure from it. Monitor your ratings of your level of satisfaction with regards to this new aspect in your life on a regular basis. (10 means to be totally fulfilled and happy and 0 is not at all happy). Record the ratings with the date you took them in your journal. Use these for guidance of how it is and how it could be improved so that you become more fulfilled and engaged in life again.

10. Once a new leisure activity, hobby or personal interest is integrated into your life, you could explore if there is space for another activity on your list. These may not take place every week, but create yourself as fulfilling and engaging a life as possible without exerting unnecessary stress. The aim is for you to enjoy!

Spotlight 4: Friendships and your relationships with others

Good friends are important as they connect us to a sense of belonging, companionship and safety. They can also be a very helpful mirror to us in times when we are uncertain about ourselves or struggling with life. A healthy friendship is about mutual valuing, exchange and support throughout all times in life, challenging as well as settled and peaceful moments. The effects of trauma and PTSD can be challenging to friendships and other relationships in your life and for many people this is a time that reveals who their genuine friends are.

The example of Antonia in chapter 14 highlighted that trauma and the effects of it frequently bring life-altering changes. People who you previously regarded as your friends may not be able to handle your situation and distance themselves, and other people who you had not even considered part of your friendship circle may move closer into your life. Your circumstances might have changed to such an extent that previous friends no longer find a place in your life or you may find that there is very little now that you still have in common. Trauma can be a 'wake-up' call for many people and your values and priorities may change and you may no longer be able to relate to aspects that you regarded as important in your life in the past. Depending on your particular circumstances, the trauma and its effects may have demanded radical changes in your life and this may have called into question your friendships and relationships to others.

This section helps you shine a spotlight on your friendships and relationships with others and provides you with an opportunity to define what is important for you now and which friendships or future friendships might form part of your healthy and positive life choices.

EXERCISE 39: REFLECTING ON YOUR FRIENDSHIPS AND RELATIONSHIPS WITH OTHERS

Find a place in your home where you can be undisturbed for at least 30 minutes and sit down with your journal.

1. Make a list of all the people in your life who you consider your friends or have a closer relationship with. Distinguish between those relationships that already were part of your life before the trauma and those that have developed since.

2. Consider first the friendships that were already part of your life before the trauma. Go through each one of these and notice the qualities of each of those friendships. What are the positive aspects of those friendships for you? What do you appreciate most in those friendships?

3. Notice if any of these friendships have changed as a result of the trauma and its effects on you? How have they changed? Consider if you have

---

changed also and how? Reflect for each of these friendships how it is for them to have you as their friend? Do you nurture and value those friendships? Do you feel nurtured and valued by your friends? Do your share a mutual understanding of each other or have you drifted apart? Do you feel invigorated and positive about your exchanges? Can you be honest and open about your feelings in these friendships? Are your friends honest and open with you? Are there any friendships which are no longer helpful or supportive to you now?

4. Now consider those friendships, if any, that have formed since the trauma. Are these different compared to your friendships before the trauma? What do you have in common and share in these friends? What do you value most about these?

5. Evaluate which friendships you feel most at ease with. Notice what it is that makes you feel this way. Is there anything else that you could bring into these friendships to improve them?

6. If you have noticed that you have no or very few friends, what could you change to attract more friends? Write down what is important for you in a friendship. Also, become aware of what you could contribute to a friendship. Make a plan of what you could do to bring more friends

into your life. Are there any friends from the past that you have neglected that you might like to be in touch with again? Could you combine your leisure activity plans in Exercise 38 with inviting new friends into your life?

Spotlight 5: Your life–work balance

You may now not be working at all as a consequence of the trauma. Equally you may be working far too much and be hiding yourself behind your work and spend too little time alone with yourself or others that might be important to you. Your happiness, wellbeing and overall satisfaction with life will depend on how well balanced your life choices are.

This section and Exercise 40 enable you to examine the balance between your personal life and your work and provide you with the opportunity to evaluate which changes you might like to make.

EXERCISE 40: REFLECTING ON YOUR LIFE-WORK BALANCE

Find a place in your home where you can be undisturbed for at least 30 minutes and sit down with your journal.

Allow yourself to reflect on your current life as objectively and honestly as you can. Imagine that this is not your life but someone else's you are observing. It is your task to ensure that this person lives a well-balanced life as fully as they can. Imagine you are their 'happiness' consultant (except that this is of course your life).

1. For a moment just reflect on this person's (your) life? What stands out most? Do you feel that this person is fulfilled in their life–work balance? If yes, then great. Consider if there is anything else they could change to make their life even more fulfilled.

2. If no, write down all the obstacles that you observe to their (your) life being in a good balance. Be as thorough as you can and don't let practical considerations (such as needing to work for the money) get in the way of you noting down the obstacles.

3. Now that you have recorded the obstacles, determine how this person's (your) life would need to change in order for them to feel happier and more balanced? What currently are the biggest obstacles that are standing in the way of these changes?

4. Imagine that it is a matter of utmost urgency (i.e. if their balance did not improve this person

would get very ill) that their life–work balance improves. What advice as their 'happiness' consultant would you give? What would need to shift first? How could this be achieved?

5. Work out a plan of the changes that would need to be made first and how long this would realistically take. Write this down. Be specific about the steps that are involved to bring about these changes. Then set a review date by when you would have to come back to re-evaluate this person's (your) life-work balance and determine what further changes might be required using the same process at that later stage.

6. Now look at this plan again and imagine this had been worked out by a lifestyle consultant to whom you paid a lot of money for this job. You might now choose to implement these changes as part of your decision to opt for positive life choices.

Summary checkpoints:

- The final stage of healing from the effects of your trauma is to reclaim control of your life. This chapter shines a spotlight on five important areas of your life:
  - Diet, nutrition and eating habits
  - Physical health, exercise and fitness
  - Leisure, hobbies and personal interests
  - Friendships and your relationship with others
  - Your life–work balance
- You are invited to evaluate to what extent you are content with and how much in control you feel in each of these areas of your life.
- You are encouraged to identify areas or habits that do not benefit your healing process, are not healthy for you and do not serve you well now.
- You can now explore what you might try to do differently to bring about more positive choices in any one or all of these particular areas of your life.
- Congratulations, you have now reached a stage in your healing process that allows you to focus on reclaiming your life!

16

Healing, letting go and moving on

'You say that you cannot bear the pain.
But you have already borne the pain. What you
have not done is seen all that you are beyond the
pain.'

Rumi

Recovery can be a lengthy process. People vary, both in their reactions to traumatic events and in the amounts of time they need for different stages of the healing process. By the time you come to this chapter, you might feel that your healing is already well on its way. Equally, you may feel that it has just begun and though you are moving along the path towards recovery there is still a long way to go.

The human spirit can find new strength in the aftermath of terrible events and rather than being broken by this you may find that it served as a 'wake-up' call for you to define what really is important in your life now. It is possible despite injury, despite losses, despite terrible tragedy to rise out of this. You may even build a completely different, far more positive and meaningful life than you have ever led before. You may become more conscious of what it truly means to be alive and each day may become more precious and valuable to you.

Transcending trauma requires that you give yourself adequate time for healing and an important and necessary period of mourning, trauma processing and genuine enquiry and truthful connection to yourself. Society currently emphasises fast cures and regards them as the most effective. In order for you to be able to heal adequately, it is important that you distance yourself from this and allow yourself to take the necessary time, whatever this is for you, to heal. You and only you can know when you are healed. Be patient with yourself and give yourself the time and space that you truly need for this.

Chapter 15 gave you some pointers towards helping you change and organise your life in a way that truly serves your healing process and that reflects your authentic needs. The healing of trauma requires most people to look deep. Deeper than they may have ever remembered looking at themselves or their lives before. Although this can be somewhat daunting and may not feel as if it fits into the fast-paced, sometimes rather superficial society we are living in, now it may be just what you need in order to heal and move on. It is important to allow whatever rises up in you as a result of the trauma. Use journaling to note it. The more you resist, deny or fight what comes up, the stronger it is going to get. Whatever rises up in you, however uncomfortable, it rises up for you to look at it, to experience it and then to process and integrate it.

This is a truly challenging path and it requires your courage. At the same time it requires compassion and patience with yourself. You may have to do this very slowly and gently because of the levels of dissociation you experience. You may not be able to go on this journey on your own but require the help of a specialist trauma therapist. Allow yourself to create for yourself whatever you need. Don't give up easily, trust to find for yourself what and who you need to help you with this process. Above all be true to yourself and your needs.

Whether you are ready now or many months from now, you can begin to think about a future for yourself and start to visualise where you would like to be, when you have integrated your traumatic experience and moved beyond it.

Visualising the future

Visualisation is a very powerful tool in the healing process. There are many stories from the medical community about people who have greatly enhanced their recovery or far exceeded anyone's expectation for their health by *visualising* themselves getting better. This is not meant to be a substitute for following sound medical advice or a bypass of the trauma processing work but an additional tool. In the safety and privacy of your own imagination, you can create an image of how you would like things to be in your future. Use the exercise below to help you with this.

EXERCISE 41: VISUALISING YOUR FUTURE

Read through the instructions a few times to familiarise yourself with the steps before carrying out the visualisation exercise. It can be repeated as often as you wish and at different stages in your recovery. You can also audio-record the instructions or have someone read them to you, so that you don't have to keep looking at the page.

1. Settle back in a chair where you can sit comfortably, with your back supported or if this is difficult because of physical disabilities adjust this to your needs. Ensure that you are undisturbed and in a place that feels safe to you. Allow yourself to begin to relax slightly. Take a few deep breaths. With each breath, exhale fully and bring the next breath in more deeply, into your diaphragm. Feel your belly pushing OUT as you breathe in fully and pulling IN as you exhale completely. Listen to your breathing. Let distracting thoughts or sounds around you just pass by – you don't have to attend to them for a moment. Close your eyes now and let any excess tension begin to drain away – from the top of your forehead down past your neck and shoulders, down your arms and hands and OUT through your fingertips. Let any excess tension

in the lower part of your body drain away now, down your tummy and thighs, past your calves and ankles, and OUT through your toes. Enjoy the feeling of being calm and relaxed.

2. Now, begin to see yourself as you would like to be in the future as you have completed more of your healing. Imagine that you are surrounded by a golden–blue light, which signifies the state of your wellbeing. Look around you. What kind of place are you in? Really feel into this image. What are you doing? What colours can you see around you? Notice what it feels like being in this setting. Are there sounds? Are the sounds clear? Soft? How are you feeling? See and sense yourself with a new self-respect and a new understanding of yourself. You are accepting yourself more fully than ever before . . . knowing that you are vulnerable as a human being and yet discovering the courage and strength you didn't know you had. Enjoy this feeling of arrival. Feel at peace with yourself. Stay with this feeling for a while.

3. The person you are meeting in your image is the progression of the person you are now. Ask the person in your image if he/she has a message to give to you now that may encourage and help you with your healing journey. Thank the person in your image for giving you this

message and for showing him/herself to you. Stay in this image as long as you like. When you are ready to leave, orient yourself back to the room you are in and know that you have the strength to move forward in your life.

This visualisation technique may be repeated as often as you wish. It is intended to bring you a sense of calm and comfort during your journey to recovery and give you a sense that there is a future.

Anniversary dates

Even for people who feel they are well on the way to overcoming their traumatic experiences or their losses, an upcoming 'anniversary' of the event can have an extremely unsettling effect. You may be taken by surprise, especially if you feel you have 'dealt with' your reactions. You may not expect to find yourself suddenly depressed or agitated again, unable to concentrate or even beginning to have dreams or flashbacks once more. The researcher Bessel van der Kolk[1] explained this succinctly, saying, 'the body keeps the score'. In other words, our subconscious memory systems mark the time and, when it gets close to the anniversary date, presents us with a series of reminders.

If some of your post-trauma reactions have returned with intensity around an anniversary time, this does not signify that you are 'not dealing' with your trauma. It should *not* be viewed as a backward step in your healing. It is important that you do not resist it or hold negative thoughts against yourself for feeling this way. Instead, try to look at anniversary reactions as one more natural step in your recovery. Once you have a framework for understanding what is happening to you, your reactions become more predictable and you can begin to feel more in control and even embracing of them.

The two weeks or so leading up to an anniversary date are likely to be the most difficult period, in terms of the return of traumatic reactions. Your anxiety level may rise, as the date comes closer and associated feelings are recalled. Once the trauma anniversary has passed, you will probably notice a dramatic reduction in symptoms. Although you may have been very upset and agitated, it probably won't take you long this time to feel your normal self again.

Anniversary reactions can also happen at other important marker dates, such as birthdays of lost loved ones or special celebrations, such as Christmas, Pesach, Rosh Hashana, Hanukkha, Eid al-Fitr, Eid al-Adha, Diwali or others.

Anniversary reactions can be managed, to reduce their impact. It is a good idea to plan some sort of symbolic ritual that will be personally meaningful to you, to help you mark the occasion. This could be as simple as lighting a candle at a particular time of day, or taking a moment of silence (alone or with others), making a donation (of money or of your volunteer time) to a particular cause, attending a service that is meaningful to you, planting a tree or a special plant, taking a walk in the park, requesting that a special piece of music be played on a radio programme, etc. The point is that you choose an action, no matter how small, that allows you to acknowledge what has happened and pay tribute to the person or thing that has been lost. In this way, too, you honour yourself for having come this far in your life, in spite of the trauma.

Native American Indians used a form of a 'blessing ritual' for such occasions, described in the book, *Good Grief Rituals*[2]. This ritual consisted of gathering a candle, a bowl of water and some white sage, the herb that is traditionally associated with wisdom. At the time or in the place you have chosen to mark the anniversary (this might be outdoors or indoors) you light the candle, dip your fingers in the water and touch your forehead, saying, 'Bless my forehead, that I may understand fully'. Next you dip your fingers in the water and touch your eyes, saying 'Bless my eyes, that I may see clearly', then you touch your lips with the water, saying 'Bless my lips, that I may speak the truth', then you dip your fingers in the water and touch your heart, saying 'Bless my heart, that I may carry strength and courage'. Now the sage is crushed between your fingers, and you inhale its pungent smell, then you wash your fingers in the bowl of water. The water is poured away, while you pause and reflect for a moment, and then the candle is blown out.

Your healing experience is unique to you!

It can take time to recover from a traumatic experience and it is important that you trust in your journey. Recovery means that you have been able to integrate your traumatic experiences into your everyday life and although the memory of them has not gone, you are able to think about your experiences without dissociating from them, feeling overwhelmed and out of control. The length of time it takes you to reach this stage will be particular to you. Every person differs in their own experience of a trauma, even if all the people at the time of the event were in exactly the same position. Likewise, each person's path to recovery is unique. However long it takes you, the most important point is that you allow yourself to recover in your own time and don't feel pushed by the expectations or advice of others.

Seeking professional help to support your healing process

Despite all your efforts, there may be times when you feel you are 'stuck' and you just can't seem to move beyond the trauma on your own (look back to the Energy Distribution Diagram in Chapter 5, page 134). This is an indicator that you probably would benefit from professional help. It is not a sign of weakness, and in fact this recognition that you might need help is a sign of your own personal strength. It indicates that you are able to take personal responsibility for your recovery and that you recognise your own limits and boundaries.

Chapter 17 of this book in the Addendum – Useful guidance gives you advice on how to seek professional help and introduces you to different forms of therapy that have been found to be effective in helping people recover from trauma. When you seek professional help it is most important that you find yourself a therapist who really understands trauma and who is properly qualified and registered with a professional body.

Whatever type of therapy or therapist you decide on, you might find it very helpful to use some of the exercises or suggestions in this book *with* your therapist during your recovery process.

Marking the journey you have made

Lastly, whether you have travelled your path of recovery on your own or with friends or a partner or with the help of a professional, the final stage is to mark the journey that you have made in a personally meaningful way.

Expressing your story through some artistic means can be a powerful healing tool. Even though you may have never done anything 'artistic' in your life, and are convinced that you have no creative talent, this exercise can still be valuable. Many trauma survivors have found that writing or creating something to represent their experiences symbolically was a vital step in their recovery.

Compiling a scrapbook of clippings and photos, finger-painting, wood-carving, drawing a series of sketches, making a sculpture out of clay, painting in crayon, acrylic, watercolour or oil, writing a short story, composing a poem, making an audio- or videotape, are all creative ways of telling your story. But they are by no means the only ways to do this – even painting a sign is an artistic task, if the intention is to help you in your healing.

Here are a few suggestions to get you started:

1. *The 'breathing line'*

When you start to explore methods of creative expression, it is best not to be too concerned about the finished product.

Just pay attention to what your senses tell you to do. The book *Managing Traumatic Stress Through Art*[3] suggests that, as a start, you pick up a pencil and draw a line to represent your breathing. Your line(s) might be short or long (quick breaths or deep breaths), curved or straight, flowing or broken.

Use the **Relaxed Breathing Technique** introduced in Exercise 20 in Chapter 9 to help you attend to your breathing. As the rate of your breathing becomes slow and relaxed, you may wish to draw it with your eyes closed. Imagine that with each breath of air you breathe new life, healing, nourishment and regeneration into every single cell of your body. By producing a simple line drawing, you are showing, on paper, how you have mastered your traumatic stress reactions through control of your breathing.

2. 'Imprint of fear'

Another exercise suggested is called the **Imprint of Fear**[3]. Select or mix several strong paint colours to represent your fear. Combine the colours you have chosen to form an abstract painting of the feelings of fear you experienced, both during and after your trauma. In a variation of this exercise, you could use the bold colours of fingerpaints to make handprints, which you place on top of each other, in different positions.

3. Collage

The collage method has been used successfully by Falklands War veterans who received post-traumatic stress therapy at the Royal Naval Psychiatric Hospital in Haslar. A collage can be made by pasting together clippings, photos, magazine cuttings/pictures or other substances, like cloth, sand, dried flowers, etc. on a hard surface such as cardboard or poster board so that the result depicts your traumatic experience. A collection of the collages produced by military personnel treated at the Haslar hospital was exhibited some years ago by the Manchester Art Gallery. The images and emotional struggles depicted in these collages were vivid and powerful. Whatever your artistic inclinations, you *can* cut and paste and use colour and texture to create a collage that depicts your journey out of trauma.

Try not to put off this task. It will help you express in a complete and genuine way the impact of the trauma on your life. Let it be a final healing task that allows you to make sense of things so that you can put them to one side and move on. Or, if you choose, it could become a more public expression that you might share with family or friends or significant others. It is a unique way to tell others what it is like to live through chaos and put yourself together again. It symbolises the completion of your journey.

'To a mind that is still, the entire universe surrenders.'

Zhuangzi

A Final Note

Congratulations! By the time you read this page you may be well on the road to recovery. You might have come quite a long way already, with the path ahead of you now visible again for you to reclaim your life. Equally, you might feel that you have only just begun to make the first tentative steps in the direction of recovery, and you might still be considering if you can find the courage and strength within yourself to make this journey.

Wherever you currently are on your journey, you are encouraged to try and keep moving along at your own pace. Finding the courage and strength in yourself to believe that you can do this and to give yourself another chance of life. A new life!

There is no doubt that this might be a challenging journey for you. You are encouraged to persevere and get the help and support you may need with this. I wish you well and trust that making a commitment to your journey of healing and inner growth can positively transform the effects of your trauma.

C. Herbert

PART THREE

ADDENDUM – USEFUL GUIDANCE

17

Seeking professional help

You may have realised while reading Chapter 2 and the rest of this book that there are many different reactions that people can experience in response to trauma. You may have noticed also that these can be quite diverse and it can be confusing that there are so many. It may have been quite difficult for you to read about all these possible reactions, especially if you are suffering from the effects of your trauma and your concentration is poor (which can be part of these reactions). You may have recognised some of these reactions in yourself, but may not have been able to relate to others. This is perfectly normal and most people wouldn't experience the whole range of reactions described. If you have been able to relate to some of these reactions, you may now be wondering what to do about them and whether you might need professional help. This chapter will introduce you to the possibility of seeking professional help and will help you consider some of the options available to you.

When should you seek professional help?

Most people will have some adverse reactions following a traumatic life event, but not every person needs professional help. Although these initial symptoms might be uncomfortable for you they can be helpful because they remind you of the experience so that you can understand, make sense of and adjust to it. For most people their initial reactions will fade and with appropriate support from their partner, family or friends they will be able to work through their traumatic experience and recover from their symptoms within about four weeks. This is usually the case if your initial symptoms were relatively mild; you know that although the trauma was horrific it was just a one-off event and you are safe again now; you have got a good support network of family, friends or work colleagues and there are no longer-term consequences arising for you from the trauma now. If this is the case for you, you probably don't need professional help. You might like to work through some of the sections in this book on managing traumatic stress that are relevant to you to help you make a full recovery.

You are likely to have made a recovery when you can talk and think about your traumatic experience without getting overly distressed; when it no longer intrudes into your mind at unwanted times; and when you feel safe and no longer under constant threat.

If your initial reactions to a trauma were quite mild and they don't shift or seem to be getting stronger, or if they were quite strong and you don't seem to be able to shake them off very easily, or they get worse you are advised to consider seeking professional help. You might also try some of the management strategies in this book to find out if these can assist you in reducing your distress. This book could be helpful but is not intended as a replacement for specialist professional help where it might be needed.

Some people don't have any reactions at all or only very mild ones after a traumatic event, and only several weeks, months or even years later start to develop uncomfortable reactions to their traumatic event. This usually happens in response to a particular trigger event that connected them to the unprocessed memories of a trauma. The trigger event in itself could be quite benign. If this applies to you the strength of your reactions might feel quite overwhelming and puzzling to you especially if you didn't know that they could be related to a trauma you experienced some time ago. Some of the management strategies in this book could be helpful for you, but if your symptoms are quite strong or don't seem to reduce easily you are advised to seek professional help.

If a recent trauma re-triggered memories of underlying developmental or childhood trauma that you haven't come to terms with yet, or if your recent trauma was very severe, involved crime, violence and intentional harm, or went on over a long period of time, it is likely that you have experienced complex trauma. This could also apply if you have experienced multiple, separate traumatic events in your life. In all of these instances you are advised to seek professional help. If you suffer from significant symptoms of dissociation

463

or are at risk of harming yourself or others you should seek professional help as soon as possible. Try and keep yourself and others safe. In all these instances this book might inform and give you some guidance but it is unlikely to be enough to help you recover from your traumatic experiences.

What is the benefit of seeking help?

There are two potential benefits to seeking help. The first is to find out more accurately the extent to which you may have been affected by a traumatic event and what trauma- or stressor-related condition you might be suffering from. The second benefit is to receive appropriate help for your specific problems.

You can seek appropriate help from either the National Health Service (NHS – UK only) or another public sector service (if your country has one); a private insurance scheme; the legal system (if you are entitled to compensation for the damages you suffered); or by finding yourself a registered private trauma psychotherapist who is experienced in this area.

Often, the best starting point is to visit your medical practitioner, who should be able to advise you on the services that are available in your local area. In England the Department of Health sponsors NICE (National Institute for Health and Care Excellence, 2013) to provide guidance and support to healthcare providers in the NHS, public sector and social care to help improve outcomes for users of their services in England. If you are reading this book in other parts of the UK or different English-speaking countries this may not apply. NICE guidelines state that you should visit your medical practitioner (in the UK, your GP) if you are still experiencing problems about four weeks after the traumatic event or if your symptoms are particularly troublesome. Your medical practitioner then is advised to refer you to mental health specialists for further assessment and treatment. In some areas of the UK you can also directly access NHS services and ask to be assessed. Depending on your locality access to this may vary and waiting times for an assessment also.

You should be referred to a mental health specialist who has sufficient training and experience in the assessment of trauma- or stress-related problems. You may be diagnosed with a number of possible conditions, including Post-Traumatic Stress Disorder.

What is Post-Traumatic Stress Disorder (PTSD)?

You may have been told by your medical practitioner, a psychiatrist, clinical psychologist or other mental healthcare professional, that you are suffering from Post-Traumatic Stress Disorder, or PTSD for short. Many people also suspect that this is what they might be suffering from through their searches on the internet.

PTSD is the term given to a particular range and combination of reactions following a trauma. It conveys to a healthcare professional which reactions you may be experiencing and how best to help you. If you continue to experience many or most of the responses described in Chapter 2 of this book for longer than a month, it is likely that your reactions will be classed as PTSD. This diagnosis will also depend on how many reactions you are experiencing in each of the four symptom clusters and how frequent, severe and disabling these are to you.

PTSD is not easy to self-diagnose because, as you probably noticed, there are rather a lot of diverse reactions that people can experience after trauma. It requires sufficient time, specialist training and experience in conducting trauma assessments and the right assessment environment and conditions to diagnose PTSD properly[1].

Medical practitioners usually have a very busy schedule and might not be able to give you the time nor have the expertise to assess your condition properly. Unfortunately, some of the trauma–related reactions that you might report mirror symptoms that might also fit into other mental health problems, such as depression or anxiety. Therefore if a medical practitioner or other mental health professional who you consult for a diagnosis has not got the time or expertise to properly check all your possible reactions you could be misdiagnosed. It is not uncommon for people to be given a diagnosis of depression or anxiety disorder when in actual fact they are suffering from PTSD. This is concerning because depression or anxiety problems are often treated with medication as a first line of intervention, whereas there is evidence that this should not be the first treatment choice for PTSD.

If you are considering approaching your medical practitioner for help with an assessment after a traumatic event, you might like to prepare a list beforehand with those reactions that you have experienced since the trauma. At the end of this chapter there is a brief checklist of potential reactions that you could list and take along to your meeting. It might also help to better prepare you for your assessment meeting with a mental health specialist.

Other Trauma- or Stressor-Related Disorders

Although you are experiencing distressing reactions in relation to a traumatic life event, you may not suffer from PTSD. There are a number of other trauma or stressor-related disorders and a specially trained mental health professional should be able to assess the specific condition or conditions you may be suffering from. Some of these will be briefly outlined here.

Acute Stress Disorder (ASD) may be diagnosed if you seek help shortly after a traumatic event for a range of quite distressing reactions, similar to symptoms of PTSD, but in your case these have been present for less than a month. Acute Stress Disorder can develop into PTSD if those symptoms persist for longer than four weeks.

An **Adjustment Disorder** may be diagnosed when you develop a range of disturbing emotional and behavioural symptoms in response to a significant life stressor which would not be considered a trauma. This could be in response to a single event (such as redundancy, retirement, divorce or break-up of a relationship, the death of a loved one, etc.) or multiple or recurrent stressors (such as marked business difficulties, a continuous, persistent painful illness, failing to obtain occupational goals, etc.). This could be diagnosed if your symptoms occurred within three months of the onset of this stressor and lasted no longer than six months after the stressor or its consequences have terminated. If your symptoms have lasted longer than this your problems might be diagnosed as **Adjustment-like disorder with prolonged duration**.

Persistent Complex Bereavement Disorder might be diagnosed if you experience prolonged, severe, persistent grief and mourning reactions in response to a traumatic death. This could be diagnosed additionally to your PTSD or on its own.

Children and young people can also be affected by trauma. There are some specific conditions affecting young children who have experienced trauma. If your child has been affected by trauma a child trauma specialist should be able to help you with this.

Complex PTSD might be diagnosed if you have experienced repeated, enduring or prolonged trauma, such as for example, domestic violence, torture, hostage taking or situations of solitary confinement. It might also be diagnosed if there has been **Developmental Trauma**, such as birth complications or early life illness necessitating longer periods of separation from primary care givers, or if there has been childhood sexual, physical or consistent emotional abuse, affecting your ability to trust and safely attach to others. In this case you may never have felt any sense of safety in your life. You may not be able to remember much of your early life or a life without trauma.

As part of your PTSD or Complex PTSD you may be diagnosed with a **Dissociative Disorder, such as Dissociative Amnesia, Depersonalisation/Derealisation Disorder or Dissociative Identity Disorder (DID),** or another dissociative condition. Dissociative disorders are usually linked to unresolved trauma, but you may not be able to remember what the trauma was because it is stored in memory systems that are not consciously accessible to you at the moment. A mental health specialist in Complex Trauma should be able to explain to you in more detail what their assessment might mean in relation to your particular circumstances and what specialist help is available to you.

Whatever the effects have been on you as a result of trauma, the findings of the assessment should be explained to you by your mental health specialist. Once you know what these are the next step is to seek appropriate professional help. It can be quite overwhelming to go through such an assessment, especially if you find it difficult to concentrate and remember. It could be helpful for you to take a pen and paper and you can then write things down that your mental health specialist shares with you and to look at it again afterwards.

Finding the right type of therapy

At the end of your assessment process your mental health specialist should explain to you what the options are for receiving therapeutic help. As a general guideline the more severe, prolonged, repeated or early in life your trauma was the more impact it is likely to have had on you and the more specialist and in-depth your road towards recovery usually is. The field of trauma psychology is rapidly growing and there are now many new psychological treatments emerging for trauma-related problems and it can be confusing to decide on what might benefit you most.

If you are seeking help within the public health sector in England for PTSD following a trauma, NICE guidelines[2] recommend that you should be offered a course of trauma-focused psychological treatment as part of the National Health Service (NHS). If your post-traumatic symptoms or your PTSD is severe this should be made available to you in the first month after the traumatic event. If your symptoms are less severe you should also be offered a course of trauma-focused psychological treatment, although this may not be within the first month after your trauma. These treatments are provided on an outpatient basis and should be in a setting that feels calming and safe to you.

Currently, NICE (2013) recommends only two trauma-focused psychological treatments for PTSD. This is because NICE recommends treatments only if they have been subjected to randomised controlled trial (RCT) research, which is a very stringent form of evaluation. Trauma-focused cognitive behavioural therapy (TF–CBT[3,4]) or eye-movement desensitisation and reprocessing (EMDR[5,6]) are the two treatments that have both had those evaluations[7] and have thus been recognised by NICE as effective treatments of PTSD. TF–CBT and EMDR are also the only psychotherapies currently recommended by the World Health Organisation (WHO)[8] for children, adolescents and adults with PTSD. You should not be offered medication as a first line of treatment in preference to trauma-focused psychological therapy[2], but medical practitioners or psychiatrists are not always aware of these guidelines.

If your PTSD has resulted from a single event with no significant other underlying previous stressors in your life you should be offered a course of between eight and twelve sessions of either TF–CBT or EMDR[2]. These sessions should normally be at least 90 minutes long, especially while you are working through aspects of the traumatic event in order to help you feel safe doing so. You should be offered therapy regardless of the time elapsed since the trauma. Your therapy should take place regularly and continuously, usually once a week, and it should be provided by the same therapist throughout. It is very important that right from the start of your therapy you feel confident and safe with the setting and the therapist who has been allocated to you.

If you have suffered from multiple traumatic events, traumatic bereavement, chronic disability resulting from the trauma or you are experiencing additional mental health conditions or have suffered also from developmental trauma, you will require more long-term trauma-focused psychological treatment[9] and this should be embedded into an overall care plan that is specially designed, taking account of your individual circumstances. You should be offered a therapist who is skilled in working with more complex trauma and PTSD and it may be important to check this before you embark on treatment.

If you have not been diagnosed with PTSD following your initial assessment but with any of the other trauma- or stressor-related disorders described above, and you are significantly affected by your symptoms, you should still be offered psychological therapy tailored to your specific condition. Your mental healthcare specialist should be able to explain what therapeutic help can be offered to you.

Although you should be entitled to timely trauma-focused psychological therapy according to the guidelines following a diagnosis, in reality this may not be so easy to access. It will depend on the way in which the treatment services within your area are organised and set up. Many public services only offer limited therapy sessions and sometimes they can have very long waiting lists. If you feel that a long waiting time would be very difficult for you to manage, you should discuss this with your mental health specialist and also your medical practitioner. If your medical practitioner is supportive and knowledgeable about PTSD and trauma-related problems it can be a great help. There may be a priority treatment service for certain difficulties or they may be able to suggest other alternatives for you while you are waiting. You might also find it helpful to work through this book while you are waiting for your therapy.

Finding the right professional help

It is very important that you find the right professional help in order to avoid complications and a potential deterioration in your condition. If you can afford to pay for yourself, have a private insurance plan or your legal compensation claim covers it, you could see a private therapist. Most medical practitioners can recommend therapists, such as clinical psychologists, psychotherapists, psychiatrists, clinical nurse specialists, community mental health nurses or others, offering private therapy in your area. It is extremely important that you seek help only from a professional who has appropriate experience in the area of traumatic stress reactions and PTSD. If this is your chosen route it is important that you ensure that your therapist is properly qualified, professionally insured and registered with one of the recognised professional bodies regulating therapy. Even if you find that your medical practitioner isn't very supportive or doesn't seem to understand, don't give up! Try a different one until you find one you're comfortable with and who can support you with this.

There are so many types of therapy available, it can be very confusing to decide on what might benefit you most. Certain forms of therapy have been found to be very effective in helping people recover from trauma. You might like to see a therapist who is trained in either trauma-focused cognitive behavioural therapy (TF-CBT) or eye movement desensitisation and reprocessing (EMDR) or both. However, it is important that you find yourself a professional who really understands trauma and who you feel comfortable working with. Depending on your type of trauma you may not feel safe with certain therapists because they may re-trigger aspects of your experience. For example, if you have been sexually assaulted and your abuser was male, you may not feel safe working with a male therapist.

When you have experienced trauma that has utterly shattered your trust it can take significant time to build a relationship that feels safe and secure with your therapist. Your therapist may also need to help you feel more stabilised before any work on your actual traumatic experiences can start and depending on your circumstances this could take a significant amount of time, sometimes requiring several months of therapy. This is why it is important for you to work with a therapist who has experience in working with more complex trauma. There are several new forms of trauma therapy emerging that are being increasingly evaluated and you may explore which type of therapy seems most suitable for your particular trauma. You may have to do some research yourself or talk to different therapists, asking them to explain how they work with trauma.

Therapists should be able to tell you about their training and experience with more complex trauma-related conditions. Although this can seem a bit overwhelming at first, it is very important that you ask for as much information as possible. Don't just accept things at face value. It is perfectly acceptable to ask professionals about their experience and qualifications. If they are properly registered and qualified they will be more than happy to show you their relevant certificates. If you don't feel comfortable with a therapist, trust your own feelings! You won't progress with your process of recovery if you feel that you can't have an honest, open and trustworthy relationship with your therapist.

If you are in doubt or the work doesn't feel safe to you, it is important for you to address this. Your therapist should take your concerns seriously and explore what might need to be changed to make therapy feel safer for you. If the issues cannot be resolved you are entitled to seek a second opinion or find a different therapist.

Finding the right trauma therapist for you can take some time and also be quite confusing. Registers of approved and qualified mental healthcare professionals should be available in most countries. It is important that you ensure that your therapist is registered with their appropriate professional body. In the UK for all practising Chartered Clinical Psychologists or Chartered Counselling Psychologists the Health and Care Professions Council (HCPC) keeps a register. These professionals would have had to have been approved by the British Psychological Society (BPS). The United Kingdom Council for Psychotherapies (UKCP) keeps a register of psychotherapists, and the British Association for Counselling and Psychotherapy (BACP) for counsellors and psychotherapists. Psychiatrists are registered with the Royal College of Psychiatrists and mental health nurses (called psychiatric nurses in some countries) have to be registered with the Nursing and Midwifery Council. If you are looking for a Cognitive Behavioural Psychotherapist (CBT) you could find one on the register of the British

Association for Behavioural and Cognitive Psychotherapy (BABCP). If you are looking for an EMDR therapist you can find one on the register of the EMDR Association for the UK and Ireland, EMDR Europe or EMDRIA. It is important for you to know that not every CBT practitioner or every EMDR psychotherapist is experienced in working with trauma and PTSD. You might have to search around until you find a therapist who has the particular qualifications and experience you need. It is worth the search because it is very important that you work with a person who you feel confident in.

There is growing awareness of the close interlinkages between mind and body in trauma[9, 10]. This has grown out of our increased understanding of the neurobiology underlying trauma due to more sophisticated screening technology used in research, such as MRIs (Magnetic Resonance Imaging) or CTs (Computed Tomography). EMDR[5,6] can be considered a body-oriented therapy. There are other body-oriented approaches that you might want to consider in conjunction with your trauma-focused psychological therapy. Most of these require further research before they can be regarded as scientifically proven, but preliminary studies seem promising[11]. Some of these approaches may not be sufficient as a standalone trauma treatment but may be helpful combined or in addition. Your chosen trauma therapist may already additionally be trained in a body-oriented approach and combine this, or may recommend that you seek out another practitioner who can support you alongside your psychological healing process. In some countries psychotherapists are not allowed to use therapeutic touch with their clients and if this is the case you would always have to find a separate body therapist.

Body-oriented approaches include Mindfulness-based therapy[12]; Compassion-focused trauma therapy[13]; Mind–Body Interventions[14], for example Sensorimotor Psychotherapy (SP[15]), Somatic Experiencing[16,17], Trauma Resiliency Model (TRM[18]), Comprehensive Resource Model[19]; Acupoint Tapping[20], such as Emotional Freedom Technique (EFT), Thought Field Therapy (TFT); Havening Techniques[21]; Pesso Boyden System Psychomotor (PBSP) Therapy[22], Trauma-Sensitive Yoga[23,24]; Acupuncture[25]; Healing Touch[26]; Calatonia and Subtle Touch Techniques[27]; Rosen Method Bodywork[28,29]; Craniosacral Therapy[30]; Matrix-Rhythm Therapy[31] and various others. Working therapeutically with animals who have been trained to assist trauma sufferers, such as with horses in Equine-Facilitated Psychotherapy (EFP)[32,33], can also be a source of healing.

Depending on the type of trauma you have experienced you may not feel comfortable to be touched by another person. Not all body-oriented approaches use direct touch and for many you don't have to undress. It is of utmost importance that you feel safe and only try approaches that feel manageable to you. Again, be very careful to use a qualified, registered and reputable practitioner who has an understanding of working with trauma.

Here is what Anja experienced and how she eventually sought help after her trauma:

I had got caught up in the London bombings while I was on a work placement in the City on the morning of Thursday, 7 July 2005. I was extremely lucky to have just missed the tube train leaving Liverpool Street Station, although felt annoyed at the time as I thought I would now be late. I then saw smoke billowing out of the tunnel that the train had just entered seconds before. I felt confused, shocked and had no idea what had happened, but knew immediately that it must have been something bad. I was terrified and then got caught up in the turmoil of many other equally shocked and confused people trying to get out of the station. I wondered what had happened to the people on the train. It was extremely scary because nobody knew what was happening. The whole transport system had stopped, emergency services arrived, London was in chaos and when I eventually got back to my hotel, I watched the news over and over again and gradually the whole picture of what had happened emerged.

I thought that I should feel extremely lucky to have missed that train. There were no feelings of elation though. Instead I felt really frightened, gloomy and even guilty about surviving and walking away when others had been killed or were badly injured. I felt I should have stayed on and helped. I couldn't contemplate ever going back on the Tube again and making another trip to my work placement, which would have finished the next day anyway. I rang my employer and told him that I wanted to come back to my regular work in Oxfordshire and not complete the last day, given the circumstances. He was totally understanding and empathic.

I returned to my home in the countryside and went to my normal work on the Monday. Everybody was so pleased to see me and they all expressed that I had been very lucky to have missed that train.

I thought at first everything would go back to normal now, but I felt totally different from before. Something had really changed in me. I had lost all my former confidence, felt numb and shut down inside. At the same time I was overalert, irritable and really jumpy all the time. My sleep was disrupted, I had terrible nightmares of explosions and fire. I had watched too many of the images of the injured people on TV and knew that that could have been me or worse. These images and that of the smoke coming out of the tunnel didn't go out of my head. I felt drained, tired and gloomy all the time. I didn't tell people because I felt they would think I was silly because I had been one of the lucky ones.

Eventually, I went to my GP and told him. He didn't have much time for me and tried to encourage me by saying that I had been fortunate to have missed that train and should be grateful to be here. He prescribed me a tranquiliser saying that this should help me calm down a bit. My feelings went on for weeks and if anything they got worse. The tranquiliser made me feel drowsy and dizzy and I didn't like those feelings as they made me feel even less in control. Eventually my best friend confronted me. She had observed that I seemed different, but hadn't been wanting to say anything. Her mum was a psychologist and when I opened up and told her what went on in me, she thought that I might have been traumatised by what had happened. She offered to come with me to see my GP again. With her help we could explain to the GP how I was still affected and that I wanted some psychological help for my symptoms. He then referred me to an NHS-based psychology service where I was assessed by a clinical psychologist, who told me that I met diagnostic criteria for PTSD and put me on a waiting list for a course of trauma-focused cognitive behavioural therapy (TF-CBT). She told me that there would be a waiting time, which could be several months unfortunately.

Once I knew what my problems were and what help I needed I searched for a private trauma therapist, as I couldn't contemplate suffering all this time until I was seen. I found a private trauma specialist who offered me a combination of TF-CBT, EMDR and mindfulness-based therapy, which I found very helpful. I managed to fully recover from my PTSD over a course of twenty sessions that were two hours in length. The final stages of my therapy involved me going back to Liverpool Station in London. This was a very moving experience which touched me deeply. I re-learnt to negotiate the London Tube and transport system without fear and was able to go into the City again, even meeting the people I had worked with during my placement.

I experienced strong emotions during some parts of my therapy and although this was hard at the time, I am pleased that my therapist helped me feel safe enough to release those feelings. I feel that therapy helped me greatly not only with coming to terms with my trauma and making a full recovery from the PTSD, but in also enabling me to appreciate life in a *different way. I don't take things for granted so easily now. I feel stronger and happier in myself and life feels much more meaningful and worth living to me and I am very grateful for being here.*

Anja

It is not uncommon, as in Anja's example, for it to take time until you seek help for your problems and to secure the professional help you need. Whatever type of therapy or therapist you decide on, some of the exercises or suggestions in this book might be helpful to work on *with* your therapist during your recovery process. Whether you have full-blown PTSD or suffer from other trauma- or stressor-related conditions, the content of this book will be equally relevant to you. As a general rule, the sooner you start working through the effects of the trauma and the more you understand what is happening to you, the better equipped you will be to take control of your recovery and healing process.

Below is a checklist to monitor your trauma reactions. You could photocopy this and score your own responses in terms of how often you have experienced any of these reactions over the course of the past month. This might help you recognise if you are still affected by a trauma and whether it could be helpful for you to seek professional help. You could then show this to your medical practitioner or your mental health specialist when you have your assessment.

Checklist for stressor- or trauma-related reactions

TYPE OF REACTIONS	FREQUENCY		
Re-experiencing the event	Never	Sometimes	Often
Unwanted thoughts or images			
Dreams			
Flashbacks			
Intense emotional distress			
Reactions to reminders			
Avoidance reactions	Never	Sometimes	Often
Avoiding thoughts, feelings or conversation about the event			
Avoiding people, places or activities that retrigger event			
Changes in mood and thought	Never	Sometimes	Often
Difficulty remembering important aspects of the event			
Negative beliefs about yourself, others or the world			

Ruminations about the cause or consequence of the event			
Lingering feelings of low mood			
Loss of interest in activities			
Feeling distant and detached			
Inability to feel positive			
Hyperarousal reactions	**Never**	**Sometimes**	**Often**
Irritability or angry outbursts			
Reckless or self-destructive behaviour			
Feeling overalert and watchful			
Startle in response to sudden movement or noise			
Concentration problems			
Sleeping difficulties			

Important summary checkpoints:

- Trauma can cause a range of diverse reactions.
- Reactions can range from mild to severe.
- Many people recover from their trauma without long-term effects and without the need for professional help.
- If reactions after a traumatic event are particularly troublesome or are still present four weeks later it would be helpful to visit a medical practitioner.
- A medical practitioner can refer for a trauma assessment with a mental health specialist.
- The mental health specialist should share their findings and what help might be needed.
- For post-traumatic Stress Disorder (PTSD) or other stressor- or trauma-related problems a course of trauma-focused psychological therapy is recommended.
- In the case of prolonged, complex or multiple traumas the course of therapy will be longer and needs to be tailored to your specific needs.
- Therapy should be conducted by an accredited and experienced trauma therapist working in the public sector or privately.
- Currently only trauma-focused cognitive behaviour therapy (TF-CBT) and eye movement desensitisation and reprocessing (EMDR)

have been evaluated in randomised control trials (RCTs) as effective treatments for PTSD.

- Medication should not be the first line of treatment for PTSD or other trauma-related problems.
- The interplay between body and mind in trauma is increasingly recognised and researched. Body-oriented approaches for PTSD might be a helpful adjunct to TF–CBT.

18

Issues for professionals and carers: vicarious traumatisation

This chapter is written specifically for professionals and carers working with trauma, as they too are affected by it. If you have bought this book because you are a trauma survivor and not a carer, professional or trauma therapist, then this chapter may be of less interest to you. It may nevertheless give you some helpful background if you are looking for a trauma therapist or engaging a carer, as you might like to check that they are sufficiently supported and have the capacity to engage with you in an empathic, caring and yet professional manner.

The privilege of being a trauma therapist

Facilitating another person's journey out of suffering, pain and trauma into recovery, healing and positive growth is probably one of the most privileged jobs one can hold in this world. It is incredibly meaningful, rich and rewarding to be able to be of service to people who have been affected by trauma and to have the ability, skills and tools to help a person rebuild their shattered trust in life and move out of the perceived tunnel of darkness into discovery of renewed inner strength and healing.

The privilege of being a trauma therapist carries with it enormous responsibility. This may not always be highlighted enough in contemporary training courses or work settings for trauma therapists. Working with trauma sufferers requires therapists to confront and cope with some of life's deepest and darkest issues. Trauma work brings us face to face with experiences that are outside most people's range of experience as well as our own. Despite increasing media coverage of the most inhumane atrocities, it is different to sit face to face with a person who has been through some of these. We are frequently required to test our own fundamental beliefs about the world and bear witness to the incredible suffering that people can inflict on each other. Trauma not only changes the people who have experienced it, it can also change the professionals who are working with it. In order to be able to remain healthy in this field of work and to be of maximum benefit to clients, trauma therapists have a responsibility to embark on their own inner healing journey, requiring them to transform any of their own unprocessed trauma experiences and to commit to a life-long process of supervision, professional development and personal growth. This helps trauma therapists to develop an inner shield of resilience and strength so that clients can feel safe enough to disclose and share the hardest parts of their experiences and their deepest feelings without fearing that they are having to protect their therapists because they may not be strong enough to hear it.

It is very important for trauma therapists to stay present, engaged and connected (mindful) with their clients during the whole of the therapeutic process. This ability is compromised in trauma therapists who have not processed their own stressful life experiences, as these can be triggered by their clients' experiences and this can cause emotional overwhelm or dissociation in the therapist. Both of these reactions compromise their ability to stay mindfully engaged and connected with their clients. If therapists' own traumas or stressful life events are being suppressed and left unprocessed it increases the therapist's likelihood of early burnout[1]. If you are a trauma sufferer and a potential client reading this, it would of course not fall within your remit nor be helpful to the therapeutic process to check your therapist's life history. It would be perfectly legitimate for you to ask though if your therapist has ever undergone therapy to work through any life issues that have been distressing for them, without the need for any further disclosure. It is helpful to know that your therapist is taking care of their own needs, and one important indicator for you would be that you feel that your therapist is empathic and stays engaged with you during your therapy and you feel safe to share your experiences.

Working with trauma can be 'emotionally infectious'

Professionals and carers who work in this field have to be careful how they respond to ever-increasing demands on services with fewer and fewer staff support structures and resources in place, as these are frequently considered by management as adding unnecessary costs. In order to remain healthy, professionals and carers need to consider the impact that this type of work might have on them. It is a common pattern for professionals to place the least emphasis on their own care and nurturing, but in the long run this may be a false economy.

There might still be stigma attached to admitting that, as professionals, we can also be affected by our work and the impact of the trauma we are having to deal with. Yet working with trauma does mean being faced repeatedly with the darker side of life, bearing witness to horrific events and shouldering serious issues, often over long periods of time. It is unavoidable that professionals and carers are 'emotionally infected'[2] by this work and sadly this is often overlooked and not sufficiently acknowledged by managers of trauma services. Therefore, in order to be able to sustain such work and at the same time remain healthy, motivated and engaged, professionals and carers must learn to develop their own nurturing strategies and put in place appropriate support structures, supervision and back-up systems.

What is vicarious traumatisation and can we avoid it?

Working with survivors of trauma inevitably affects professionals and carers. Vicarious or secondary traumatisation[3] has been described as 'the transformation of the therapist's inner experience as a result of empathic engagement with survivor clients and their trauma material.'[4]

Vicarious traumatisation is thus the unavoidable by-product of working with trauma survivors in a caring and empathic way. It is the natural consequence of caring for and helping traumatised people and it is important not to see it as a sign of weakness.

If vicarious traumatisation can't be avoided, trauma professionals and carers need to learn to accept and recognise it as an integral part of their trauma work and devise adaptive coping strategies and resources in order to sustain long-term, healthy working practices in this field.

How to recognise it

Trauma work can change professionals and carers working within this field. It can damage, unsettle, throw us off our chosen path or change us as a person, as in Vera's case.

Vera was a qualified clinical psychologist, who had been working in the field of Adult Mental Health for five years when she started to get an increasing amount of referrals of clients who had been involved in traumas. For years her workload had been high generally and this did not change now. Vera tried to approach her trauma work in the same way as she had always approached her other work. She put in long hours, was a very caring and committed therapist, but the atmosphere in her department was quite anonymous, with everyone minding their own business, and she received very little support from her colleagues. After a while Vera started to notice that something inside her had changed. There were times when she found herself carrying distressing, traumatising images in her head, which her clients had shared in the session. This did not only happen during work time but also in the evenings and at night. She felt embarrassed because she thought that as a therapist she ought to be able to handle these thoughts. She didn't really feel comfortable with her colleagues and therefore had nobody to share her concerns with, not even her supervisor who worked in the same department. She tried to ignore them by telling herself that she should know better and that this, after all, was an unavoidable part of her work. A few months later Vera got a visit from her long-standing friend, Eva, who she had last seen a year previously. Eva suggested various outings and activities together but Vera found herself quite switched off and couldn't summon up the energy to do very much. She felt exhausted and was unable to experience any sense of pleasure or joy in any of the things they did together. On many occasions she noticed thoughts or images relating to her client's traumatic experiences intruding into her mind. Everything else around her seemed so trivial compared to what these people had had to suffer. Eva noticed that Vera had really changed.

She felt that Vera had become very cynical and that she had lost her natural enthusiasm for life. The previous year she had been very active and had engaged in many activities outside work, but this year it all seemed different. Eva's feedback eventually helped Vera to look for some professional help and support for herself.

Vera

As demonstrated in Vera's example above, the effect of vicarious traumatisation tends to develop gradually over time and it is often easy not to notice that you are being affected by it until something happens to highlight changes in your personality and lifestyle. You might want to reflect if anything has changed for you since you have been working with trauma. Here are some signs to watch out for:

- Reduced energy, exhaustion, lack of motivation and feeling that you have no time for yourself.
- Disconnection from others – other people don't really understand you; you don't feel close to people any more. Difficulties with your partner or with other close relationships.
- Emotional blunting – finding it difficult to experience emotions; not being able to laugh or cry as you used to; not caring. Difficulty empathising with your clients. Being less self-reflective and less able to sort out your own feelings.

- Questioning your career choice, feeling ineffectual.
- Errors in maintaining professional boundaries, failure to set limits, a general sense of failure and resentment.
- Social withdrawal, loss of interest in social activities.
- Feelings of despair and hopelessness, a bleakness in your outlook.
- Feelings of weakness, shame or guilt, often because your own problems seem comparatively minor compared with those of your clients.
- Loss of belief in the justice of life or in a sense of balance between good and bad, resulting in cynicism and bitterness.
- Heightened sense of danger, feeling less secure, scanning for danger, including for violence or aggression, in your environment.
- Sleeping problems and nightmares. Difficulties in concentrating and making decisions; not listening to others; confusion and disturbance of organisational skills.
- Lowered immune functioning, repeated colds, infections, less resilience in warding off illness
- Lack of self-control, increased anger, impatience, strained relationships with others.
- Loss of trust in others.
- Alterations in sensory experiences, e.g. intrusive imagery and flashbacks.

Other changes to look out for:

- Changes to your inner sense of identity and equilibrium, i.e. you find it harder to experience and integrate strong feelings or to maintain an inner sense of connection with others or to feel grounded and anchored within yourself.
- Changes to your world view and spirituality, i.e. you have lost or changed your philosophy of life, your values and beliefs about others and the external world.

If you notice any of the aforementioned changes in yourself, it could be helpful to share them with another person and to identify ways in which you could reverse or control the impact of some of them. You should not feel it is a sign of weakness if you do experience any of these responses, but an important signal that you need to do something to redress the balance in your work and life and identify and change those factors that are harmful to you.

How to help yourself

It is often the case that people working as caring profession-als are not very good at self-care. However, in order to be genuinely helpful to your clients you have a responsibility to take proper care of yourself. Therapists who are 'burnt out' or give their clients the impression that they shouldn't 'burden' them with their feelings because they seem too exhausted and needy themselves are not going to benefit their clients and will give a poor service.

Although, as a trauma professional you may not be able to avoid being affected by vicarious traumatisation, you can avoid being controlled or damaged by it. The most important means of preventing the negative side effects of vicarious traumatisation is therapeutic self-awareness of the trauma therapist[5]. In order to minimise the damaging effects of vicarious traumatisation this would include being aware of possible contributing factors in your environment. Generally speaking, these might include[4]:

- the nature of the trauma work
- the organisational context in which this work takes place
- the social and cultural context in which your work takes place
- individual factors
- professional factors

More specifically, working with trauma can be especially difficult when:

- there is no provision for staff respite (e.g. shared coverage, adequate time off).
- staff carry unrealistically high case loads.
- there is not enough adequately qualified supervision available.
- the organisation fails to recognise the value of trauma work or the impact that it might have on professionals.
- the organisation fails to work with staff to identify and address signs of vicarious traumatisation.
- the organisation does not provide opportunities for continuing education.
- holidays are inadequate.
- personal therapy for therapists is not supported.
- professionals also have to cope with stressful personal circumstances.
- professionals feel reluctant or create obstacles to using supervision and consultation, seeking education or taking vacations.
- professionals are new or under-qualified for this work.
- professionals carry unrealistically high expectations of themselves as therapists.

Now you are aware of the potential risk factors, identify for yourself:

1. which of those may apply to you
2. what you could do to change them
3. how and when you will make these changes

Assess your needs and note down in the table below how you have addressed, and how you will address in the future, the potential effects of stress:

Your needs:	What do you already do?	What changes would you like to make from now on?
Taking care of yourself		
Engaging in your own therapeutic growth process		
Arranging specialist supervision for your particular type of trauma work		

Nurturing activities		
Holidays and other escapes		
Creating meaning in your work and life		
Challenging negative beliefs and assumptions		
Social activities		

Take some time to work out which areas you will need to change in both your work and private life. It would be helpful to find yourself a 'working partner', maybe a professional colleague or a specialist supervisor, with whom you could discuss your planned changes and monitor your progress.

You may also want to explore whether engaging in your own therapeutic healing and inner growth work could be of benefit now, as your work with trauma clients may have triggered unprocessed stressful life experiences in you. Seeking help yourself is a not a sign of 'weakness' or failure but rather a very positive step. It indicates that you are committed to 'walking your own talk' and strong enough to role-model to yourself that you can take good care of your needs and look after yourself. It will make you a stronger and more resilient trauma therapist and enable you to sustain working in this field healthily.

Special issues for other trauma care response groups

Although the main focus of this chapter is on the effect of vicarious traumatisation on healthcare professionals and carers, trauma work can have an equally profound effect on other trauma care response groups, such as first responders, emergency and rescue services, community welfare services, humanitarian aid organisations, and other voluntary or fund-aided helpers. When people are working outside their normal range of duties, the danger of vicarious traumatisation increases.

Organisations vary in the range of support they provide for their personnel, but generally, the more back-up and support your organisation provides for you and the more you take personal responsibility for maintaining a good balance in your life, the better shielded you are from the potentially damaging effects of trauma work.

Although dealing with traumatic events will be part of your daily experience if you work for the emergency services or for another front-line carer group, there will still be certain events that will affect you more than others. These are likely to be details of events that feel distressing to you personally or incidents that have a more disturbing impact on you and members of your colleague groups, especially if they involve violent deaths. Moreover, it has been found that the cumulative effect of having to deal with different traumas over and over again can lead to vicarious traumatisation or burnout, especially if there are not enough support strategies or resources that you can draw on to build your resilience. Frequently, in unsupportive settings of this kind, people self-medicate with alcohol or other addictive substances in an attempt to down-regulate their feelings and sensations. While this might offer relief in the short-term, this is not a helpful strategy as it artificially masks the effect that the work has on you and weakens rather than strengthens your inner resources.

It may be difficult for you to disclose to your colleagues or managers the changes that you are noticing in yourself especially if your culture would perceive this as a sign of 'personal weakness'. Nevertheless, if you feel after reading this chapter that you are negatively affected by your work it may be important for you to do something about it rather than suffer in silence. It is not a sign of personal weakness if you are suffering from vicarious traumatisation as a result of your work engagement. It is a sign that something in your work–life balance isn't working to afford you sufficient respite time, support, training or supervision for you to be able to recover in between your work assignments. It is also possible that some of your own unprocessed past stressful life experiences are triggered by some events that you are witnessing as part of your work. This may intensify the distress that you are experiencing to some of the incidents that you are dealing with as part of your work and can increase your risk of vicarious traumatisation.

If you think you are affected by vicarious traumatisation it is important that you seek help from people either at work who you can trust, through your medical practitioner or privately. It might be helpful for you to undergo a course of trauma-focused psychological therapy to support you with this. As a general rule, the sooner you notice signs of vicarious traumatisation and make positive changes to your life–work balance and/or seek professional help the easier it will be for you to recover.

- If you belong to one of these trauma-care response groups and you are experiencing any signs of vicarious traumatisation or other reactions, you may find it helpful to read and work through the rest of this book.
- If your reactions persist, you would be advised to seek help either from people at work who

you can trust, through your medical practitioner or privately.

- It might be helpful for you seek out a trauma specialist, who can offer you individually tailored professional help to support you with this.

Summary checkpoints:

- It is a great privilege being a trauma professional and facilitating another person's recovery and journey into healing and positive growth.
- Being a trauma therapist carries with it the responsibility of looking after your own well-being and personal development to build inner resilience to sustain working healthily in this field.
- Trauma work can be 'emotionally infectious' and vicarious traumatisation is an inevitable consequence of working in this field.
- As a trauma professional, carer or trauma-care response worker you probably can't avoid being 'infected' by vicarious traumatisation, but you can avoid being controlled or damaged by it.
- The damaging side effects of vicarious trauma-tisation tend to develop gradually over time

and you may not notice them until something happens that highlights changes in your personality and lifestyle.

- The most important means of preventing the negative side effects of vicarious traumatisation is self-awareness:
  - Familiarise yourself with the signs and symptoms of the negative side effects of vicarious traumatisation.
  - Minimise the damaging effects by developing awareness of possible risk factors in your work environment and your overall life–work balance.
- If you are affected it is not a sign of weakness; it is a sign that something in your work–life balance isn't working to afford you sufficient respite time, support, training or supervision for you to be able to recover in between your work assignments.
- The sooner you notice signs of vicarious traumatisation and make positive changes to your life–work balance and/or seek professional help the easier it will be for you to recover and rebuild your resilience.

Resources

Useful books

For Post-Traumatic Stress Disorder (PTSD)
If you want a less extensive, readable guide on understanding trauma:

Claudia Herbert (2017, fully revised 3rd edition) *New understanding of your reactions to Trauma: A booklet for survivors of trauma and their families.* Oxford, UK: Merkaba Publishing.

This first psychological self-help guide written on trauma in the UK (1996) has been translated into several other languages, including Japanese, Turkish, Ukrainian, Polish, Spanish and now fully revised.

A comprehensive and more detailed self-help book for both single-incident and prolonged, repeated trauma (complex trauma, like childhood sexual abuse):

Glenn, R. Schiraldi (2016) – *The Post-Taumatic Stress Disorder Sourcebook – A guide to Healing, Recovery, and Growth.* New York: McGraw Hill Education

A very helpful book on complex PTSD:
Pete Walker (2014). *Complex Ptsd: From Surviving to Thriving.* USA: Azure Coyote Publishing

Four more useful and topical books:
Williams, M.B. and Poijula, S. (2013). *The PTSD Workbook. Simple, Effective Techniques for Overcoming Traumatic Stress Symptoms.* Oakland, CA: New Harbinger Publications

Levine, P. A. (2010). *IN AN Unspoken Voice. How the Body Releases Trauma and Restores Goodness.* California: North Atlantic Books

A compassion-focused approach to recovering from trauma:
Deborah Lee (2012). *Recovering from Trauma using Compassion Focused Therapy.* London: Constable & Robinson

Body-Oriented Help for PTSD:
Miller, R.C., Schoomaker, A. and Schoomaker, E. (2015). *iRest Program for Healing PTSD: A Proven-Effective Approach to Using Yoga Nidra Meditation and Deep Relaxation Techniques to Overcome Trauma.* Oakland, CA: New Harbinger Publications

For Loss and Grieving
Childs-Gowell, E. (1995). *GOOD GRIEF RITUALS: Tools for Healing.* New York: Station Hill Press

Richardson, J. (2016). *The Cure for Sorrow: A Book of Blessings for Times of Grief.* Wanton Orlando, Florida: Gospeller Press

For Sexual Difficulties

Keesling, B. (2006). *Sexual Healing: The Complete Guide to Overcoming Common Sexual Problems*. Alameda, CA: Hunter House Publishers

Healing your Sexuality after Sexual Abuse:

Maltz, W. (2012 – 3rd Edition). *The Sexual Healing Journey: A Guide for Survivors of Sexual Abuse*. New York: Harper Collins Publishers

Healing the trauma of infidelity:

Ortman, D. (2009). *Transcending Post-Infidelity Stress Disorder (PISD): The Six Stages of Healing*. New York: Crown Publishing Group

Cognitive Therapy

An international bestseller and classic, which contains much useful information:

Burns, D.D. (2009 – revised and updated). *Feeling Good: The New Mood Therapy*. New York: Avon Books

Another international bestseller which explains many helpful strategies that can be used to change the way you feel:

Greenberger, D. and Padesky, C.A. (2016 – 2nd Edition). *Mind Over Mood: Change How You Feel by Changing the Way You Think*. London: The Guilford Press

Eye Movement Desensitisation and Reprocessing (EMDR)
Shapiro, F. & Forrest, M.S. (2016 – updated edition).
*EMDR. The Breakthrough Therapy for Overcoming Anxiety,
Stress, and Trauma.* New York: Basic Books

Useful addresses

United Kingdom

Specialist trauma services are available within the National
Health Service and privately. Your first port of call should
be your medical practitioner, who should be able to advise
you on the services that are available in your area. You can
also directly approach the NHS through NHS choices and
find a psychological therapies service (IAPT) in your geo-
graphical area to which you can self-refer.

You can visit the website of the UK Psychological Trauma
Society (UKPTS) http://www.ukpts.co.uk to find a list of
several trauma services in the UK.

PTSD UK (http://www.ptsduk.org), a charity dedicated to
raising awareness of PTSD, also publishes a list to help you
find a private or NHS service that can offer you trauma
treatment in your area.

The Oxford Development Centre – Centre for Trauma
Healing and Growth is one of the longest established private
specialist trauma therapy services (since 1997) in the UK and

incorporates The Cotswold Centre for Trauma Healing. You can find their website on: http://www.oxdev.co.uk Other professional organisations that publish a register of accredited therapists may be able to advise on finding a Registered Trauma Specialist are:

The British Association for Behavioural and Cognitive Psychotherapies (BABCP) – website: http://www.babcp.com

The British Psychological Society (BPS) – website: http://www.bps.org.uk

United Kingdom Council for Psychotherapy (UKCP) – website: https://www.psychotherapy.org.uk

British Association for Counselling & Psychotherapy (BACP) – website: https://www.bacp.co.uk

Health & Care Professions Council (HCPC) – website: https://hcpc-uk.co.uk

United Kingdom Psychological Trauma Society (UKPTS) – website: http://ukpts.co.uk

USA

American Psychological Association – PTSD
Website: https://www.apa.org/about/offices/directorates/guidelines/ptsd.pdf

National Center for PTSD – VA Mental Health
Crisis Resources for Veterans, Families and Friends, including children with PTSD Parent
Website: https://www.ptsd.va.gov/public/family/resources_family_friends.asp

International Society for Traumatic Stress Studies (ISTSS)
Find-a-Clinician Service for USA, Canada, and International, Assessment and Resource Materials
Website: https://www.istss.org

CANADA

Canadian Psychological Association – Traumatic Stress Section
Website: http://www.cpa.ca/aboutcpa.cpasections/trarmaticstress/

TEMA.CA

'Canada's Leading Provider of Peer Support, Family Assistance, etc. for Public Safety & Military Personnel Dealing with Mental Health Injuries.'
Resources and Crisis Centers are listed by Province. U.S. Addiction/Rehab. Centers included.
Website: https://www.tema.ca/resource-links

Canadian Resource Centre for Victims of Crime – Canadian Resources for Treatment of Post-Traumatic Stress Disorder Resources listed by Province, including Health and Social Service Centres and Private Practitioners with rates.
Website: http://www.trauma-ptsd.com/en/ressources

MOBILE APP:

PTSD COACH CANADA – Mobile Application
From Veterans Affairs Canada 'to help learn about and manage symptoms that occur after trauma.'
Website: http://www.veterans.gc.ca/eng/stay-connected/mobile-app/ptsd-coach-canada

References for this book

Chapter 1 – When trauma strikes

1   Janoff-Bulman, R. (1992). *Shattered Assumptions*. New York: Free Press
2   American Psychiatric Association (APA – 2013). *Diagnostic and Statistical Manual of Mental Disorders* (5th ed.; DSM-5). Washington, DC: APA
3   Hodgkinson, P. and Stewart, M. (1991). *Coping with Catastrophe*. London: Routledge
4   Ortman, D. (2009). *Transcending Post-Infidelity Stress Disorder: The Six Stages of Healing*. New York: Crown Publishing
5   Shaw, L., Tacconelli E., Watson, R. and Herbert, C. (2015). *Living Confidently with HIV – A Self-Help Book For People Living With HIV*. Oxford: UK, Amazon Kindle, I-book, Blurb http://www.blurb.co.uk/bookstore/invited/6038557/e4d80465f2694f469e28932fc31153abad9e6e83
6   Meister, R., Princip, M., Schmid, J.-P., Schnyder, U., Barth, J., Znoj, H., Herbert, C. and Von Känel, R. (2013) – Myocardial Infarction – Stress PRevention INTervention (MI-SPRINT) to reduce the incidence of posttraumatic stress after acute myocardial infarction through trauma-focussed psychological counseling: study protocol for a randomised controlled trial. *Trials*, **14** (329), 3-11. DOI: 10.1186/1745-6215-14-329
7   Adapted and updated with permission from: Tyler, P. (1998). *'Upsetting Things'. PTSD assessment scale for clients*. Personal Communication. Clwyd, Wales: Psychological Services

8   Herbert, C. (2002). A CBT-based therapeutic alternative to working with complex client problems, *European Journal of Psychotherapy, Counselling and Health,* **5**(2), 135–144

9   Herbert, C. (2006). Healing from Complex Trauma: An integrative 3-system's approach. In J. Corrigal, H. Payne and H. Wilkinson (2006). *About a Body: Working with the embodied mind in psychotherapy.* London and New York: Routledge, Taylor Francis Group

10   Foa, E.B., Keane, T.M., Friedman, M.J., and Cohen, J.A. (2009). *Effective treatments for PTSD: Practice Guidelines of the International Society for Traumatic Stress Studies.* New York: Guilford Press

11   Collard, P. (2003). Interview with Dr Claudia Herbert. *Counselling Psychology Quarterly,* **16**(3), 187–193

12   Herbert, C. (2005) 'Towards New Competencies in Trauma Work' – invited guest lecture at the Chester Trauma Conference, University College Chester, Chester, UK

13   Kahl, K.G., Winter, L., Schweiger, U. (2012). The third wave of cognitive behavioural therapies: what is new and what is effective? *Current Opinion in Psychiatry,* **25** (6), 522–528. DOI: 10.1097/YCO.0b013e328358e531

Chapter 2 – Understanding your reactions

1   Kilpatrick, D.G., Resnick, H.S., Milanak, M.E., Miller, M.W., Keyes, K.M. and Friedman, M.J. (2013). National Estimates of Exposure to Traumatic Events and PTSD Prevalence using DSM-IV and DSM-5 Criteria. *Journal of Traumatic Stress,* **26**, 537–547

2   Kessler, R.C. Chiu, W.T., Demler, O., Merikangas, K.R., and Walters, E.E. (2005). Prevalence, severity, and comorbidity of 12-month DSM-IV disorders in the National Comorbidity Survey Replications. *Archives of General Psychiatry,* **62**(6). 617–627 http://www.hcp.med.harvard.edu/ncs/publications.php

3   Galea, S., Nandi, A. and Vlahov, D. (2005). The Epidemiology of Post-Traumatic Stress Disorder after Disasters. *Epidemiologic Reviews,* **27**, 78–91

4   Green, M. (2015). *AFTERSHOCK: The Untold Story of Surviving Peace.* London: Portobello Books

5   American Psychiatric Association (APA - 2013). *Diagnostic and Statistical Manual of Mental Disorders* (5th ed.; DSM-5). Washington, DC: APA

6   Selye, H. (1946). The general adaptation syndrome and the diseases of adaptation. *Journal of Clinical Endocrinology,* **6**, 117-230

7   Walker, P. (2014). *Complex PTSD: From Surviving to Thriving.* US: Azure Coyote Publishing

8   Spoormaker, V.I., Montgomery, P. (2008). Disturbed sleep in post-traumatic stress disorder: Secondary symptom or core feature? *Sleep Medicine Reviews,* **12**(3), 169-184

Chapter 3 - Understanding the reactions of families and loved ones

1   Herbert, C. (1996, 2000(2nd edition), 2017). *New understanding of your reactions to trauma: A guide for survivors of trauma and their families.* Newly updated and revised edition of 'Understanding your reactions to trauma'. Oxford, UK: Merkaba Publishing

Chapter 4 - Moving towards your path of recovery

1   Rosenbloom, D. and Williams, M.B. (2010). *Life after Trauma: A Workbook for Healing.* New York: Guilford Press

2   Williams, M.B. and Poijula, S. (2013). *The PTSD Workbook.* Second Edition. Oakland, CA: New Harbinger Publications

3   Herbert, C. and Didonna, F. (2006). *Capire e superare il trauma – Una guida per comprendere e fronteggiarre i traumi psichici.* Gardolo, Italy: Edizioni Erickson

4   Herbert. C. (2004). 'Installation of a Safe Place Protocol for use with clients who have no pre-existing concepts of safety' – Clinical practice session presented at the 5th EMDR European Congress, Stockholm, Sweden

5   Pennebaker, J.W. (2004). *Writing to Heal: A Guided Journal for Recovering from Trauma and Emotional Upheaval.* Denver, CO: Center for Journal Therapy

6   Pennebaker, J.W., Mehl, M.R., and Niederhoffer, K.G. (2003). Psychological aspects of natural language use: Our words, our selves. *Annual Review of Psychology*, **54**, 547–577

7   Pennebaker, J.W. and Evans, J.F. (2014). *Expressive Writing: Words that Heal*. Enumclaw, WA: Idyll Arbor

Chapter 5 – Your life before the trauma

1   Herbert C. (1998). 'The use of Energy Distribution Monitoring to affect schema-shifts in trauma', *Presentation at the Annual Congress of the European Association for Behavioural and Cognitive Therapies (EABCT)*, September 1998, Cork, Ireland

2   Erikson, E.H. (1963). *Childhood and Society*. 2nd Edition. New York: W.W. Norton

3   Herbert, C. (2009). 'Working with PTSD, Complex Trauma and Dissociative Identity Disorder (DID)'. Invitation to present a 'Meet the Expert Session' at the 39th Annual Congress for the *European Association for Behavioural and Cognitive Therapies (EABCT)*, September 2009, Dubrovnik, Croatia

4   Panksepp, J. (1998) – The Periconscious Substrates of Consciousness: Affective States and the Evolutionary Origins of Self. *Journal of Consciousness Studies*, **5**, No. 5–6, 1998, pp. 566–82

Chapter 6 – Methods to soothe your disturbed nervous system

1   Porges, S.W. (2011). *The polyvagal theory: Neurophysiological foundations of emotion, attachment, communication, self-regulation*. New York: W.W. Norton

2   Panksepp, J. (2004). *Affective Neuroscience: The Foundations of Human and Animal Emotions*. New York: Oxford University Press

3   Schwarz, L. and Corrigan, F. (2016). *The Comprehensive Resource Model (CRM): Effective Techniques for the Treatment of Complex PTSD*. London: Routledge

4   Corrigan, F.M. (2014). *Defense Responses: Frozen, Suppressed, Truncated, Obstructed, and Malfunctioning*. In U.F. Lanius, S.L. Paulsen and F.M. Corrigan

5 Cloitre, M., Cohen, L.R. and Koenen, K.C. (2006). *Treating survivors of childhood abuse. Psychotherapy for the interrupted life.* New York: The Guilford Press

6 Ogden, P., Minton, K. and Pain, C. (2006). *Trauma and the Body: A Sensory Motor Approach to Therapy.* New York: W.W. Norton

7 Siegel, D.J. (2010). *The mindful therapist: A clinician's guide to mindsight and neural integration.* New York: W.W. Norton

8 Hanson, R. (2010, October). Confronting the negative bias (online newsletter). http://rickhanson.net/your-wise-brain/how-your-brain-makes-you-easily-intimidated

9 Miller-Karas, E. (2015). *Building Resilience to Trauma. The Trauma Community Resiliency Models.* New York and London: Routledge, Taylor & Francis Group

Chapter 8 – Managing your intrusive, re-experiencing reactions

1 Wegner, D. (1989). *White Bears and Other Unwanted Thoughts: Suppression, Obsession and the Psychology of Mental Control.* New York: Viking

2 Weathers, F.W., Litz, B.T., Herman, D.S., Huska, J.A. and Keane, T.M. (1993). The PTSD Checklist (PCL): Reliablity, validity, and diagnostic utility. Paper presented at the 9th Annual Conference of the ISTSS, San Antonio

3 Weathers, F. W., Litz, B. T., Keane, T. M., Palmieri, P. A., Marx, B. P., and Schnurr, P. P. (2014, February 5). PTSD Checklist for DSM-5 (PCL-5). National Center for PTSD

4 Meichenbaum, D. (1994). *Treating Post-Traumatic Stress Disorder, A handbook and practice manual for therapy.* Chichester, UK: Wiley

5 Schwarz, L. and Corrigan, F. (2016). *The Comprehensive Resource Model (CRM): Effective Techniques for the Treatment of Complex PTSD.* London: Routledge

6 Dolan, Y.M.(1991). *Resolving Sexual Abuse: Solution-focused Therapy and Eriksonian Hypnosis for Adult Survivors.* New York: W.W. Norton

7 Herbert, C. (2004) – 'Neither good nor bad – just perfect as you are! Establishing healthy affect control in clients diagnosed

with personality disorders or complex trauma through the repair of early attachment problems' – Workshop at the European Association for Behavioural and Cognitive Therapies (EABCT) – 34th Annual Congress – UMIST, Manchester, UK

Chapter 9 – Managing your arousal reactions

1   Breathnach, S.B. (1995). *Simple Abundance a Day Book of Comfort and Joy*. New York: Warner Books
2   Bower, S.A. and Bower, G.H. (1976). *Asserting Yourself: A Practical Guide for Positive Change*.Reading, Mass.: Addison-Wesley

Chapter 10 – Managing your avoidance reactions

1   Cushing, H. (2016). *Hope: How Yoga Heals The Scars of Trauma*. Hobart, Australia: Ganges Yoga

Chapter 11 – Managing negative changes in mood and thought patterns

1   Kabat-Zinn, J. (1994). *Wherever you go there you are: Mindfulness Meditation for Everyday Life*. London: Piatkus
2   Kornfield, J. (2002). *A Path with Heart*. London: Rider & Co
3   Williams, M. and Penman, D. (2011). *Mindfulness – a practical guide to Finding Peace in a Frantic World*. London: Piatkus
4   Burns, D.D. (1980, revised 2000). *Feeling Good: The New Mood Therapy*. New York: Avon Books

Chapter 12 – Guilt, shame, self-blame and self-respect

1   Thompson, J. (1993). '*The origins of guilt*', personal communication. Traumatic Stress Clinic. London: Middlesex Hospital
2   Miller, A. (1984). *For your Own Good*. Toronto: Collins Publishers
3   Walker, P. (2014). *Complex PTSD: From Surviving to Thriving*. USA: Azure Coyote Publishing
4   Scurfield, R.M. (2006). *War Trauma: Lessons Unlearned, from*

Vietnam to Iraq. (HC) (A Vietnam Trilogy). New York: Algora Publishing

5   Shiraldi, G.R. (2000, updated and revised 2016). *The Post-Traumatic Stress Disorder Sourcebook.* New York: McGraw Hill Education

6   Bodin, L., Bodin Lamboy, N. and Graciet, J. (2016) – *The Book of Ho'oponopono – The Hawaiian Practice of Forgiveness and Healing.* Rochester, Vermont: Destiny Books

7   Janoff-Bulman, R. (1992). *Shattered Assumptions, towards a New Psychology of Trauma.* New York: Free Press

Chapter 16 – Healing, letting go and moving on

1   Van der Kolk, B. (1994). 'The Body keeps the Score: Memory and the evolving psychology of post traumatic stress'. *Harvard Review of Psychiatry,* **1**, 253-256

2   Childs-Gowell, E. (1992). *Good Grief Rituals: Tools for Healing.* New York: Station Hill Press

3   Cohen, B.,M., Barnes, M-M. and Rankin, A.B. (1995). *Managing Traumatic Stress Through Art: Drawing from the Center.* Lutherville, Md: The Sidran Press

Chapter 17 – Seeking professional help

1   Friedman, M.J. (2003). *Post Traumatic Stress Disorder, The Latest Assessments and Treatment Strategies.* Kansas City, MO, US: Compact Clinicals

2   National Institute for Health and Care Excellence (2005). *Posttraumatic Stress Disorder(PTSD): The Treatment of PTSD in adults and children.* London, UK: NICE guidelines (CG26)

3   Foa, E.B., Keane, T.M., Friedman, M.J., and Cohen, J.A. (2009). *Effective treatments for PTSD: Practice Guidelines of the International Society for Traumatic Stress Studies.* New York: Guilford Press

4   Ehlers, A., Clark, D. M. (2000). A cognitive model of post-traumatic stress disorder. *Behaviour Research and Therapy,* **38**, 319-345

5   Shapiro, F. (1989). Eye movement desensitization: A new treatment for post-traumatic stress disorder. *Journal of Behavior Therapy and Experimental Psychiatry*, **20**(3), 211-217

6   Shapiro, F. (1995). *Eye movement desensitization and reprocessing: Basic principles, protocols and procedures.* New York: Guilford Press

7   Bisson, J., Roberts, N.P., Andrew, M., Cooper, R. and Lewis, C. (2013). Psychological therapies for chronic post-traumatic stress disorder (PTSD) in adults. *Cochrane Database of Systematic Reviews* 2013, DOI: 10.1002/14651858.CD003388. pub4

8   World Health Organization (2013). *Guidelines for the management of conditions that are specifically related to stress.* Geneva, WHO

9   Herbert, C. (2006). Healing from Complex Trauma: An integrative 3-system's approach. In J. Corrigal, H. Payne and H. Wilkinson (2006). *About a Body: Working with the embodied mind in psychotherapy.* London and New York: Routledge, Taylor Francis Group

10   Van der Kolk, B. (2014). The Body Keeps The Score. Mind, Brain and Body in the Transformation of Trauma. New York: Penguin Group

11   Bloch-Atefi, A. and Smith, J. (2014). *The effectiveness of body-oriented psychotherapy: A review of the literature.* Melbourne: PACFA.

12   Follette, V., Palm, K.M., Pearson, A.N. (2006). Mindfulness and Trauma: Implications for Treatment. *Journal of Rational-Emotive & Cognitive-Behaviour Therapy*, **24**(1), 45-61. DOI:10.1007/s10942-006-0025-2

13   Lee, D. and James, S. (2012). *The Compassionate Mind Approach to Recovering from Trauma using Compassion Focused Therapy.* London: Robinson

14   Gordon, J.S., Staples, J.K., Blyta, A., Bytyqi, M., and Wilson, A.T. (2008). Treatment of posttraumatic stress disorder in postwar Kosovar adolescents using mind-body skills groups: A randomised controlled trial. *Journal of Clinical Psychiatry*, **69**(9), 1469-1476

15   Ogden, P., and Minton, K. (2000). Sensorimotor psychotherapy: One method for processing traumatic memory. *Traumatology*, **6**(3), 149-173

16   Levine, P.A. (2010). *In an Unspoken Voice: How the Body Releases Trauma and Restores Goodness.* Berkely, CA: North Atlantic Books

17 Payne, P., Levine, P. A., Crane-Gordreau, M.A. (2015). Somatic experiencing: using interoception and proprioception as core elements of trauma therapy. *Frontiers in Psychology*, **6** (93), 1-18. DOI:10.3389/fpsyg.2015.00093

18 Miller-Karas, E. (2015). *Building Resilience to Trauma: The Trauma and Community Resiliency Models*. New York: Routledge

19 Schwarz, L. and Corrigan, F. (2016). The Comprehensive Resource Model (CRM): Effective Techniques for the Treatment of Complex PTSD. London: Routledge

20 Church, D., and Feinstein, D. (2013). Energy psychology in the treatment of PTSD: Psychobiology and clinical principles. In T. Van Leeuwen, and M. Brouwer. (Eds.), *Psychology of trauma* (pp. 211 - 224). Hauppage, NY: Nova Science Publishers

21 Ruden, R.A. (2005). A neurological basis for the observed peripheral sensory modulation of emotional responses. *Traumatology*, **11**(3), 145-158

22 Slaninova, G. and Pidimová, P. (2014). Pesso Boyden System Psychomotor as a method of work with battered victims. *Procedia - Social and Behavioral Sciences*, **112**, 387–394

23 Van der Kolk, B.A., Stone, L., West, J., Rhodes, A., Emerson, D., Suvak, M., Spinazzola, J. (2014). Yoga as an Adjunctive Treatment for Posttraumatic Stress Disorder: A Randomised Controlled Trial. *Journal of Clinical Psychiatry*. **75**(0), 1-7

24 Cushing, H. (2016). *Hope: How Yoga Heals The Scars Of Trauma*. Hobart, Australia: Ganges Yoga

25 Hollifield, M., Sinclair-Lian, N., Warner, T.D. and Hammerschlag, R. (2007). Acupuncture for Posttraumatic Stress Disorder – A Randomised Controlled Pilot Trial. *The Journal of Nervous and Mental Disease*. **195**(6), 504-513

26 Jain, S., McMahon, G.F., Hasen, P., Kozub, M.P., Porter, V., King, R., and Guarneri, E.M. (2012). Healing Touch with Guided Imagery for PTSD in returning active duty military: A randomised controlled trial. *Military medicine*, **177**(9), 1015-1021

27 Ribeiro-Blanchard, A.J., Rios, A.M.G. and Seixa, L.P. (2010). The Body in Psychotherapy: Calatonia and Subtle Touch Techniques. In Jones, R. (Ed) *Body, Mind, and Healing After Jung: A Space of Questions*. London: Routledge

28 Rosen, M. and Bremer, S. (2003). Rosen Method Bodywork:

Accessing the Unconscious through Touch. Berkeley, CA: North Atlantic Books

29 Salibian, A. (2015). Trauma Therapy with Rosen Method Bodywork. *Rosen Method International Journal*, **8**(1), 4–33

30 Kern, M. (2005). *Wisdom in the Body: The Craniosacral Approach to Essential Health*. Berkeley, CA: North Atlantic Books

31 Randoll, U.G. (2014). *The Matrix Concept. Fundamentals of Matrix Rhythm Therapy*. Bad Koetzting, Germany: Verlag Systemische Medizin Ag

32 Schultz, P.N., Remick–Barlow, G.A. and Robbins, L. (2007). Equine-assisted psychotherapy: a mental health promotion/intervention modality for children who have experienced intra-family violence. *Health and Social Care in the Community*, **15**(3), 265–271

33 Lentini, J.A. and Knox, M. (2009). A Qualitative and Quantitative Review of Equine Facilitated Psychotherapy (EFP) with Children and Adolescents. *The Open Complementary Medicine Journal*, **1**, 51–57

Chapter 18 – Issues for professionals and carers: vicarious traumatisation

1 Hawkins, P. and Shohet, R. (2000). *Supervision in the helping professions: an individual, group and organizational approach*. Buckingham: Open University Press

2 McCann, L. and Pearlman, L.A. (1990). Vicarious traumatization: a framework for understanding the psychological effects of working with victims. *Journal of Traumatic Stress*, **3**(1), 131–149

3 C.R. Figley (Ed) (1995). *Compassion fatigue, coping with secondary traumatic stress disorder in those who treat the traumatised*. New York: Brunner & Mazel

4 Saakvitne, K.W. and Pearlman, L.A. (1995). *Transforming the pain. A workbook on vicarious traumatization*. New York and London: W.W. Norton

5 Pross, C. (2006). Burnout, vicarious traumatization and its prevention. What is burnout, what is vicarious traumatization? *Torture*, **16**(1), 1–97

Index

THE
IMPR⟳VEMENT
ZONE

Looking for life inspiration?

The Improvement Zone has it all, from **expert advice** on how to advance your **career** and boost your **business**, to improving your **relationships**, revitalising your **health** and developing your **mind**.

Whatever your goals, head to our website now.

www.improvementzone.co.uk